PLACES TO GO WITH CHILDREN IN *New England*

DIANE BAIR
AND
PAMELA WRIGHT

Completely Revised and Expanded

CHRONICLE BOOKS
SAN FRANCISCO

For Charlotte, Connor, Sadie, and Jared

Printed in the United States of America.

Second Edition.

Library of Congress Cataloging-in-Publication Data:
Bair, Diane.
    Places to go with children in New England / by Diane Bair and Pamela Wright.
      p.   cm.
     "Completely revised and updated"—Cover.
     Includes index.
     ISBN 0-8118-0429-1
     1. New England—Guidebooks. 2. Children—Travel—New England—Guidebooks. 3. Family recreation—New England—Guidebooks. I. Wright, Pamela. 1953–   . II. Title.
F2.3.B34   1994
917.404'43—dc20   93-40370
                                            CIP

Design and illustration: Karen Smidth
Composition: Words & Deeds

Distributed in Canada by Raincoast Books, 112 East Third Ave., Vancouver, B.C. V5T 1C8

10 9 8 7 6 5 4 3 2 1

Chronicle Books
275 Fifth Street
San Francisco, CA 94103

Contents

Introduction

It's one of the secrets of parenthood that no one tells you: having kids is a great excuse for being a kid again yourself. You can blow bubbles, walk on stilts, swing from the monkey bars—in general, have the time of your life—and meanwhile everyone thinks, "Such a wonderful parent!" What a coup.

Traveling with children is even better. Oh, sure, there are those maddening moments when you're in the middle of nowhere and someone needs a potty, or your two-year-old crashes—publicly, of course—after a day of Too Much Fun. Not to mention those times when you're ready to leave Josh and Jessie on the side of the interstate if you hear, "She's on my side!" one more time. But ultimately the things you'll remember about family trips (we hope) are the Pleasant Moments: marveling at a gorgeous sunset, en famille, on a lonely stretch of beach; seeing your daughter's face when she lands her first trout; watching the little one's gleeful grin as he whirls past you on an antique carousel.

This book is full of places with special-memory potential. We've focused on attractions that are uniquely New England, such as boat cruises where kids can play "lobsterman for a day," places where you can beachcomb for starfish and horseshoe crabs, old cemeteries where you can make grave rubbings, medieval castles to visit and play "knight in shining armor," and places where you can not only pet the animals but help milk cows and shear sheep. The emphasis is on interactive fun, places where kids can really get involved in the action, not just watch. And we looked for places where grown-ups will enjoy themselves. After all, it's your precious leisure time, too.

Obviously, not every destination in this book will appeal to every child; you know your kids better than we do. Not every child can handle a Newport mansion, for example. So we went out of our way to find historic attractions with an element of kid appeal—a museum with a treasure trove of old toys, for example, or a landmark house where kids can play 18th-century games while you check out the antiques. And, for the sake of balance, we included places that offer no redeeming educational value whatsoever but kids unabashedly adore: amusement parks, water-slides, kiddie rides, mega video arcades, restaurants where your food will be served by someone in an animal suit.

We invite you to get into the spirit of it all and enjoy. Rediscover the fun-loving kid inside you, reconnect with your own children, and have a great time discovering New England.

BOSTON

Steeped in tradition yet pulsing with the beat of a modern city, Boston is one of the most popular tourist destinations in the world. Stroll the cobblestone streets of Beacon Hill or hop on the "T" (short for MBTA, the subway system) to experience the color and diversity that make Boston unique. Savor high tea at the Ritz, or slurp oysters at a raw bar in Quincy Market. Take the children for a relaxing ride on a swan boat, or brave the bargain-hungry throngs at Filene's Basement. You'll soon learn why Bostonians love their city. Just listen to some of the locals:

"Even though I grew up here, walking the Freedom Trail always stirs my imagination. It conjures up visions of Paul Revere's ride, the Boston Tea Party, the Revolution—it makes you feel a part of history."

"Boston is a visual, sensory treat. Nothing feels as wonderful as walking down Marlborough Street surrounded by beautiful brownstones and dogwoods in bloom."

You've heard the phrase, "Pahk your cah in Hahvahd yahd?" Don't even consider it. Boston's maze of narrow, one-way streets is best navigated by foot, trolley, or subway—not by car. There wouldn't be any place to park, anyway. Don your most comfortable shoes (forget fashion; given Boston's climate, comfort beats style every time), and start walking. When little feet get tired, board the "T." Boston's subway system is clean and modern and will get you to all major points of interest in the city.

DOWNTOWN

⚛ Museum of Science

Science Park; (617) 723-2500. Tues.-Thurs., Sat. and Sun., 9-5; Fri., 9-9. Museum, Omni Theater, and laser show admission: adults, $6.50; 4-14, $4.50. Planetarium admission: adults, $6; under 4, free.

You won't want to miss this world-renowned museum, with more than 400 participatory exhibits. Walk beside a three-story-high tyrannosaurus rex, see live animal and physical science demonstrations, or test your wits in the computer center. There's always a special exhibit going on, featuring child-pleasing themes like "Backyard Monsters," with huge robotic bugs. The museum's Omnimax theater boasts the world's largest projection system and a dome screen 76 feet in diameter. It's the perfect venue for multiimage presentations that have included "Tropical Rainforest," "Antarctica," and "Mountain Gorilla"—guaranteed to astonish kids young and old. Little kids adore the Touch Room, a child-scaled space filled with "neat stuff" that just happens to illustrate scientific principles.

⌇ Museum of Fine Arts

465 Huntington Ave.; (617) 267-9300. Tues. and Thurs.-Sun., 10-4:45; Wed., 10-9:45; Thurs. and Fri., West Wing only, 5-9:45. Family Place: Oct.-June, first Sun. each month, 11-4. Children's Room: June-Aug., Tues.-Thurs., 3:30-4:45; Sept.-May, Wed.-Fri., 3:30-4:45. Adults, $7; 6-17, $3.50. Under 6, free. All fees reduced by $1 Thurs. and Fri. eves. Free to all, Wed., 4-9:45. Family Place: free with museum admission. Children's Room: free.

You'll probably be attracted to the Fine Arts for its terrific collections of Chinese, Japanese, Indian, Egyptian, Greek, Roman, European, and American art; happily, the kids can get a lot out of this wonderful museum as well. In the Children's Room, geared to age 6 to 12, drop-in workshops highlight the museum's collections through dramatics, art projects, poetry, and music. (Kids only here; you can tour the museum while they're busy with projects.) In the Family Place you can all get into the act, by setting out on a museum scavenger hunt, for example. You'll meet at the Family Place, then explore the museum together. There's also a self-guided tour for families—pick up a booklet at the Information Desk.

Special Note: May is Museum-Goers' Month in Boston. More than 40 area museums participate, with special events and exhibits, free days, and more—a real bonus for museum hoppers.

⌇ Faneuil Hall Marketplace

Merchants Row; (617) 242-5642.

First, let's get this straight: it's pronounced "fan-yool" hall, or is it "fan-il?" Whatever. If you visit Boston, you'll end up here at some point—it's practically the law. There are street performers galore, and they're good (they have to be—they audition for this plum position) and they include clowns and mimes, harpists and guitarists and jugglers. And of course, there's lots of shopping and food, with more than 170 shops and restaurants within four refurbished buildings. This colorful, festive area has become a model for the restoration and conversion of older urban areas into centers for shopping, dining, and entertainment. Little kids will want to check out the huge Disney store; older ones will have a grand old time picking out the coolest souvenir T-shirt from among hundreds of possibilities. And once they discover there's a whole hall filled with nothing but delectable edibles—look out.

Special Note: While at Faneuil Hall, stop by the Bostix Booth to see what's happening in the arts around town; buy half-price, day-of-performance tickets here.

ꙮ Beantown Trolley

Eleven tours daily, 9-6; (617) 236-2148. Adults, $14; children, $5; under 5, free. Good starting points: Sheraton Boston Hotel, Dalton St., or Park St., in front of Boston Common.

The best thing about this narrated bus tour? You can get on and off to explore, anytime you wish, and catch up with another bus later. The worst thing? Some of the terrible puns the drivers tell—although the kids will love them. Along with the bad jokes there are plenty of interesting factoids and anecdotes about the city, and some of them are even true. Other tour companies include Boston Trolley Tours, (617) 427-TOUR; Old Town Trolley Tours, (617) 269-7010; and Horse and Carriage Tours, (617) 523-5256.

ꙮ Boston Common

Bounded by Beacon, Charles, Boylston, Tremont, and Park streets.

It's the oldest public park in the United States, occupying 48 acres in the city's busy downtown area. In colonial days the area was pastureland for animals and training ground for the militia. Today you're likely to find street musicians, art exhibits, political demonstrations, food vendors, even outdoor concerts. Pick up maps and information at the Visitor's Information Center located on the hilly east side. This is also the starting point for Boston's Freedom Trail.

ꙮ Freedom Trail

If you really want to see downtown Boston, put on some sensible shoes and follow the red-brick road. Boston's Freedom Trail is a self-guided, 2.5-mile walking tour of 16 historic sites. A bold red stripe on the sidewalk, beginning at the Boston Common Visitor's Information Center, leads visitors through the downtown financial and shopping district to Faneuil Hall, through the North End, and into Charlestown.

Depending on how fast you walk, how may sites you see, and how long you stay at each site, the Trail can take anywhere from two hours to a full day to complete. Maps can be found at Visitor's Information Centers located throughout the city. Freedom Trail sites include: the State House, Park Street Church, Granary Burying Ground, King's Chapel, Ben Franklin's statue and the site of the first public school, the Old Corner Bookstore, Old South Meeting House, the Old State House, the Boston Massacre Site, Faneuil Hall, the Paul Revere House, Old North Church, Copp's Hill Burial Ground, the U.S.S. *Constitution,* and Bunker Hill Monument. You might want to pick and choose sites along the tour to tailor it to your family's interest.

⅋ Boston-By-Little-Feet

Starts at the statue of Samuel Adams in front of Faneuil Hall (Congress St. side) on Sun. at 2 P.M. throughout the summer, rain or shine; (617) 367-2345. Per person, $5. Children must be accompanied by an adult.

This is a nifty idea, and we highly recommend it—it's an hour-long guided tour designed for children aged six through twelve. It covers a major portion of the Freedom Trail and introduces kids to Boston history and architecture in a fun, participatory style. It's a great way to introduce kids to the city of Boston.

⅋ Boston Public Garden

Swan boats: Mid-April–mid-Sept. Adults, $1.25; 12 and under, $.75.

An oasis of tranquility in the middle of a bustling city, the Public Garden is a wonderful place to relax and catch your breath before the next stop on your agenda. Sure to grab your attention—if you visit in season—are the swan boats. Do take a 12-minute ride and enjoy. This is the venue of Robert McCloskey's *Make Way for Ducklings,* the classic children's story of a mallard family looking for a home. (The kids can even pose for a picture with bronze replicas of same.) In winter, the frozen lagoon is a public ice skating rink; skate rentals are available at $2.50 a day.

⅋ Wheelock Family Theater

180 The Riverway; (617) 734-4760. Late Oct.–May. Performances Fri., 7:30 P.M.; matinees Sat. and Sun., 3 P.M. Tickets, $8-$9 (evening performances); $9-$10 (matinees).

Catch a performance of *The Secret Garden, Aladdin,* or whatever child-pleasing production is playing here. The theater, run by Wheelock College, is a great place to introduce kids aged three and up to the magic of the stage.

 **WATERFRONT**

⚛ Boston Tea Party Ship and Museum
Congress St. Bridge; (617) 338-1773. Daily, 9 A.M.-dusk. Adults, $6; 5-15, $3.

Relive one of the most colorful chapters in our country's history. Kids will love tossing a bundle of tea into the harbor below (and pulling it back up again, of course) as they relive the notorious rebellion aboard a full-size reproduction of one of the famous Tea Party ships. The adjacent museum houses colonial artifacts and exhibits.

⚛ Children's Museum of Boston
Museum Wharf, 300 Congress St.; (617) 426-6500. Tues., Thurs., Sat. and Sun., 10-5; Fri., 10-9; closed Mon. except holidays. Adults, $7; 2-15, $6; 1-year-olds, $2; under 1, free. Fri., 5-9 P.M., $1 for everyone.

This multilevel space is fairly bursting with wonderful things to do; if the world were designed by kids, it would probably look a lot like the Children's Museum. Want to explore a Japanese house, appear on your own TV show, make giant bubbles, or put bones together to make a skeleton? It all happens here, and that's just a sampling, along with traveling exhibits and special events. Many events are tied in with holidays and celebrate cultural diversity.

A special play space is set aside for toddlers and preschoolers, where they can climb, play, and put together puzzles without the distraction of big kids. Tip: The recycling center has lots of neat stuff (cheap) that's great for at-home craft projects.

⚛ Computer Museum
Museum Wharf, 300 Congress St.; (617) 423-6758. Tues.-Sun., 10-5; Fri., 10-9; closed Mon. except holidays. Adults, $7; 5-17, $5; Sun., 3-5 P.M., admission half-price.

Right next door to the Children's Museum, the Computer Museum is a user-friendly spot with enough activity to keep children happy and enough gee-whiz technology to impress the most jaded adult. Much is interactive: hold a conversation with a computer, change the look of your face, design a new car…you'll find the lastest in computer technology here, as well as early, vintage computers. The changing exhibits are always intriguing, and have included "Robots and Other Smart Machines," "Design Your Own Racing Bike" (with computer graphics), and a walk-through computer.

New England Aquarium
*Central Wharf; (617) 973-5200. Mon.-Wed. and Fri., 9-5; Thurs.,
9-8; Sat., Sun., and holidays, 9-6. Adults, $7.50; 3-11, $3.50; under 3,
free.*

The world's largest circular, glass-enclosed tank—housing its own
coral reef—brings sharks, turtles, and hundreds of underwater creatures
within inches of your face. If your children are like most, they'll get a real
thrill out of walking through the tunnel of sharks at feeding time (adults
generally find it gruesome) or hand-dunking for crabs, shells, and starfish
at the Tidal Pool. Outdoors, see harbor seals Rigel, Cecil, Trumpet,
Smoke, Lana, and Amelia. Dolphin and sea lion shows are included in the
price of admission.

HarborWalk
15 State St.; (617) 242-5642. Daily.

Get in touch with Boston's shoreline on this two-mile, self-guided
tour. Visit the National Park Service Visitor's Center at 15 State Street for
a map and brochure that includes tidbits on Boston's maritime history.
Sites along the way include New England Aquarium, the Children's Museum, and the Boston Tea Party Ship. Are you ready, Reeboks? Start
walkin'....

Boston Harbor Islands
Tired of city sounds and sights? Consider a short ferry trip to one
or more of the islands that make up the Boston Harbor Island State Park.
There are more than 30 islands altogether, and most are included in the
state park. Spend a day exploring an old fort, swimming in an ocean cove,
hiking along wooded trails, and berry picking; each island has its own
unique character. Several cruise companies will take you by ferry boat
from Boston's waterfront piers to Georges Island. (See "Boat Cruises"
listing, below.) From there, take a free water taxi to the other islands.

◤ BACK BAY

John Hancock Observatory
*Copley Square; (617) 572-6000. Mon.-Sat., 9 A.M.-11 P.M.; Sun., 10
A.M.-11 P.M. Adults, $2.75; 5-17, $2.*

New England's tallest building offers sweeping views from its 60th
floor. A multimedia presentation simulates a helicopter tour of the city.

⇉ Skywalk
Prudential Center, 50th floor, 800 Boylston St.; (617) 236-3318. Mon.-Sat., 10-10; Sun., 12-10. Adults, $2.75; 5-15, $1.50.

Get a 360-degree view of Boston and beyond from this 52-story building. Signs on the wall indicate points of interest.

⇉ Where's Boston?
Copley Place, 100 Huntington Ave.; (617) 267-4949. Daily, shows on the hour. Free.

This multimedia show gives a quick, all-around introduction to the city's sights, sounds, and people. Stop in before you begin your visit to Boston.

⇉ Mapparium
175 Huntington Ave.; (617) 450-2000. Tues.-Sat., 9:30-4. Free.

Inside the headquarters of the First Church of Christ, Scientist, you'll find a walk-through glass globe, an intriguing sight for adults as well as kids.

◣ BEACON HILL

⇉ The State House
Beacon St.; Mon.-Fri., 10-4. Free.

Samuel Adams laid the cornerstone for this gold-domed Boston landmark. Sitting atop Beacon Hill, the State House is now the seat of Massachusetts government. Two tours are offered; older children might enjoy the Legislative Process Tour that covers how laws are made; a historical/architectural tour features the Hall of Flags and House and Senate rooms. Be sure to pick up the special booklet for children at the tour desk.

⇉ Granary Burying Ground
Tremont St., next to Park Street Church; (617) 542-3071. Daily, 8-4. Free.

Step back into history and recall the lives and times of several American heroes. This is the final resting place of John Hancock, Samuel Adams, Robert Treat Paine, the parents of Ben Franklin, and Paul Revere. Some say the grave of Mother Goose is also here.

⇉ Black Heritage Trail
This walking tour commemorates the history of Boston's 19th-century black community, which settled in this part of Beacon Hill. The trail

begins at the African Meeting House (8 Smith Center), the oldest black church building still standing in the United States, and continues through Beacon Hill with stops at the Smith Court Residences, Abiel Smith School, the George Middleton House, Robert Gould Shaw and the 54th Regiment Memorial, the Phillips School, the home of John J. Smith, the Charles Street Meeting Houses, the Lewis and Harriet Hayden House, and Coburn's Gaming House. Pick up maps and information at Visitor's Information Centers throughout the city.

NORTH END

౨ᢃ Paul Revere House
19 North Square; (617) 523-2338. Daily, 9:30-4:15; closed Mon., Jan.- March. Adults, $2; 5-17, $.75.

Visit Boston without stopping by the Paul Revere House? Unthinkable. The famous patriot was living in this very house when he took his famous ride, shouting, "The British are coming!" This house is the oldest building in Boston (built around 1680) and contains many original furnishings.

౨ᢃ Haymarket Square
Haymarket St., adjacent to Quincy Market, behind the Bostonian Hotel. Fri. and Sat., dawn to dusk.

If you're near Boston's North End on Friday or Saturday, you won't be able to miss this open-air farmer's market. Push your way through the crowds and hear the staccato sales pitch of the vendors, amid the color and aroma of fresh produce, fish, and flowers. Bargains abound, especially at the end of the day. You might find fresh oysters on the half shell for a quarter a piece, or succulent peaches for a buck a bag.

౨ᢃ Feasts and Festivals
North End (Hanover, Salem, and Prince streets), weekends throughout the summer.

The narrow streets of the North End, Boston's "Little Italy," come alive with celebration in summer, in honor of the saints. The statues are decorated, and the streets are blocked off to make way for pushcarts laden with pizza, sausages, pastries, Italian ices, and other treats. Add parades, music, and song and you have a colorful and lively outdoor festival. Walk over and join the fun. (See "Annual Events" section for more.)

⚝ Scenic Strolls
Newbury Street and Beacon Hill

Boston is a walker's paradise. You've probably visited several of the city's attractions on foot, or plan to; the following are suggestions for rambling along, with no particular itinerary in mind. After spending some time in Boston, you'll no doubt discover your own favorite spots to sit back and savor the city. Newbury Street, from Arlington Avenue to Massachusetts Avenue, is lined with antique shops, boutiques, unique stores of every kind (some not so unique), and restaurants. Sit at an outdoor cafe, visit an art gallery, window shop and people watch. If you have time, meander down Marlborough Street (our pick as the most beautiful street in Boston); stroll down Commonwealth Avenue, a tree-lined promenade of parks; or walk over to Copley Square, where you'll see the impressive Trinity Church and the Copley Square fountain.

There's no other place in the country quite like Beacon Hill. The very first Bostonians resided here, and it's still regarded as a highly desirable residential location. This is a neighborhood of charm and antiquity, full of 18th- and 19th-century townhouses, cobblestone streets, courtyard gardens, brick walkways, and gas-lit lanterns. The best way to see it all is to wear comfortable shoes (most of the area is steep), start at Charles and Beacon streets, and meander. You'll also find the Bull & Finch Pub, model for the TV show "Cheers," on Charles Street.

⚝ Charles River Esplanade and Hatch Shell

Located off Storrow Drive, the Esplanade is a hub of activity when good weather beckons Bostonians outdoors. Join them and you'll see why this stretch along the river is perfect for walking or roller skating, bicycling (along the Paul Dudley White bike trail), or simply grabbing a picnic and a park bench and watching the sailboats and sculls zigzag up the Charles. On summer evenings, the action centers at the Hatch Shell, where there's often an outdoor concert or (on Friday night) free movie screening, under the stars. This is also the site of Boston's giant July 4th fireworks gala, with dazzling pyrotechnics set to music by the Boston Pops.

⚝ Boat Cruises

Discover a humpback whale playground, visit the Boston Harbor Islands, or board a ship that will take you to the tip of Cape Cod and back again. A number of cruise companies offer several options for folks who want a view of Boston from the water. All depart from points along

Boston's waterfront piers; call ahead for schedules and rates. A good option for families: the 55-minute, narrated cruise of Boston's inner harbor offered by Bay State Cruise Co. ($5 for adults, $3 for kids). Departing from Long Wharf, it's just the right length for kids. Call (617) 723-7800. Other good trips are offered by A.C. Cruise Line, (617) 426-8419; Boston Harbor Cruises, (617) 227-4321 (no charge for kids under 12 on some of their tours); Boston Harbor Whale Watch, (617) 345-9866; and New England Aquarium Whale Watch, (617) 973-5281.

≈₿ Sailing

Community Boating, Storrow Dr., Boston; (617) 523-1038. Mid-June–third week in Aug., weekdays, 1 P.M.-sunset; weekends and holidays, 9 A.M.-sunset.

If you're a sailing family, you've probably spotted the Tech dinghies and other craft dotting the Charles River. With Boston on one side and Cambridge on the other, it looks plenty inviting. You can join 'em even if you didn't bring a boat. Community Boating, off Storrow Drive on the Esplanade in Boston, offers two-and seven-day memberships (or longer), at $50 and $70 respectively, allowing you the use of a 16-foot Mercury sailboat. It's a great deal and a super place to sail, with great views to port and starboard.

≈₿ Boston Sports

There may not be a kid alive who wouldn't enjoy an afternoon cheering the Red Sox at classic Fenway Park, a hot dog in one hand and scorecard in the other. Would you rather see the Celts or the "Broons?" Maybe the hapless Pats? Just pick your favorite spectator sport— Beantown is well known for its championship teams (not to mention enthusiastic fans). For tickets and information, call the following numbers: Boston Red Sox, (617) 267-1700; Boston Celtics, (617) 523-3030 (if the Celts are your dream team, good luck; tickets are hard to come by); Boston Bruins, (617) 523-3223; and New England Patriots (Sullivan Stadium, Foxboro), (508) 543-1776.

≈₿ Boston Children's Theatre

Call (617) 424-6634. Adults and children, $5 to $8.50.

See classic children's tales, such as *Aladdin and His Wonderful Lamp* and *Cinderella,* performed at venues in and around Boston and Cape Cod (most often at New England Life Hall in Copley Square, Boston). Call for a current schedule.

⁓ John F. Kennedy Library

Off Morrissey Blvd., next to U-Mass.-Boston, Dorchester; (617) 929-4523. Daily, 9-5. Closed major holidays. Adults, $5; 6-15, $1; under 6, free.

This I. M. Pei–designed museum/library, set on the waterfront, is the nation's memorial to President Kennedy. Featured is a 30-minute film about the president, along with a collection of personal items, letters, and family photographs, with special exhibits. The assassination is handled gently but matter-of-factly.

⁓ Franklin Park Zoo

Franklin Park, off Blue Hill Ave., Dorchester; (617) 442-4896. Daily, 9-5 (grounds close at 4:30). Adults, $5; 4-11, $2.50; under 4, free.

Just outside the city, this state-of-the-art zoo is something special. The centerpiece is a dazzling three-acre African Tropical Rainforest pavilion. A few of the other features are an aviary, a children's petting zoo, a barnyard area, and a waterfowl pond. Many scheduled special events include the annual "Zoo Bash," when Sesame Street characters join the fun with songs, shows, and lots of photo opportunities.

⁓ New England Sports Museum

100 CambridgeSide Place, CambridgeSide Galleria; (617) 78-SPORT. Mon.-Sat., 10-9:30; Sun., 12-6. Adults, $6; 4-7, $4.50.

Sports fanatics in your family might enjoy a visit to the Sports Museum, now located in the CambridgeSide Galleria shopping mall. You'll relive some of the greatest moments in New England sports history here, and pose beside life-size statues of Bobby Orr, Larry Bird, and Carl Yastrzemski. Watch the magic of Bob Cousy's fast-break and Ted Williams's perfect swing on film.

⁓ Bunker Hill Monument

Monument Ave., Charlestown; (617) 242-5641. Daily, 9-5. Free.

This towering obelisk marks the site of the first major battle of the American Revolution. Poised on the summit of Breed's Hill, this 220-foot monument was built to honor those who died on June 17, 1775. Older children will love climbing the 294 steps to the top; join them and you'll be rewarded with a great view of Boston, not to mention a good workout.

◊ U.S.S. *Constitution* and Museum

Charlestown Navy Yard, Charlestown; (617) 426-1812. Year-round,
daily, 9-5. Adults, $3; 6-16, $1.50; under 6, free.

A visit to *Old Ironsides* can be an intriguing experience for families.
The ship, originally launched in Boston in 1797, is the oldest commissioned warship afloat in the world. Climb aboard for a tour, guided by one
of the ship's active-duty sailors, and you'll learn all about life at sea. Kids
love peeking into the nooks and crannies and climbing the ladderlike
steps. Even better, at the Constitution Museum children can play sailor-
for-a-day: there are several interactive exhibits and even a computer simulator that allows you to be ship's captain.

◊ Bunker Hill Pavilion

55 Constitution Rd., Charlestown; (617) 241-7575. Daily, April-May,
9:30-4; June-Aug., 9:30-5; Sept.-Oct., 9:30-4. Adults, $3; under 16,
$1.50. Family rate (2 adults, up to 4 children age 16 and under), $8.

During your visit to the U.S.S. *Constitution* stop by the Bunker Hill
Pavilion. Catch "The Whites of Their Eyes," one of the liveliest half-hour
history lessons you're likely to encounter. This multimedia presentation
on the Battle of Bunker Hill is both entertaining and informative. You'll
find yourself rooting for the badly outnumbered colonists who fought
bravely until the ammunition was gone—an example of stubborn Yankee
pride in action.

◊ Museum of Transportation and Larz Anderson Park

15 Newton St., Brookline; (617) 522-6547. Park: year-round, daily.
Museum: early April–Aug., Wed.-Sun., 10-5; Sept.-Feb., Sat. and Sun.,
10-5. Adults, $4; 12 and under, $2.

Larz Anderson Park, located about 15 minutes west of Boston, is a
lovely urban oasis where you'll always find children somersaulting on the
vast lawn or skipping rocks on the pond. In winter, the rolling hills are a
favorite sledding spot for local kids, and you'll get a great view of the
Boston skyline in the distance. Don't leave without a visit to the Transportation Museum, also on the grounds. Kids can climb on cars and mo-
torcycles, test their wits on the scavenger hunt auto quiz, or try out an
antique bicycle. Special events might include a Model T Convention or
Ferrari Fun Day; special exhibits feature subjects like "Wild in the
Streets," a celebration of "muscle" cars enhanced with Beach Boys music
and surfing videos, and "100 Years of the American Automobile."

꩜ Puppet Showplace Theater
32 Station St., Brookline; (617) 731-6400. Sept.-June, Sat. and Sun., 1 and 3 P.M.; July and Aug., performances also on Wed. and Thurs. at 1 P.M. Tickets, $5.

Fairies, folk tales, fun, and fantasy all await you at Puppet Showplace Theater in Brookline (a short "T" ride from Boston). Shows are designed for children age five and up.

꩜ Tot Stop
41 Foster St., off Massachusetts Ave., E. Arlington; (617) 643-8687. Mon.-Thurs. and Sat., 9:30-5:30; Fri., 9:30-8. Closed Sun. Per child, all day, $6; family maximum, $14; siblings under 9 mo., free. Friday (Pizza Night), $2 after 5:30.

Tykes up to age six or so love Tot Stop, with three tiers of fun things to do and explore. This indoor play space has a sandbox, slides, a barn with lots of nooks and crannies, toys (including pedal tractors, always a hit), games, and areas propped for make-believe play. An area is gated off for toddlers. Friday night pizza parties are a fun way to spend an evening out with small fry; pay reduced admission and order a pizza. Mom and dad can get reacquainted while the little ones run around to their hearts' content. There's another, smaller Tot Stop at Museum Place in Salem; there, pizza night is Thursday and features are similar (it has a ball crawl, as well). The Salem Tot Stop is open seven days a week; call (508) 741-4913.

꩜ Blue Hills State Reservation and Trailside Museum
Rte. 138, 10 miles south of Boston, Milton; (617) 698-1802, (617) 333-0690. Museum: Wed.-Sun., 10-5. Adults, $3; children, $1.50; under 3, free.

Just south of Boston, this unique area boasts a series of massive granite domes (monadnocks) rising more than 635 feet. A network of trails leads to a panoramic overlook on Great Blue Hill. Some of these trails are rugged; if your group includes young children or inexperienced hikers, stick to the lowlands of this vast area. Houghton's Pond is a popular swimming spot, while Ponkapoag Pond is best for fishing. A trailside museum operated by the Massachusetts Audubon Society features the natural history of the Blue Hills, including native animals, a Native American wigwam, a crawl-through log, and more. Cross-country skiing in winter.

❄ Motion Odyssey Movie (M.O.M.)

Jordan's Furniture, 100 Stockwell Dr., Avon; (508) 580-1335. Mon.-Fri., 11-9; Sat., 10-9; Sun., 12-6. Adults, $4; children, $3 (40-inch height requirement).

Sounds odd, we admit. But this promotion-minded furniture store is drawing crowds with this attraction, best explained as a motion-simulated movie "ride." There's even a snack bar. Net profits from M.O.M. go to charity.

❄ Stone Zoo

149 Pond St., exits 34N and 35S off I-93, Stoneham; (617) 438-5100. Daily, 10-4. Adults, $2; children, $1; under 4, free.

Recently renovated, the Stone Zoo is much improved, and it's now a nice, inexpensive oasis for families. A short hop north of Boston on I-93, the zoo boasts a tropical rainforest exhibit with a huge aviary and a South American Grasslands exhibit featuring lovable llamas. Kids adore the polar bear exhibit—home of Major, the zoo's mascot—and the waterfowl at the wetlands exhibit. Plan your visit around one of the special events for children, such as the "Kids Run Wild" road race.

▶ RESTAURANTS

❄ Quincy Market

Faneuil Hall Marketplace, Merchants Row; (617) 242-5642.

Between the numerous food stalls and pushcart vendors you can find every imaginable foodstuff here. Some of it's great, some of it is just alright, but it all makes great grazing. Stay away if you hate crowds. Grab a table in the center courtyard, or sit outside on benches. Now, if you're looking for a real sit-down restaurant at Faneuil Hall, consider...

❄ Durgin Park

Faneuil Hall Marketplace; (617) 227-2038. Daily, lunch and dinner.

Touristy? Yes. But this has been a Boston landmark since 1827. You'll get real Yankee cooking here—pot roast, succotash, Indian pudding—all served family style. Not for shy types; you'll be seated at long tables next to other diners, and the waitstaff will give you a hard time if you don't finish your vegetables. At one time, the waitstaff was downright crabby, which some patrons adored and others apparently didn't; these days, Durgin Park is trying a more friendly approach.

≋ Serendipity 3
Faneuil Hall Marketplace; (617) 523-2339. Daily, lunch and dinner.

You'll have fun here, especially when you try to navigate the eclectic menu. Burgers, sandwiches, and finger food are the mainstays. Save room for dessert: Serendipity is famous for ice cream concoctions and other sinful goodies. The Victorian setting is fun, too. Best night to go: Thursday, when Bonaparte, our favorite magician, performs table-side feats. Now that's a treat.

≋ Hard Rock Cafe
131 Clarendon St.; (617) 424-7625. Daily, 11 A.M.–2 A.M.

Yeah, we know, it's not the only Hard Rock on the planet. But hey, the Boston venue of this chain is the only one billed as "Massachusetts Institute of Rock" (not to be confused with the other Massachusetts Institute). All the classic rock memorabilia you'd expect are here, along with good burgers and pie a la mode. If there's a preteen in your group, expect to spring for a T-shirt.

≋ Imperial Tea House
70 Beach St.; (617) 426-8439. Daily, 9 A.M.–2 A.M. Dim sum served 'til 3 P.M.

For children who love to eat with their fingers, we've got just the place. This airy restaurant in the heart of Chinatown is known for its dim sum, served at lunch. Choose whatever looks good—say, spicy shrimp or pork dumplings—then nibble happily 'til the next tempting cartful rolls by. You'll be charged per serving; most items are less than two dollars. Even the pickiest eaters should find something appealing.

≋ La Piccola Venezia
60 Salem St., North End; (617) 227-0765. Daily, 11:30-10.

It's tiny, homey, authentic, and the staff will treat you like family. What better way to get into the spirit of the North End? Italian restaurants come and go but this is a perennial favorite, offering good food at great prices. Such hard-to-find Italian specialties as salt cod, whelk, and tripe are listed on the blackboard, as well as "macaroni and gravy" (pasta and sauce) in several varieties.

≋ Pizzeria Regina
11½ Thatcher; (617) 227-0765. Daily, lunch and dinner; Sun., 2-11 P.M.

Not just a pizza place but a Boston landmark. Families have been coming here for more than 40 years to enjoy the thin-crust pizza and soft drinks by the pitcher. Regina's is now a chain, but locals agree that this is the only real Regina's, by far the best of the bunch. Another great place for pizza is Santarpio's, at 111 Chelsea St., near Logan Airport, in East Boston. Not the easiest place to find, but the pizza is out of this world. Call (617) 567-9468 for directions.

LEXINGTON AND CONCORD AREA

Prepare to soak up some 1775 spirit—and lots of history—when you retrace Paul Revere's famous ride. This is where the American Revolution began. As you stand on North Bridge, it seems you can still hear that first "shot heard 'round the world," and as you walk Battle Creek, you just might feel the presence of patriots long gone.

The historical landmarks are the big attractions in this area. But when children tire of history lessons, there are plenty of other things to do. Visit the top-notch Children's Discovery Museums in nearby Acton, hike to Thoreau's cabin on lovely Walden Pond, or canoe the calm waters of the Concord River. A visit to this area is a popular day trip from Boston, but if you come from that direction try to avoid morning and evening rush hour traffic, as it can be horrendous. In fact, locals joke that if Paul Revere were to make the ride today, he'd probably be delayed and opt to call John Hancock and Samuel Adams from his car phone. ("Sam? Hi, it's me, Paul. I'm stuck in traffic. The British are coming!") Or maybe he'd just send a fax.

ᲛᲒ Minuteman Statue and Battle Green

This is the spot where the events began in the early morning of April 19, 1775. The mounting tension between the British occupiers and the independence-seeking rebels finally erupted at a place now known as Battle Green. Leading the Minutemen onto the green was Captain John Parker, immortalized by the Minuteman Statue. Captain Parker's rallying cry: "Stand your ground, don't fire unless fired upon; but if they mean to have a war, let it begin here!"

ᲛᲒ Museum of Our National Heritage

33 Marrett Rd., Rtes. 2A and 4, Lexington; (617) 861-6560. Mon.-Sat., 10-5; Sun., 1-5. Free.

The focus here is on the development of the United States, with changing exhibits and films featuring the dramatic events and turning points that shaped our history.

⅍ Minuteman National Historical Park
Off Rte. 2A; (508) 369-6944. April-Dec., daily. Free.

This 750-acre park spans three towns: Lexington, Lincoln, and Concord. Stop wherever you like—there are several visitor's centers in the park, each with maps and helpful staff to guide you. (A good place to start is Battle Road Visitor's Center, run by the National Park Service, with exhibits, films, and a diorama of what happened that fateful day in 1775.) Be sure to visit the reconstructed North Bridge, where the shot heard 'round the world was fired.

⅍ The Wayside
455 Lexington Rd., Concord; (508) 369-6975. Daily, late June–early Sept. Tours: Tues., 1, 2:30, and 4 P.M.; Wed., Fri., and Sun., 1:15, 2:15, and 3:15. Fri.-Tues., 8:30-5. Adults, $1; 6 and under, free.

Follow Battle Road (Route 2A) into Concord, and you'll see a number of historic houses. Young readers will enjoy visiting The Wayside, the 19th-century home of Nathaniel Hawthorne, the Alcotts, and Margaret Sidney, author of the *Five Little Peppers* series. In nearby Orchard House, Louisa May Alcott wrote *Little Women.*

⅍ Sleepy Hollow Cemetery
Rte. 62, Bedford St., Concord.

Visit the gravesites of famous people, with some heavy hitters buried along Author's Ridge: they include Thoreau, Emerson, Hawthorne, and the Alcotts.

⅍ Walden Pond
Rte. 126, Concord.

Round out your trip to the Lexington and Concord area with a stop at Walden Pond, and you'll see why Henry David Thoreau (along with Don Henley) was so moved by its beauty. This freshwater kettle pond has been around a long time, dug out of the landscape by an Ice Age glacier. At the north end of the pond, you'll find a wooded walking path that will lead you to the site of Thoreau's cabin. This is where he lived and wrote from 1845 to 1847. Pack a lunch and bring your swimsuits—across the pond, in the 150-acre Walden Pond State Reservation, is a large picnic area and swimming beach.

⅍ Canoeing
Rte. 62, Main St., Concord; (508) 369-9438. Weekdays, $6.65/hr. or $26/day; weekends, $7.85/hr. or $36/day.

The calm, flat waters of the Concord River and its tributary the Sudbury are favorites for family canoeing. Stop by the put-in spot at Southbridge Boat House in Concord, where you can rent canoes by the hour or day.

⚜ Drumlin Farm Wildlife Sanctuary

South Great Rd., off Rte. 117, Lincoln; (617) 259-9807. Grounds open 9-5; closed Mon., except major holidays. Adults, $5; children, $3.50.

Drumlin Farm, owned by the Massachusetts Audubon Society, is a great back-to-nature escape. The 180-acre property is made up of pastures, fields, ponds, and woodlands. The best part is that farm animals live here, in several barns, as do wild animals native to the region. Special events include Harvest Days, Bird Seed Day, and school vacation week activities.

The Audubon Shop has lots of neat and also environmentally correct stuff, like binoculars, bird-feeders, games, and books.

⚜ Discovery Museums

177 Main St., Rte. 27, Acton; (508) 264-4200. During school year: Tues., Thurs., and Fri., 1-4:30; Sat. and Sun., 9-4:30. Children's Discovery Museum open 9-4:30 Wed., Science Discovery Museum open 1-6 Wed. Summer hours: Tues.-Sun., 9-4:30. Per person, $5; both museums, same day, $8; under 1, free.

What a find: two wonderful hands-on museums, right next door to each other in the town of Acton. This is no secret to local children, though. They love the cozy Children's Discovery Museum, housed in a 100-year-old Victorian. Best enjoyed by kids age one to eight, it has delightful things to explore everywhere, in rooms, hallways, even closets. Tots will like climbing aboard the Discovery Ship, constructing wondrous structures in the Lego room, setting off a roomful of chain reactions, and listening to the sounds of a humpback whale. There are 10 exhibit areas in all—an afternoon's worth of fun and learning.

Located behind the Children's Discovery Museum is the architecturally unique Science Discovery Museum, for kids age six and up. The spacious, colorful building is full of interactive science exhibits. Build dams and waterfalls in the Water Discovery Room, make patterns with sound waves, shout in the echo tube...there are hundreds of things to explore. Kids have so much fun they don't realize how much they're learning about science and technology.

∾ Lowell Heritage State Park and National Historical Park

Market Mills, Lowell; (508) 937-9300. Daily, 8:30-5.

Travel a maze of canalways on river barges or hop an antique trolley to the 19th-century mill complexes as you learn about life during the American Industrial Revolution. As you tour the restored textile mills, you'll meet the mill girls and canal workers who first set the revolution in motion. The American Industrial Revolution began when Frances Cabot Lowell brought the power loom design to the United States from England. Situated on the Merrimack River at Pawtucket Falls, the town of Lowell had enough waterpower to create a cloth manufacturing industry. Walk the Esplanade along the river, stop by Market Mills with its changing displays and shops, or attend one of the special family programs held throughout the summer.

∾ The Butterfly Place

120 Tyngsboro Rd., Westford; (508) 392-0955. Mid-April–Halloween, daily, 10-5. Per person, $5.

Your kids will be awestruck by nature's beauty here, surrounded by hundreds of colorful butterflies. This 3,100-square-foot atrium is a living museum of North American species. Watch them in action here, where you'll see the most activity on sunny days, when butterflies are busiest.

▶ RESTAURANTS

∾ Willow Pond

745 Lexington Rd., Rte. 2A, Concord; (508) 369-6529. Mon.-Sat., 11-11; Sun., 12-11.

What's a rowdy roadhouse like this doing in an upscale town like Concord? Well, for starters, it's serving interesting things like fried frog's legs and amazingly inexpensive boiled lobster dinners. Kids get a kick out of the decor—including stuffed wildlife specimens and World War I relics—and the laid-back atmosphere of the place. And the frog's legs. Promise you won't tell a soul about this area's best-kept dining secret.

∾ Michael's

208 Fitchburg Tpke., Concord; (508) 371-1114. Daily, 11:30-10.

This small, busy Italian place serves lotsa pasta—try the chicken-broccoli ziti—along with steaks, chicken, and salads. It's friendly, reliable, and the portions are large enough for sharing.

NORTH SHORE

Beautiful beaches, picturesque seaside towns, a colorful history—these elements make the North Shore a popular destination for families. Of course, some people drive 30 miles from Boston just to sample the delectable Ipswich clams.

Many visitors are attracted by Salem, the Witch City. If you're among them, you won't have to look hard to find traces of Salem's grim past. (Even its high school athletic teams are called the Salem Witches.) Salem has an official witch, Laurie Cabot, and museums that recount the events of the "Witch Hysteria" of 1692 in vivid detail.

Venture beyond Salem and you'll find nautical Marblehead, referred to as the Yachting Capital of the East and boasting a beautiful harbor; artistic Bearskin Neck in Rockport, home of the most-painted motif in America; two very different castles; and some of the best beaches in New England. You'll also find lots of magic.

⛄ Le Grand David and His Own Spectacular Magic Company
286 Cabot St., Beverly; (508) 927-3677. Year-round, shows every Sun. at 3 P.M. (doors open at 2:15). Adults, $10; 11 and under, $8.

Enter the beautifully restored Cabot Street Cinema Theater and leave reality behind. Le Grand David and his troupe will delight you with comedy, pageantry, and fast-paced fun. The 2.5-hour show will be a bit long for the very young, but school-aged children will enjoy figuring out how to pluck rabbits from the air and how to make someone levitate (especially useful if one has siblings). Sit up front if you can. More nice surprises are a hand-painted puppet theater with performing puppets, magicians' props on display, and clowns bearing goodies.

⛄ North Shore Music Theatre
Dunham Rd., Beverly; (508) 922-8500. Children's performances Mon.-Fri., 9:45 and 11:45 A.M. Ticket prices vary; usually around $6.

By night, Broadway revivals, pop singers, and comedians take center stage here. But by day, professional productions of children's plays and concerts are featured, such as *Peter and the Wolf, Snow White and the Seven Dwarfs,* and *Dinosaur Rock.* It's a theater in the round, so almost every seat is a good one.

❧ Lynch Park

55 Ober St., Beverly; (508) 922-0720. Memorial Day–Labor Day.

This waterfront park has it all: a small beach, two wooden playscapes (one for toddlers), picnic tables, a big grassy field for kite flying and Frisbee tossing, and a snack bar. (It features Dick & June's ice cream, the local favorite.) Family concerts are held here most summer weekends in front of the bandshell. Take a minute to meander, and admire the beautiful rose garden.

❧ Peabody & Essex Museum

East India Sq., Salem; (508) 745-9500. Mon.-Wed., Fri.-Sat., 10-5; Thurs., 10-9; Sun., 12-5. Adults, $6; 6-18, $3.50. Family rate: $15.

World-renowned collections of maritime art and history and of Asian and Pacific art and artifacts are housed here, making the Peabody Museum an intriguing place to visit. Children will enjoy the special events and programs geared toward them. Past programs have included a maritime music festival, Morris dancing and sea shanty performances, sailor's knot-tying demonstrations, kite making, and a Doll's Day event, based on the annual Japanese holiday. Call for a schedule of events.

❧ Harbor Sweets Chocolate Factory

85 Leavitt St., Salem; (508) 745-7648. Sept.-Nov. and before holidays, 8:30-4:30. (Best time to visit: before noon.)

We promise: this is the sweetest tour in town. See candy dippers create "Sweet Sloops," "Barque Sarah," and other favorites. And yes, there are free samples, which will only tempt you to take home a carload.

❧ Salem Witch Museum

Washington Sq., off Washington St., Salem; (508) 744-1692. Sept.-June, daily, 10-5; July and Aug., 10-7. Adults, $4; 6-14, $2.50.

The tour buses parked out front will clue you in—this is the place. Probably one of the oddest "museums" you'll ever visit, this multisensory presentation recreates the witch hysteria of 1692 with 13 stage sets, eerie music, and voice-overs. It draws no conclusions about the chilling events but asks visitors to "be the judge." Outside the museum, you'll notice a large statue of a figure that looks like a witch. It's not—it's Roger Conant, one of the first settlers of Salem, garbed in a flowing cape. Nonetheless, most kids prefer to think of him as a witch and willingly pose for pictures beside him.

How can you not like a place that implores you to "Stop in for a spell?"

⅋ Witch Dungeon Museum

16 Lynde St., Salem; (508) 744-9812. May-Nov., daily, 10-5. Adults, $4; 6-14, $2.50.

Featured here are a live reenactment of a witch trial and a guided tour of a recreated dungeon (and you thought the Witch Museum sounded creepy). It's pretty scary, not a good idea for small children.

⅋ Salem Wax Museum of Witches and Seafarers

Derby St., Salem; (508) 740-2929. July-Oct., daily, 10-6; Nov., Dec., April, and June, 10-4:30; Jan.-March, Sat. and Sun., 10-4:30. Adults, $4; under 14, $2.50.

Salem's newest contender for the title "Most Bewitching," this attraction explores the city's colorful past with 50 lifelike wax figures. Startlingly well-made, they're set in 13 tableaux, enhanced by music, sound, and lighting effects. Adding to the appeal of Salem Wax Museum are an interactive area where kids can learn how wax figures are made, make a grave-stone rubbing from headstone replicas, try out a 17th-century jail cell, and learn to tie nautical knots.

⅋ House of Seven Gables

54 Turner St., Salem; (508) 744-0991. Year-round, except first 10 days of Jan., Thanksgiving, Christmas, and New Year's Day. Daily, 9:30-5 except Thurs., 9:30-8. Adults, $6.50; 6-12, $3; 13-17, $4. Combination ticket with Pioneer Village: adults, $9.50; 6-12, $5; 13-17, $6.50.

Of interest to older children and adults who have enjoyed Nathaniel Hawthorne's classic novel, this tour includes several houses: the "Gables" (1668); Hawthorne's birthplace (1750); Hathaway House (1682); Retire Beckett House (1655), and period gardens. A museum shop and coffee shop are also on the grounds. The site is not stroller accessible; bring a backpack for baby.

⅋ Salem Willows

173 Fort Ave., Salem; (508) 745-0251. April-Sept., Mon.-Sat., 10-9; Sun., 11-9. Free.

It may be a little scruffy around the edges these days, but how can you not appreciate a place that claims to be the original home of saltwater taffy? This seaside park, shaded with willow trees, has a carnival-type charm all its own. Play skeeball or have your fortune told by a mechanical gypsy in the old-fashioned arcade, or take a ferry ride around Salem Harbor. There are kiddie rides for small fry, including tiny tugboats and a 1920s carousel. And then there's the food. You could bring your own healthful picnic, but why miss an excuse to dig into fried clams, cotton candy, or—for the truly adventurous—a chop suey sandwich. Or stake out a picnic table and indulge in some classic New England cuisine: a lobster roll and onion rings, washed down with a raspberry-lime rickey.

⛵ Pioneer Village

Forest River Park, West St., Salem; (508) 745-0525. Mon.-Sat., 10-5; Sun., 12-5. Adults, $4.50; 13-17, $3.50; 6-12, $2.50. Family rate, $12. Combination tickets available at House of Seven Gables.

Living history museums are all the rage these days, and this is America's oldest. It's an authentic recreation of Salem in 1630 when Salem was a Puritan fishing village, some 60 years before the witchcraft hysteria. Early buildings, gardens, and animals create the feel of life in the 17th century; you'll be guided by costumed interpreters and see demonstrations of crafts and day-to-day activities of the time. Special events are held throughout the summer. Combine your visit with some outdoor fun (swimming, picnicking) at Forest River Park, adjacent to Pioneer Village.

⛵ Salem Trolley

Essex St. mall at National Park Service Visitor's Center; (508) 744-5469. April-Nov., hourly, 10-5; July-Oct., every half-hour, 10-5. Adults, $8; 5-12, $3; 12-18,$7. Family rate (2 adults, 2 kids), $20.

Hop the trolley for a one-hour tour of the city's attractions. Salem Trolley stops at several of them, including museums, the House of Seven Gables, Salem Willows, and Pickering Wharf. Get on and off as often as you like.

⛵ Kid's Cove

Humphrey St., Swampscott. Open 'til sunset.

This large wooden playscape is a local favorite, open to the public. It's a great destination when kids need to stretch their legs and parents need a break from playing tourist. Park along Humphrey Street and bring a picnic lunch (or pick up sandwiches at a nearby deli). Rest rooms (usually open) are located in the adjacent field house.

⛵ Jeremiah Lee Mansion

16 Washington St., Marblehead; (617) 631-1069.

As this book goes to press, the Marblehead Historical Society is developing a children's museum within this 1768 Georgian mansion. Once the home of a wealthy shipowner, its claim to fame is the fact that presidents George Washington, John Adams, and Andrew Jackson slept here.

Exhibits geared to kids will include Indian and colonial artifacts and period toys, clothing, and utensils from the 1880s. A hands-on approach is
planned that sounds promising. Combine your visit with a walk around
Marblehead's Old Town, heading toward the busy harbor on Front Street.
(See "Scenic Strolls," below.)

☙ Endicott Park

*Forest St., Danvers; (508) 774-0864, 774-6518. Year-round, 9 A.M.-
dark.*

This former estate property, now owned by the town of Danvers, is
another great place to play. The 164-acre recreation area was the site of a
working farm (Endicott Estate) during the early 20th century. The original buildings are still there, but the attraction for kids is a large, inviting
playscape. Wander over to the children's barnyard and meet horses, sheep,
and turkeys (at last visit—each time there's a new addition). You'll also
find walking and fitness trails and a fishing pond. Rest rooms are located
in the carriage house across from the barn.

☙ Myopia Polo

*Rte. 1A, exit 20N off Rte. 129 North, Hamilton; (508) 356-7797. Late
May–Oct., Sun., 3 P.M. (grounds open at 1 for picnickers). Adults, $5; 12
and under, free.*

Bring the kids to a polo match? Are we joking, or what? Not at all.
While polo's image is genteel, the sport itself is a rough-and-tumble
competition in which bumping is allowed and players traverse the field
atop 1,000-pound horses traveling at 30 miles an hour. There's plenty of
action, and the horses (called ponies) are beautiful. To get into the spirit
bring along a gourmet picnic (this isn't the place for fast-food cartons) and
cheer the Myopia team from the grassy sidelines. At half-time, go out on
the field and help tromp down the divots of turf kicked up by the horses
(kids love to do this). A different—and pleasant—way to spend a Sunday
afternoon.

☙ Wenham Museum

*132 Main St., Rte. 1A, Wenham; (508) 468-2377. Daily, 11-4; Sat.,
1-4; Sun., 2-5. Adults, $3; 6-14, $1.*

This gem of a museum—actually the Claflin-Richards House (c. 1660)
and connected buildings—houses some exhibits of special interest to
children. These include a world-famous doll collection (more than 5,000
dolls!), toys, and incredibly intricate dollhouses. Special events and exhibits have included a teddy bear parade, a hands-on blocks exhibit, a kite
exhibit, and a demonstration of how to turn "junk" into sculpture.

Call ahead for current information. Have lunch or tea across the street at the Wenham Tea House and make it a really special afternoon.

✿ Crane Beach and Castle Hill

Argilla Rd. off Rte. 1A, Ipswich; (508) 356-4354.

With 1,400 acres and five miles of white sand, Crane Beach is considered by many to be the North Shore's best. Swaying sea oats, graceful dunes, and sailboats bobbing in the distance are just a few of the features that make Crane Beach so popular. Although the water never seems to get warm, children (and warm-blooded adults) don't seem to mind. But you will mind the dreaded greenhead, a pesky fly that often infests the area in—wouldn't you know it?—midsummer. The Crane Reservation Staff posts a greenhead warning at the gate if the flies are bad, so once you pay the nonrefundable (and stiff) parking fee, you take your chances. Bathhouses, a snack bar, and lifeguards are on the premises.

Up on the hill you'll see Castle Hill, a 59-room English Stuart-style mansion, built for plumbing magnate Richard T. Crane in 1927. You can tour the castle or, even better, attend one of the children's events scheduled during the summer. These include lawn concerts, an Independence Day celebration, a Halloween party, and Christmas programs. Call (508) 356-7774 for details.

✿ Goodale Orchards

Argilla Rd. off Rte. 1A, Ipswich; (508) 356-5366. Mid-May–Dec., daily, 9-6. Open Sat. and Sun. in April.

A trip to Ipswich wouldn't be complete without a visit to Goodale's. Besides selling one of the world's best treats (a fresh cider donut with a cup of just-pressed cider), Goodale Orchards offers pick-your-own produce. Pick your own strawberries from mid-June through July. Raspberries are ready to be picked in July, and blueberries are ripe from mid-July through mid-August. (Dates vary due to weather and crop conditions.) In the fall, pick a peck of apples and select a potential jack-o'-lantern from the piles of pumpkins. You can also watch cider being pressed or take a free hayride through the orchard. Kids love meeting the farm's animals, including horses, goats, turkeys, and Vietnamese pot-bellied piglets. Check out the goodies in Goodale's barn store, featuring farm-grown produce, cider, preserves, cheese, and delicious fresh-baked pies.

✿ New England Alive

163 High St., Rtes. 1A and 133, Ipswich; (508) 356-7013. Daily, May-Oct., Mon.-Fri., 9:30-5; Sat. and Sun., 9:30-6. Open April-Nov., weather permitting. Adults, $5; 2-12, $3; under 2, free.

Stroke a scaly snake, nuzzle a baby chick, or feed a kid goat from the palm of your hand. This small petting farm is a favorite with North Shore children and a fun destination for a picnic. Meet such native New England wildlife as a bobcat, red fox, coyote, black bear, and more. There's also a collection of native and exotic snakes. Most of the animals here were found injured and were brought to owner Lyle Jensen to be nursed back to health. Jensen gives informational demonstrations, too, and will happily chat about any of the residents here.

⅋ Massachusetts Audubon Society

87 Perkins Row, Ipswich; (508) 887-9264.

This site is Massachusetts Audubon's largest sanctuary, covering about 2,000 acres of meadow, swamp, islands, ponds, and part of the Ipswich River, along with an observation tower. It offers a great selection of family programs; a recent spring line-up included "Nature Detectives" for kids six to eight; "Sense of Wonder Walks" for tots and their families; a bat-house building workshop and a maple-sugaring tour. All programs are held at the Ipswich River Sanctuary Barn. Preregistration is required; call for information and fees.

⅋ North American Wolf Foundation

Wolf Hollow, Rte. 133, Ipswich; (508) 356-0216. Sat. and Sun, 1-5; presentations at 1:30 and 3:30. Adults, $3.50; children, $2.

Did the wolf get a bad rap in "Little Red Riding Hood?" Those who study them think wolves are generally misunderstood—here's a chance to learn about gray wolves and their habits in their natural environment.

⅋ Willowdale State Forest

Linebrook Rd., Ipswich.

This 2,400-acre forest has hiking trails, both marked and unmarked, and canoeing on the Ipswich River. Canoes may be rented from Foote Bros., Topsfield Rd., Ipswich; (508) 356-9771.

⅋ Bradley Palmer State Park

Rte. 1, Topsfield; (508) 887-5931.

Take a respite from the beach as well as the summer heat at this pleasant, relatively undeveloped state park. Hike along woodsy trails (the park has 20 miles of them marked) and enjoy a picnic among the pines. In summer, a giant fountain provides a place for kids to splash and play. Adults watch the action from a grassy slope nearby. This is a popular and very beautiful site for cross-country skiing in winter.

❄ Wingaersheek Beach

Exit 13 off Rte. 128, Gloucester; (508) 283-1601. Memorial Day–Labor Day.

Looking for a perfect family beach? Wingaersheek has sand bars and warm, shallow inlets. Small children will be content to plop right down in the warm water, while older ones will enjoy rock climbing and swimming in the calm waters. Arrive early (by nine on summer weekends) to secure a parking space. Eats are available at the snack bar. Other beaches to try in Gloucester: Good Harbor Beach and Stage Fort Park. The latter has a beach that's small but offers a playground area.

❄ Hammond Castle Museum

80 Hesperus Ave., off Rte. 127, Gloucester; (508) 283-2080. May–July 4th, Tues.-Sun., 10-5; July 4th–Oct., daily, 10-5; Nov.-May, Sat. and Sun., 10-5. (Call first; special events may affect hours.) Adults, $5.50; 6-12, $3.50.

Like a fairy tale come to life, Hammond Castle has a moat and drawbridge, parapets and turrets, even an indoor reflecting pool. This recreated version was built in 1926 as the home of inventor John Hayes Hammond, Jr., and houses his unique collection of Roman, medieval, and Renaissance art—not to mention a huge, working, 8,200-pipe organ. Children especially enjoy the tiny suits of armor (man size, in their time) and the winding passageways. (The castle is not stroller accessible, so bring a backpack for baby.) Visit on a rainy day for an added element of spookiness, or during Halloween week when the castle becomes a truly awesome haunted house.

❄ The Schooner *Adventure*

Harbor Loop off Rte 127N (next to Gloucester Marine Railways Corp., Gloucester; (508) 281-8079. Tues.-Sun., 10-4. Admission, $3; $5 maximum for families.

Come aboard this 121-foot schooner and get a taste of shipboard life without leaving the berth. Built in nearby Essex in 1926, the two-masted *Adventure* is the real thing, complete with a large spoked wheel, tiny bunks, and shipboard galley. Kids can play captain at the wheel, poke around nooks and crannies, and learn seaworthy skills like knot tying and sail rigging.

❄ Whale Watching

Gloucester is a great place to get out on the water and learn about the gentle giants. Although the whales don't always cooperate, local cruise companies claim sighting records of over 90 percent, and some guarantee you'll see whales—that's how confident they are. On-board naturalists provide narration. Children—always the first to spot a whale's tail in the distance—squeal with delight as playful humpbacks leap into the air or pass near the boat. Bring a pair of binoculars, and bring warmer clothes than you think will be necessary (it's always cool out there) and rubber-soled shoes. Cruises leave daily from Gloucester's waterfront. Companies to call: Cape Ann Whale Watch, Rose's Wharf, 415 Main St., (508) 283-5110; Captain Bill's Whale Watch, Captain Carlos Restaurant, 33 Harbor Loop, (508) 283-6995; Seven Seas Whale Watch, Seven Seas Wharf, Rte. 127, (508) 283-1776; and Yankee Whale Watch, 75 Essex Ave., 1-800-WHALING.

✂ The Paper House

52 Pigeon Hill St. (look for the sign on Rte. 127), Pigeon Cove in Rockport; (508) 546-2629. July and Aug., daily, 10-5 or by appointment. Adults, $1; 6-14, $.50; under 6, free.

Kids are really into recycling these days, and this 1922 house is a recycler's dream home. The entire cottage—even the furniture—is made from old newspapers, rolled and varnished. A half-hour spent at this odd abode should inspire some interesting projects at home.

✂ Halibut State Park

Gott Ave. off Rte. 127, Rockport; (508) 546-2997. Daily, May-Oct., sunrise-sunset.

Pack a picnic basket, don your sneakers, and enjoy this beautiful spot overlooking Ipswich Bay. Once a granite quarry, this is now a prime spot for tide pooling and blueberry picking. Brochures will direct you on a self-guided walking tour.

✂ Maudslay State Park

Curzon's Mill Rd., Newburyport; (508) 465-7223. Year-round.

Once a private estate, this 450-acre park features 16 miles of hiking and nature trails. In summer, the Children's Theater-in-Residence performs outdoors here; two recent innovative pieces were *Black Elk Speaks* and *Punch and Judy's New World Almanac.* Watch for the summer arts festival, with plays, music, face painting, hayrides, and such regional big-name troupes as Vermont's Bread & Circus Puppets. Call (508) 465-2572 for a schedule of events.

⚜ Parker River Wildlife Refuge

Plum Island (take Water St. to Plum Island Tpke., then turn right to Sunset Blvd.), Newburyport; (508) 465-5753. Year-round, daily, one-half hour before sunrise to one-half hour after sunset. Parking fee, $5; $1 for visitors walking or biking.

Birdwatchers flock to this tranquil spot, where more than 300 species have been sighted. (Peak migration is from March to early June.) The refuge also offers miles of beach that's great for strolling, though too rough for swimming, and nature trails. The two-mile Hellcat Swamp trail is a standout; a boardwalk takes you past varied habitats of birds and other wildlife. Branch off from the trail to an observation tower where an easy climb will reward you with sweeping vistas of the marsh.

Special Note: The beaches and dunes area here is sometimes closed, to allow piping plovers and least terns to rest in peace. The trails will still be open.

⚜ Salisbury Beach

Rte. 1-A, exit 58 off I-95, Salisbury. Rides open Memorial Day–Labor Day, 12-10; arcades and shops open Memorial Day–Labor Day, 10 A.M.– midnight, and Labor Day–Dec. with reduced hours.

Since the 1800s, this little strip of beach has attracted fun seekers and, more recently, folks en route to Maine looking for a break from the car. One of the last of the seaside amusement parks, and suffering from a seedy reputation for a few years, Salisbury Beach is being rediscovered as a family-friendly destination. And it should be: it has a beach, kiddie rides, arcade games, and, thrilling for tots, a giant inflatable clown you can bounce on. (Find him at Pirate Fun Park, one of the family-run businesses that predominate here.) To go along with these pursuits, of course, the right treats are essential, like fried dough, homemade fudge, fried clams, and ice cream. Wednesday is Kiddie's Day, when children-only discounts are offered; Friday nights, there are fireworks, and Sundays, you're likely to see strolling musicians, a puppet show, or a petting zoo.

⚜ Scenic Strolls—Marblehead Harbor and Bearskin Neck

Marblehead's scenic harbor is a sightseer's delight. Park your car in the waterfront lot on Front Street and explore the winding streets of quaint Old Town. Crocker Park, off Front Street, offers a great view of Marblehead Harbor. On weekends, watch sailing regattas from Castle

Rock. Marbleheaders so love to sail that some continue to do so all winter; the sport is appropriately called "frostbiting."

Rockport was a sleepy fishing village until artists discovered it after the Civil War. Today, Rockport's Bearskin Neck is a thriving arts center. Even if you've never visited Bearskin Neck before, chances are it will look familiar: the fisherman's shanty overlooking Rockport Harbor, called Motif #1, has been depicted by artists more than any other building in the United States. Plan to eat in one of the casual-but-good seafood restaurants overlooking the harbor.

RESTAURANTS

☆ Woodman's

121 Main St., Rte. 133, Essex; (508) 768-6451. Daily, in season, 11-10.

Just as much as Filene's Basement is famous for shopping, Woodman's is famous for clams. Billing itself as the birthplace of the fried clam, Woodman's also offers steamers, lobster-in-the-rough, chowder, and other (mostly fried) seafood. Noisy, rustic, and self-serve, this is the place most North Shore tots go for their first restaurant meal (prop the car seat on the booth). One steamer clam can keep baby amused for hours.

☆ Prince Restaurant

517 Broadway, Rte. 1, Saugus; (617) 233-9950. Sun.-Thurs., 11-11; Sat., 11-midnight.

Located on Route 1 north of Boston, the Prince is hard to miss—its facade features a giant leaning tower. (Route 1 is not known for understatement.) Inside, the place is massive, as are the servings of pasta and made-to-order pizzas. You can tell they love kids: children's shows featuring Calvin the Clown are presented four times a week. Calvin also pops up frequently during school vacation weeks. (Hours vary, so it's best to call first.) Reservations are encouraged.

☆ Bonkers Fun House Pizza

Lowell St., Peabody; (508) 535-8355. Sun.-Thurs., 10:30-8:30; Fri. and Sat., 10:30-9:30.

Is this a restaurant or an amusement park? Both, actually, but we can guess which category will delight the young ones in your party. There's a small Ferris wheel, a carousel, arcade games, a miniature train, a mechanical elephant, and more. The food is just as much fun—all the kid-faves like pizza, hot dogs, and frozen yogurt. Not the most romantic place in town, but then, you may get a moment to yourselves while the kids are happily immersed in the action.

❦ Winter Island Grill

50 Winter Island Rd., off Fort St., Salem; (508) 744-0203. Daily, April-Oct., 7 A.M.-9 P.M.; Fri.-Sat., 7 A.M.-10 P.M.

On a warm evening in summer or fall, this is a great place to unwind. The restaurant itself isn't much to look at—it's a concrete block clam shack, formerly an airplane hangar—but the view from Salem Neck is spectacular. Kids can climb a grassy hill or explore the small, rocky beach while the grown-ups linger over dinner. (You'll probably want to eat outside, not in.) All this, and the food is very good—including beer-battered fried shrimp, fried clams, grilled fish, lobster, steamers, seafood rolls, grilled chicken, and burgers. There's also a makeshift raw bar (on weekends) and a children's menu.

SOUTH SHORE AND SOUTH OF BOSTON

Why make a stop when you're halfway to Cape Cod from Boston? For most families, the answer is Plymouth Rock. Sooner or later, nearly every child is carted to the spot where, in the autumn of 1620, the pilgrims first set foot in the New World.

Unfortunately, not much remains of this rock that seems giant size in the minds of school children. Indeed, it once was giant—over 3,000 pounds of Plymouth Rock have been chipped away by tourists. Today the rock is protected, and much of it remains underground.

Happily, there's more to Plymouth than a mostly buried rock. Plimoth Plantation is a favorite destination, and the *Mayflower II* awaits. Set aside time to visit some other South-of-Boston attractions, too, including a tiny town filled with a host of unique museums and 2,000 toy trains.

❦ Plimoth Plantation

Rte. 3A, Plymouth; (508) 746-1622. Pilgrim Village: April-Nov., daily, 9-5. Wampahoag Homesite: April-Nov., daily, 9-5. Admission (includes Plimoth Plantation, Wampahoag Homesite, Craft Center, and Mayflower II): *adults, $18.50; 5-12, $11; under 5, free.*

If you jumped into a time machine and set the dial to "Plymouth Colony, 17th Century," you'd be zapped to a place like this. Plimoth Plantation is no cutesy Pilgrim Theme Park—it's a living museum, peopled by folks posing as real Pilgrims to recreate life in the Plymouth

Colony. Portraying characters based on actual Pilgrims—each carefully researched by the Plantation—the Pilgrims perform the chores of every-day life in 1627. As in real life, chores change with the seasons. Busy as they are, the Pilgrims take time to chat with visitors. They're really good at staying in character, too; if your child asks them about Nintendo or even Barbie dolls, they'll act totally clueless. Of course, kids love this.

Also on the grounds is the Wampahoag Homesite, where you'll see Indians (portrayed by Native Americans) perform their daily tasks in a recreated setting. Seeing these two very different cultures presented side by side provides a history lesson your children won't forget. The Craft Center features demonstrations of pottery making, furniture building, basket weaving, or cloth weaving. Don't miss the museum shop, with its good selection of children's books, craft kits, and Pilgrim-themed paraphernalia.

ᘓ Mayflower II
State Pier, Plymouth Harbor; (508) 746-1622. April-Nov., daily, 9-5; July and Aug., 9-7. Mayflower II *only: adults, $5.75; 5-12, $3.75.*

Berthed at the State Pier in Plymouth, the *Mayflower II* is Plimoth Plantation's full-scale reproduction of the ship that carried the Pilgrims in 1620. Climb aboard the gangway and you'll meet *Mayflower* passengers, realistically portrayed by Plimoth Plantation staffers. The stories they tell about the hardships of the voyage will capture your attention and make an impression on your kids that no textbook could match.

ᘓ Plymouth National Wax Museum
16 Carver St., Plymouth (across the street from Plymouth Rock); (508) 746-6468. Mar.-Nov., daily, 9-5. Adults, $5; 5-12, $2.

Wax museums tend to be a little creepy, maybe because of the deathly pallor of the characters' faces, and this one is no exception. But it is educational—sort of—depicting the Pilgrim story through 27 lifelike scenes. Special lighting, sound effects, and animation add to the experience; a good rainy-day activity.

ᘓ Cranberry World Visitor's Center
Water St., Plymouth; (508) 747-2350. May-Nov., daily, 9:30-5. Free.

If your kids are world-class juice drinkers, they probably help keep this place in business. Sponsored by Ocean Spray Cranberries, Inc., Cranberry World is filled with exhibits tracing the history and development of the cranberry industry. (If you've driven around this area, you may have noticed some scarlet fields—those are cranberry bogs.) You'll see antique and modern harvesting tools and machinery and learn everything you ever wanted to know (and probably more) about this native American fruit. Children will enjoy sampling the numerous cranberry beverage combinations.

⚛ Jenney Grist Mill

Town Brook Park at Jenney Pond, Plymouth; (800) 564-1636, (508) 747-3715. Memorial Day–Labor Day, 9-9; Labor Day–Memorial Day, 10-5. Adults, $2.50; children, $2 (includes free bag of corn meal and a postcard).

This recreated grist mill operates the same way the original did more than 300 years ago, using water power to produce corn meal. Watch the milling process, then wander aound the little cluster of shops. The Gourmet Ice Cream Shop definitely merits a visit.

⚛ Plymouth Beach

Rte. 3, Plymouth.

Right on the open ocean, this 3.5-mile, sandy beach offers views of Saquish Neck to the northeast and Manomet Bluffs to the southeast. Plymouth Beach has lifeguards, concessions, and a bathhouse.

⚛ Duxbury Beach

Rte. 3A to Rte. 139 N., Canal St., Duxbury. Memorial Day–Labor Day, 8-8.

Probably the nicest beach in the area, this five-mile stretch of sand is privately owned but leased to the town. It's clean, well maintained, and alcohol-free. Lifeguards are posted; bathhouses, a concession stand, and a luncheonette are on the grounds.

⚛ A&D Toy-Train Village

49 Plymouth St., Middleborough; (508) 947-5303. Year-round, Fri.-Mon., 11-5; July, Aug., and Dec., daily, 11-5. Open during Massachusetts public school vacations and holidays, except Easter, July 4th, Thanksgiving, and Christmas Day. Christmas Festival from mid-Nov.–first week in Jan. Adults, $5; 4-12, $3.50.

There's a certain magic about toy trains; they bring out the little kid in everyone. This charming, family-run museum celebrates the toy train with more than 2,000 on exhibit. Some are strictly for looking, including models made of candy, china, and lead crystal. And, there are 52 operating trains, in seven gauges. Children love pushing the buttons (a number of trains are visitor-activated) to set the toy trains in motion. Plan to spend an hour or so here, with a stop at the gift shop. Special children's days and theme weekends are scheduled, including a very nice Christmas display; call ahead for information. If you're bringing a toddler, ask if the "little tykes" ride-on train will be operating.

᪲ Nantasket Beach

Nantasket Ave., Rte. 228 exit off Rte. 2, Hull; (617) 925-4905. Year-round.

This three-mile stretch of fine, hard-packed sand draws crowds from all over the Boston area and the South Shore. Swimmers, sun worshipers, surfers (there's often a pounding surf), joggers, shell seekers, and, of course, beach-loving families congregate here. Bathhouses and refreshments are available, and lifeguards are posted. At the mainland end of the beach is the Carousel Under the Clock.

᪲ Carousel Under the Clock

George Washington Blvd., Nantasket Beach, Hull; (617) 925-0472. Daily, May-Sept., 10-10. Per ride, $1.50.

Paragon Park, Hull's landmark amusement park, is long gone. But happily its 1928 carousel remains. Enjoy.

᪲ Hull Lifesaving Museum

1117 Nantasket Ave., Hull; (617) 925-LIFE. Year-round, Wed.-Sun., 12-5. Adults, $3; 5-17, $1.50.

Quick, put on a Coast Guard uniform and hop in the dinghy to rescue your friends...at this hands-on museum, kids learn what rescuers did when ships and boats were in trouble off the shores of Hull (at one time, the only entrance to Boston Harbor). Children can climb to the loft and talk to each other using telegraph keys in the radio room, maneuver boats and blocks over a floor map of Boston Harbor, or make signal code flags out of construction paper. Throughout the year special demonstrations are held—children might be asked to go for a mock rescue ride or to pull the ropes in on a safety buoy.

Special Note: A free shuttle service operates from Nantasket Pier and the carousel to Hull Village attractions, including the Lifesaving Museum. The shuttle runs July 4th–Labor Day from 11:30 to 5:30. Call (617) 925-LIFE for information.

᪲ Myles Standish State Forest

Rtes. 3, 44, and 58, South Carver; (508) 866-2526.

This 15,000-acre preserve is a beautiful spot for a picnic. Enjoy an after-lunch hike or swim (at College and Fearings ponds) or, provided you bring the gear, go fishing or camping.

~ Wompatuck State Reservation

Rte. 228, Hingham; (508) 749-7160.

This 3,000-acre state park offers hiking, fishing, and camping. Don't be surprised if you share the trails with horses—this is a popular place for trail riding.

~ Hiking

In addition to the destinations mentioned above, this area offers some delightful places to hike. Family favorites are: South Shore Natural Science Center, Jacob's Lane, Norwell, offering nature trails (including a trail for the visually disabled), (508) 659-2559; and World's End Reservation, Martin's Lane, Hingham, designed by Frederick Law Olmsted, (508) 749-5780.

~ Boat Cruises

Catch a codfish, spot a whale, or just relax aboard one of the excursion boats that cruise out of Plymouth Harbor. Or, cruise from Hull to Long Wharf in downtown Boston, or to George's Island, Boston's most popular harbor island. For information, call these companies: Captain John Boats (deep-sea fishing, whale watching), departing from Town Wharf, Plymouth, (508) 746-2643; Cape Cod Cruises (Plymouth Harbor cruises, sunset cruises), departing from Mayflower State Pier, (508) 747-2400; Massachusetts Whale Watching (whales, seabirds, ecology), departing from Center Town Wharf, Plymouth, (508) 833-0181; or Bay State Cruise Company, (Hull to Boston, Hull to George's Island, Harbor Islands, whale watching), departing from Nantasket Pier and other sites in Hull, (617) 723-7800.

~ Kendall Whaling Museum

27 Everett St., Sharon; (617) 784-5642. Tues.-Sat., 10-5. Closed major holidays. Adults, $2; children, $1; under 5, free.

Inspired by your whale-watch trip? Here you'll find nine galleries of maritime artifacts and memorabilia, from paintings to navigational instruments. Most interesting for kids are the ship models, figureheads, and whaling gear.

~ Wonder Museum

26 Chestnut St., Foxborough; (508) 543-1184. Tues.-Sat., 10-5; Sun., 1-5. Closed holidays. Admission, $3.

The wonders of science, art, math, and nature are presented here, in a lively, participatory style. A complex pendulum, a hot-air balloon, a walk-in kaleidoscope, an anatomy room, and a talking mynah bird (Max) are highlights. You'll also find a toddler room and special events and exhibits.

RESTAURANTS

☜ Isaac's on the Waterfront

114 Water St., Plymouth; (508) 830-0001. Daily, 11:30-11.

No question about it, this is the place to go in Plymouth. The view can't be beat, with the *Mayflower II* on the right and Plymouth's fishing fleet on the left. Virtually every table at this contemporary, multilevel restaurant has a view. (In good weather, head for the outdoor deck.) Of course, fresh seafood is featured on the menu—it's good, and not pricey. Chicken, beef, and pasta dishes (try the fettucine Neptune) round out the menu, and a children's menu is offered.

☜ The Clam Box

789 Quincy Shore Dr., Quincy; (617) 773-6677. Daily, March-Nov., 11 A.M.–midnight.

This glorified clam shack is a local institution. It draws throngs of beach goers from Wollaston Beach, across the street, and regulars who've been coming here for a clam fix for more than 20 years. Forget the umbrellaed tables outside—too noisy—and head in to the atrium-style dining area, to indulge in tasty fried clams, lobster rolls, shish kabobs, Greek salads, even fried oysters and (gasp!) fried lobster. Ice cream and fried dough, too, if you really want to send that cholesterol count through the roof. (At least they use vegetable oil in the Fryolators.)

NEW BEDFORD AND FALL RIVER AREA

About an hour south of Boston, this region has a colorful past. New Bedford was once the Whaling Capital of the World, and its revitalized waterfront offers plenty of evidence—from sea captains' homes to Seaman's Bethel, the mariner's chapel described in Herman Melville's *Moby Dick.* He wrote of the city as home to "patrician-like" houses and "opulent" parks and gardens. "All these brave houses and flowery gardens came up from the Atlantic, Pacific, and Indian Oceans," he wrote, "One and all they were harpooned and dragged up hither from the bottom of the sea." Although the idea of killing whales is repugnant today, the whaling industry made New Bedford quite prosperous in the 19th century. Now, the city is a major commercial fishing port, but making one's fortune as a fisherman is a lot tougher. The Whaling Museum is the town's most popular attraction, and many visitors find that New Bedford's revitalized downtown is a nice place to knock around.

Fall River, on the Rhode Island border, was once a mill town, made famous by the Lizzie Borden ax-murder case. (Did she or didn't she? Scholars are still debating this one.) Today, factory-outlet stores are the big draw—along with the World War II navy ships at Battleship Cove. Whatever you discover here, you'll most likely be surprised at how much this "untouristy" area offers to those who seek it out.

⚒ Whaling Museum

18 Johnny Cake Hill, New Bedford; (508) 997-0046. Daily, 9-5; Sun., 1-5; July and Aug., daily, 9-5; Sun., 11-5. Adults, $3.50; 6-14, $2.50.

New Bedford's intriguing past is revealed in this nifty museum. Children love climbing aboard the *Lagoda,* a half-scale replica of a square-rigged whaling ship. (At 89 feet long, it's the largest ship model in the world.) The museum also has an impressive collection of scrimshaw. You'll marvel at the intricate detail of these designs, engraved on the teeth of sperm whales or on pieces of whalebone. Whalemen usually whittled these as gifts for their mothers, wives, or sweethearts. The display "Down to the Sea for Fish" chronicles the tough life of men who fish for a living; "Windows on Centre Street" will point you toward other whaling-related sites along the waterfront area, on a walking tour through historic New Bedford.

⚒ New Bedford Fire Museum

Bedford St., New Bedford; (508) 992-2162. Memorial Day–Labor Day, Mon.-Fri., 9:30-3:30. Adults, $2; 6-16, $1; under 6, free.

This fire museum is even more child-friendly than most. Downstairs, you'll find (surprisingly) a 1930s Barnum & Bailey circus miniature. Upstairs, there's a fire fighter's pole to slide down, and firemens' helmets, boots, and coats to try on, a bell to ring, and (with parental supervision) real fire trucks to climb aboard. Memorabilia dates back to the early 1900s.

⚒ Battleship *Massachusetts*

Exit 5 off I-95, Battleship Cove, Fall River; (508) 678-1100. Year-round, daily, 9-5; Sat. and Sun., 10-5. Adults, $8; children, $4.

Admittedly, this attraction won't set everyone's hearts aflutter, but if this is your kind of thing, you'll love it. Climb aboard World War II warships and P.T. boats, and check out the submarine *Lionfish.* There's a collection of World War II–related memorabilia, too, as well as a gift shop and snack bar.

೫೪ H.M.S. *Bounty*

State Pier, Battleship Cove, Fall River; (508) 676-8226. July–mid-Oct.,
Sun.-Thurs., 10-6; Fri. and Sat., 10-8. Call to confirm closing times.
Adults, $4; 4-11, $2; under 4, free.

The newest waterfront attraction here, just a short walk from the
battleship *Massachusetts,* is the H.M.S. *Bounty* replica. This 169-foot-long,
three-masted Tall Ship was built for the 1962 movie *Mutiny on the Bounty.*
It was donated to the Fall River Chamber Foundation by media mogul
Ted Turner and TBS Properties. The ship is a replica of the British mer-
chant vessel commanded in 1789 by Lieutenant Commander William
Bligh. Visit this ship and recall the dramatic tale of the real *Bounty.*

೫೪ Fall River Carousel

Two Central St., Battleship Cove, Fall River; (508) 324-4300. May–Labor
Day, daily, 10-10; Oct.-April, Sat. and Sun., 11-6. Per ride, $.75; book of
10 tickets, $6.

Pick your favorite steed and take a whirl on this restored 1920s carousel.

೫೪ Marine Museum

70 Water St., Battleship Cove, Fall River; (508) 674-3533. Wed.-Fri., 9-
4; Sat., Sun., and holidays, 12-4. Adults, $3; children, $2.

Young seafarers will get a kick out of this, as will anyone who's ever
tried to put together a model ship (and how do they get those glass
bottles around them, anyway?). More than 150 ship models are on display
here; the centerpiece is the 28-foot-long *Titanic* replica.

೫೪ Horseneck Beach State Reservation

Rte. 88, Westport Point; (508) 636-8816.

Here you'll find more than 500 acres on the water's edge and enough
activity to keep the most energetic bunch happy—including swimming,
fishing, canoeing, boating, and picnicking.

೫೪ Children's Museum in Dartmouth

276 Gulf Rd., exit 12S off I-95, South Dartmouth; (508) 993-3361.
Tues.-Sat., 10-5; Sun., 1-5. Open first Fri. of every month 'til 8. Closed
Mon. except during school vacations, holidays, and early Sept. Admission,
$3.75; under 1, free. Free, first Fri. every month, 5-8.

A little out of the way, this museum is worth a visit anyway if there's
a toddler or young child in your bunch. Walk into a kaleidoscope, create a
puppet show, or build the world's largest Lego creation. The animal petting area is also popular; animals are housed in cages, but museum staff

members will bring them out to visit. During a recent visit, changing exhibits included a "Bubbles" area, a coral reef display, and a collection of teddy bears. Outside, you'll find a playground and nature trails to explore. The museum owns 60 acres of sanctuary land, made up of salt marsh, meadows, and forest.

🐾 Capron Park & Zoo

Rte. 123, County St., Attleboro; (508) 222-3047. Year-round, 10-5. Adults, $1.50; children, free.

Here's a find within a find: Inside this 63-acre park is a five-acre zoo housing everything from mice to polar bears, about 90 specimens in all. Exhibits have a pro-conservation message. A picnic area and playground are on the grounds, too.

RESTAURANTS

🐾 Freestone's

41 Williams St., New Bedford; (508) 993-7477. Daily, 11-11.

This is a rare find—a fun, funky restaurant that likes kids. While the older kids and adults in your party are enjoying the contemporary artwork displayed, the little ones will be busy playing connect-the-dots on their menus; small fry receive a mug of crayons and a take-home kid's menu as soon as you're seated. The children's menu features the usual nonthreatening line-up; adults have lots of choices, sometimes including a killer praline-pumpkin pie.

🐾 Big Top Kiddie Playland

35 Mariano Bishop Blvd., Fall River Shopping Plaza, Fall River; (508) 675-4800. Mon.-Wed., 10:30-9; Thurs.-Sun., 10-9.

Animated animal shows, a ball crawl, video games, mechanical rides, pizza—sound familiar? It's not a Chuck E. Cheese (though it used to be), but it packs the same kid-pleasing punch. Besides pizza, the menu offers grinders, nachos, and the like. You buy tokens to operate the rides and games. Tip: Go during the week to avoid the multitudes of pint-sized people and their parents.

CENTRAL MASSACHUSETTS

This region may lack ocean views and salt air, but visiting families don't seem to care. They're too busy enjoying the museums, parks, and attractions here. Take Springfield, for example: where else can you spend one day at a musket shoot and the next practicing your jump shot at the Basketball Hall of Fame? If there's a dinophile in your group, you'll want to put both the Springfield Science Museum and Dinosaur Land in South Hadley on your list of must-sees.

Worcester, the second-largest city in Massachusetts, boasts two destinations kids can't resist: Higgins Armory Museum and New England Science Center. And, if you're willing to roam a bit, there's plenty more to see and do, from antique marionettes to state-of-the-art roller coasters. Beyond the big cities, you'll find rural towns dotted with farms and antique shops.

⊰ଃ Springfield Science Museum

State and Chestnut streets, Springfield; (413) 739-3871. Thurs.-Sun., 12-4. Admission (includes all four museums in the complex, the Science Museum, the Connecticut Valley Historical Museum, George Walter Vincent Smith Art Museum, and the Museum of Fine Arts): adults, $4; 6-18, $1; under 6, free.

Part of a quadrangle of museums, Springfield's lively Science Museum was designed with families in mind. At the hands-on Exploration Center, for example, visitors learn to identify wildlife by playing games and responding to audio clues. At Turtle Pond, turtles "talk" to you (on audio tape) as you look through eye-level portholes and watch them swim. Other areas include Dinosaur Hall (where you'll see a full-size replica of tyrannosaurus rex and can walk inside a giant dinosaur footprint), African Hall, with a huge African elephant, and a planetarium.

⊰ଃ The Dr. Seuss Memorial

Is there a child or parent alive who hasn't been tickled by that wily Cat in the Hat? Few details are available at press time, but a Dr. Seuss Memorial is slated to join the Springfield Science Museum, above, and the other museums at the quadrangle. Call (413) 739-3871 for information.

⊰ଃ Basketball Hall of Fame

1150 W. Columbus Ave., adjacent to I-91, Springfield; (413) 781-6500. Sept.-June, daily, 9-5; July–Labor Day, 9-6. Adults, $6; 7-14, $3; under 7, free.

Don't expect hushed voices and "do not touch" signs at this Hall of Fame. When you enter the door, you join the great American game of basketball, which was invented in Springfield in 1891 by Dr. James Naismith. Participation is the key to this fun-filled sports museum. Visit the "How High is Up?" exhibit, where you can test your leaping ability as you try to hit panels hung from the ceiling. Try your skill at basket scoring in the Spaulding Shoot Out, the most popular spot here, where budding hoopsters shoot at baskets of varying heights while on a moving sidewalk. There's lots more, including video highlights of the great games, a special-effects motion picture that puts viewers in the middle of a game, and a peek at what some of today's famous NBA players keep in their lockers.

Forest Park

Summer Ave., Springfield; (413) 787-6434 (park), (413) 733-2251 (zoo). Park: daily 'til dusk. Zoo: April-Oct., Mon.-Sat., 10-4; Sun. and holidays, 10-5; Nov.-March, Wed.-Sun., 10-3. Adults, $2.50; 5-12, $1.50; 4 and under, $.50.

This delightful city park boasts several fun features. You can rent paddle boats and pedal your way around Porter Lake, duckling style; then pay a visit to the Children's Zoo in the middle of the park, to see wild and domestic animals from New England's woods and farmyards and such exotic species as a South American capabara, emus, and wallabies. There's also a petting area with goats and sheep. If you want more action take a trail ride on horseback ($10 per half-hour) or a pony ride ($1) from Forest Park Stable. Other options include swimmming, tennis, hiking, and picnicking.

Holyoke Children's Museum

444 Dwight St., Holyoke; (413) 536-KIDS. Tues.-Sat., 10-4:30; Sun., 12-5. Admission $3; under 1, free.

This engaging museum houses three permanent exhibits that win rave reviews from small fry. At Paperworks, kids can create handmade paper out of recycled paper pulp (which is especially appropriate here, since Holyoke was once a leading paper producer). Cityscape is a child-size Main Street, with a half-dozen or so businesses to try out including a TV studio, health center, architect's office, and bodega (Latin market). Kids love The Scientific Company exhibit, offering exciting ways to explore scientific principles with bubbles, shadows, and objects in motion. If there's a toddler in your group, you'll appreciate the Tot Lot, where little ones can play without encountering rambunctious older kids. There's also a picnic area (and some indoor tables) in the complex, along with the Volleyball Hall of Fame and the 1920s Mountain Park Carousel.

Robert Barrett Fishway

Holyoke Dam, Holyoke; (413) 536-9428. Mid-May–June, Wed.-Sun., 9-5.

Watch migrating salmon and shad on the fish elevator—that's what they call it, all right—at Holyoke Dam on the Connecticut River. Peep through the viewing windows or view from the observation platform over-looking the dam.

~~ Mount Tom State Reservation

I-91N to exit 17W, then Rte. 141 to W. Holyoke; (413) 527-4805.
Reservation: year-round. Museum: Memorial Day–Labor Day; Sept.-Oct.,
Fri.-Sun. $5 per car.

Just minutes from downtown Holyoke, this area is worth exploring.
You'll find over 30 miles of hiking trails, offering beautiful views of the
Pioneer Valley. The Reservation Headquarters has trail maps. There's also
a small nature museum, with collections of rocks, insects, butterflies, and
birds, and a playground. You can cross-country ski and ice skate (on Lake
Bray) in winter.

~~ Mount Tom Ski Area

Rte. 5, exit 17-A off I-91N, Holyoke; (413) 536-0416. Open Nov.-March,
depending on snowfall. Lift tickets: adults, $19, weekdays and night skiing;
$25, weekend days and holidays. Age 12 and under, $2 discount on all
tickets.

Many local kids get their "ski legs" here. With just 16 slopes and
trails, served by eight lifts, it's not a huge operation. But that suits many
families just fine. Features include 100 percent snow-making and a family-friendly, discounted 3.5-hour "Right Time" lift ticket, usable any time of
day. Junior ski school (for age six to 14) is offered weekends and by the
week during Christmas vacation and school vacation week in February.

In summer, Mount Tom turns wet and wild with a 9,000-square-foot
wave pool, an Alpine slide, and a twisty "Flash Flood" waterslide.

~~ Old Sturbridge Village

Rte. 20W, Sturbridge; (508) 347-3362. Year-round, Tues.-Sun., 10-4.
Adults, $15; 6-15, $7; under 6, free. (Tickets good for two consecutive days.)

What was it like to be a child growing up in rural New England more
than 150 years ago? Children will have a good time finding out at Old
Sturbridge Village, a living history museum that recreates life in a rural
New England town, circa 1830s. The Village includes residences, craft
shops, meetinghouses, mills, and a working farm. Everywhere you look,
you'll see costumed interpreters busily engaged in early-19th-century
chores and pursuits. You'll see a printer, blacksmith, tinsmith, and others
plying their trades in authentically restored buildings (transported to the
village from throughout New England). Visit Freeman Farm, where you'll
discover how much work, especially teamwork, was involved in raising
crops and livestock, and in simply preparing meals for the family.

Since this is a rural community, many of the daily activities will change with the seasons. Spring brings sheep shearing, for example, and autumn means a turkey shoot and an early-19th-century Thanksgiving dinner. If you can, plan your visit to coincide with one of the special participatory weekends scheduled throughout the year. Parades, musket shoots, children's activities—these will make your trip to Old Sturbridge Village more involving and more fun.

⚒ Brimfield State Forest
Rte. 20, Brimfield; (413) 245-9966.

This hilly forest is a favorite destination among hikers, with lovely views from several points along Mount Waddaquadduck. Cool off with a dip in the pond or fish for trout in fast-flowing streams. Cross-country skiing in winter.

⚒ Dinosaur Land
Amherst Rd., off Rte. 116, South Hadley; (413) 467-9566. Year-round, daily, weather permitting, 9-5. Adults, $3.50; 12 and under, $1.50.

Dino-fanatics won't want to miss this—it's a quarry of dinosaur tracks made by prehistoric animals who once roamed these riverbanks and cliffs north of Springfield. Over 5,000 footprints have been quarried here. The oldest item is a 500-million-year-old trilobite fossil. An indoor museum features a collection of fossils, footprints, and related artifacts. Check out the gift shop for fossils, footprints, and dinosaur bones (all real) and dinosaur models.

⚒ McCray's Country Creamery Petting Zoo
14 Alvord St., South Hadley; (413) 533-0775. Year-round, daily, 9-9.

This working farm is the home of two child-pleasing features: a petting zoo and an ice cream shop. Meet horses, goats, sheep, ducklings, rabbits, pigs, and peacocks. Take a 20-minute hayride around the grounds (adults, $2; kids, $1) to work up an appetite. Then sit at a picnic table and enjoy a homemade double-dip ice cream cone (there are inside tables, too). Ahh, simple pleasures.

⚒ Red-wind Meadow Farm Trout Hatchery
500 Sunderland Rd., Amherst; (413) 549-4118. Memorial Day–Labor Day, Mon.-Fri., 9-4; Sat. and Sun., 9-5. Sept. and Oct., Sat. and Sun., 9-5, weather permitting. Per person, $2, or $5 per family; $4.25 per lb. for all the trout you catch.

Few things are as thrilling to a young child as catching a fish. You can rent rods here, buy a bucket of worms, and fish all day for trout (rainbow, brook, and brown), large-mouth bass, sunfish, perch, and cat-fish. Staff members will provide pointers. Kids can learn a new sport—and maybe bring home the family dinner.

❦ Toy Cupboard Theatre and Museums

57 East George Hill Rd., off Main St., South Lancaster; (508) 365-9519. Performances year-round, Sun., 2 P.M. Museum open until 5 P.M. Sun. and by appt. Adults, $3; children, $2.

For some creative, homespun entertainment, visit Herbert Hosmer, his protegé Paul, and their friendly gang of hand puppets and mari-onettes. For more than 50 years, Hosmer, a retired teacher, has been run-ning the Toy Cupboard Puppet Theatre and delighting young audiences with his interpretations of favorite fairy tales and children's stories. It's a toss-up as to who enjoys the show most—Hosmer or his audiences. Whether there's a crowd of two or 52, the show goes on. Afterward, check out Hosmer's collection of toys and dollhouses, more than 40 furnished houses of all periods.

❦ Erving State Forest

Off Rte. 2, Erving; (508) 544-3939.

Swim in pretty Laurel Lake or fish for trout in the lake or streams. There's also a two-mile hiking trail and a half-mile nature walk, both marked. Cross-country skiing in winter.

❦ Riverside Park

Rte. 159, Main St., Agawam; (413) 786-9300. Mid-April–mid-Oct., Sun.-Thurs., 11-11; Fri.-Sat., 11-midnight. Admission, $18.99; under 54 inches tall, $10.99.

This rollicking amusement park has wild rides, corny family enter-tainment, costumed characters, and cotton candy, all sure to throw the kids into spasms of delight. Roller-coaster fans will groove on the Cy-clone, one of the largest in the country, or the tummy-testing, steel-loop Black Widow. Gentler souls will appreciate the 150-foot Ferris wheel, the carousel, and antique cars. Don't miss the "Just for Kids" sing-along. NASCAR auto racing competitions are held on Saturday nights.

❦ Higgins Armory Museum

100 Barber Ave., Rte. 12N off I-90, exit 1, Worcester; (508) 853-6015. Year-round, Tues.-Sat., 10-4; Sun., 12-4. July and Aug., Mon.-Sat., 10-4; Sun., 12-4. Adults, $4.25; 6-16, $3.25; under 6, free.

This may be the only place in the country where your dream of being a knight in shining armor can come true. At this wonderfully unique museum, kids (adults, too!) can try on an authentic suit of armor in the Participatory Gallery. There's even armor for dogs. The action includes demonstrations of arms and armor, games, crafts, and special events. Knightly culture is presented in a sound and light show. The collections of medieval and Renaissance armor and related artifacts are fascinating.

⚞ New England Science Center

222 Harrington Way, off Rte. 9, Worcester; (508) 791-9211. Year-round, Mon.-Sat., 10-5; Sun., 12-5. Adults, $4.50; 3-16, $3.50. Train rides, $1.

Exploration is the name of the game here. Set on 59 acres of woodlands, this three-story museum offers hands-on science exhibits, indoor and outdoor zoos, an observatory, a planetarium, a nature trail, a preschooler's area, even a working narrow-gauge train, the *Explorer Express.* Recent exhibits have featured Native American stories, earth activities, and an "Underwater Safari."

⚞ Wachusett Mountain

Rte. 140, Mountain Rd., Princeton; 1-800-SKI-1234. Lift tickets: adults, $25 weekdays, $29.50 weekends; juniors (10 and under), $22 weekdays, $24 weekends; age 5 and under, $5.

Location, location, location. That's the best thing about Wachusett Mountain. Ski here, an hour or so from Boston, and you avoid the often-brutal traffic heading to points North. Obviously snow-making is important here, and they've got it, 100 percent from top to bottom. Features include night skiing (add $5 to the cost of your lift ticket and ski until 10 P.M.), NASCAR racing, a nursery, and the acclaimed SKIwee teaching program for kids aged three to 12. Children will have fun learning to navigate the Bamboo Bridge and Hoola Hoops in the Polar Playground; new-to-the-sport adults will feel comfortable in the beginner's area. Those features make Wachusett Mountain—with 18 trails and five lifts—a great place to learn to ski.

⚞ Farmland Petting Zoo

Redstone Hall Rd., off Rte. 62, Sterling; (508) 422-6666. Memorial Day–Oct., Thurs.-Sun., 10-5, weather permitting. Adults, $3; 12 and under, $2.

This is a megavariety petting zoo, with pot-bellied pigs, llamas, Scotch Highland cattle, and more than 100 more animals to pet and feed.

Go on a hayride (free) or a pony ride, and be sure to bring a picnic lunch; you can eat alongside the animals.

⤳ Southwick's Wild Animal Farm

Off Rte. 16, Mendon; (508) 883-9182. May–mid-Oct., daily, 10-5. Circus shows at 12 and 4 daily. Adults, $7.50; 3-12, $5; under 3, free.

Dedicated to the preservation of rare and endangered species, this farm houses the largest collection of wild animals in New England. Meet lions, tigers, and bears, plus a baby giraffe, ostriches, and several varieties of birds. Catch the antics of clowns and trained elephants at the circus show. Make new friends—both furry and feathered types—at the petting area, ride a pony, and learn about them all through exhibits and demonstrations.

⤳ Whalom Amusement Park

Rte. 13, Lunenburg; (508) 342-3707. Easter–Columbus Day, Fri. and Sat., 12-10; Thurs.-Sun., 12-9. Admission, $3; all-day ride pass, $10; Kiddie Land Pass, $7.

Fifty acres of fun: rides, midway games, kiddie rides, waterslides, miniature golf, train rides, even a beach. We nominate as most thrilling ride the Comet roller coaster. We bet this is the only place in New England where you'll see Madonna and Michael Jackson (okay, so they're marionettes) sharing the same stage. Catch their performances and other, live shows throughout the day. Rent an aqua bike or paddle boat and get some exercise, pedaling or paddling around Whalom Lake. Whalom Park offers lots of old-fashioned fun, and it's inexpensive to boot.

⤳ Turner Falls Fish Viewing Facility

Fish Ave., Turner Falls; (413) 659-3714. Mid-May–June, Wed.-Sun., 9-5.

The name says it all…watch the annual migration of salmon and shad through underground viewing windows. The staff—and informational exhibits—will fill you in on all the facts.

⤳ Maple Sugaring

Sweeten up your winter with a visit to a sugar house. Massachusetts has more than 100 of them (several in this area), open for demonstrations from February through early April. They give samples, too. Call the Massachusetts Maple Producers at (413) 628-3912 for a free directory. A recorded message gives updates daily in season.

ᤰ Hiking

If you guessed this area offers some great hiking, you're right, and it's especially rewarding during fall foliage season. Places to go include Chesterfield Gorge, off Rte. 153, in Chesterfield (a 30-foot gorge near the headwaters of Westfield River); Laughing Brook Education Center and Wildlife Sanctuary, 789 Main St., Hampden (nature and walking trails, and an animal exhibit); and Northfield Mountain Recreation and Environmental Center, Rte. 2A, Northfield (mile-long nature trail ringing Northfield Mountain).

ᤰ Horseback Riding

Saddle up at Ridge Valley Stables, Rte. 140, Grafton, (508) 839-3038; Grafton Stables & School, 137 Upton Rd., also in Grafton, (508) 839-6367; or Holiday Acres Equestrian Center, 333 Main St., Rutland, (508) 886-6896.

ᤰ Boat Cruise/*Quinnetukut II* Riverboat

Rte. 63, Northfield; (413) 659-3714. Late May–mid-Oct., Wed.-Sun. Adults, $7; 14 and under, $3. Reservations recommended.

Cruise the Connecticut River, between the towns of Gill and Northfield, on this 1.5-hour interpretive tour. Narration covers local history, geology, and eco-facts, enhancing the leisurely trip.

◣ RESTAURANTS

ᤰ Bub's Bar-B-Que

Rte. 116, Sunderland; (413) 259-1254. Mon.-Sat., 5-10 P.M.; Sun., 1-10 P.M.

This is a real down-and-dirty rib joint, very casual and often very busy. If you're not into red meat, that's okay—there's chicken, swordfish, salmon, catfish, shrimp or whatever the current catch is, and even barbecued baked beans. Other tasty side dishes include dirty rice, collard greens, and dilled potato salad. The down side is that you can wait in line awhile, especially if you hit the place on Friday or Saturday night. The up side is that if the kids are rowdy no one is likely to notice.

ᤰ Gramp's

216 Lyman St., Holyoke; (413) 534-1996. Mon.-Fri., 7 A.M.–3 P.M.

This local favorite features great sandwiches and serves breakfast all day long. Try a roast beef melt or a Reuben, with soup or salad. No children's menu here, but most kids opt for a stack of Gramp's pancakes.

❧ Red Rose Pizzeria

1060 Main St., Springfield; (413) 739-8510. Tues.-Sat., 11 A.M.-midnight; Sun., 11-11.

Try the best pizza in Springfield, after you watch it being made right in front of you. Red Rose pizza makers toss dough into the air in an open kitchen. You can also get pasta, grinders, and eggplant dishes (the eggplant Parmesan is superb). There's no children's menu, but the folks at Red Rose don't mind if you order, say, a plate of ziti and split it.

❧ Weintraub's Restaurant & Delicatessen

126 Water St., Worcester; (508) 756-7870. Mon., 8-4; Tues.-Sun., 8 A.M.- 9 P.M.

Voted best deli in New England by *Yankee Magazine*—need we say more? With so many possible choices and combinations, even the finicky will join the Clean Plate Club.

❧ Worcester Diners

True, diners are fairly small, and the sounds of one whiny child can really resonate, but if you're willing to take that chance, and you love classic diners, Worcester's got 'em. Dining cars were once manufactured here, and there are still more than a dozen functioning as diners to choose from. We haven't tried them all, so we can't vouch for their quality, but would they have lasted so long if they didn't send out some mean Blue Plate Specials?

THE BERKSHIRES

The far western region of Massachusetts, called the Berkshires (short for Berkshire Hills,) is an area as graceful as its name implies. Blessed with beautiful countryside and charming Main Streets, the area offers a wealth of cultural and recreational activity. Plan to take it slow and savor the pleasures of the Berkshires. Enjoy a picnic on the lawn of Tanglewood as the Boston Symphony Orchestra provides background music. Visit a magnificent natural marble bridge with "graffiti" dating back to 1740. Or ride horseback through a forest of brilliant fall foliage. Even if you take a wrong turn along the way (and you probably will—it's easy to be distracted by the view), so what? You're bound to discover something special around the next curve in the road.

⚄ Hancock Shaker Village

Rte. 20, Pittsfield; (413) 443-0188. May-Oct., daily, 9:30-5. Adults, $10; 6-17, $5. Family rate: $25 for two adults and all accompanying children under 18.

Hancock was one of 18 communities founded by the Shaker sect in the 18th century. Although the last of the Hancock Shakers left the church family in 1960, this museum is a permanent memorial to the Shaker way of life. Twenty buildings have been restored on the site, including an unusual (but amazingly practical) round stone barn. You'll see farm animals, herb gardens, and craft demonstrations. In the Family Discovery Room, kids can try on bonnets and shoes, write with a quill pen, and get a taste of a child's life in an 18th-century Shaker community. You might be treated to a Shaker music program—children especially enjoy the dance demonstrations, and everyone joins in. Guided tours are scheduled daily; plan to spend about two hours here, depending on the ages and attention spans of your kids. Light meals and snacks are available.

⚄ Berkshire Museum

Rte. 7, Pittsfield; (413) 443-7171. Sept.-June., Tues.-Sat., 10-5; Sun., 1-5. July and Aug., daily, 10-5; Sun., 1-5. Adults, $3; 12-18, $1; 12 and under, free. Free to all Wed. and Sat, 10-12.

If Alexandra likes science museums but Christopher prefers art while Mom and Dad are history buffs, you've found the perfect museum. This one has something for everybody, and an aquarium to boot. Young children will be absorbed by the "Animals of the World in Miniature" exhibit. Special tours are offered for children.

⚄ Pittsfield State Forest

Cascade St., Pittsfield; (413) 442-8992.

This mountainous area offers plenty to see and explore, including caves, waterfalls, and cascades. Many species of mammals live here, and occasionally even a black bear or coyote is spotted. There are 30 miles of hiking trails, including several short ones. Drop a line in Berry Pond (which is stocked) or swim in the stream at Lulu Brook picnic area. Ten miles of cross-country ski trails are maintained in winter.

⚄ Natural Bridge State Park

Rte. 8 (.5 miles from town center), North Adams; (413) 663-6392. May-Oct., daily, 10-8; Sat. and Sun., 10-6.

The highlight of this tiny state park is a natural marble bridge, the only one of its kind in the United States. The bridge extends across a gorge 60 feet above ground. It was formed when flowing water and ice gradually eroded the many layers of rock covering the marble, at the rate of one foot every 2,500 years. (Obviously, someone was keeping track.) Now, deep chasms are sculpted into the rock. Some of the walls of the chasms sport graffiti dating back to 1740. Picnic tables and rest rooms are available.

⅔ Western Gateway Heritage State Park

B & M Freightyard, Rte. 8, North Adams; (413) 663-8059. Daily, 10-4:30. Free; donations appreciated.

This collection of historical attractions, specialty shops, and restaurants is located in a restored railroad freightyard. Admittedly it's a pleasant place to stroll around in, but we're including it in this book for a more specific reason: "The Tunnel Experience." This intriguing display, located inside a set of railroad boxcars, has lots of kid appeal. Through sight-and-sound effects, visitors learn what it was like to dig the Hoosaic Tunnel during the mid-1800s. Explosions, dripping water, and the rapping of pickaxes against stone all recreate the drama of this undertaking. Nearly 200 workers died while digging the tunnel, which eventually linked the East, the Great Lakes, and the West. Tales of train wrecks and ghosts add to the experience. Junior conductors will enjoy taking a ride through the park on the Tot Train.

⅔ Mount Greylock

Access road (Notch Rd.) off Rte. 2 between North Adams and Williamstown, North Adams; (413) 743-1591.

The pinnacle of Massachusetts, Mount Greylock, can be reached by car. The nine-mile drive takes about a half-hour and rewards you with a five-state view. If you're visiting the Berkshires during fall foliage season, you won't want to miss it. At the top of the mountain, the Appalachian Mountain Club offers hikes, sunset walks, slide shows, exhibits, and evening campfires. You can spend the night at Bascom Lodge, run by the club. Meals and snacks are also available.

⅔ Tanglewood Music Festival

Rte. 183, West St., Lenox; (413) 637-1940, (617) 266-1492. June-Sept. Call in advance for ticket information.

This 210-acre estate is world famous as the summer home of the Boston Symphony Orchestra. Bring a picnic and spread out on a blanket to enjoy classical music under a star-filled sky. Or, go earlier in the day and catch the BSO's rehearsal—a good option for families with young children, and the least costly way to go.

⁂ Pleasant Valley Sanctuary
472 West Mountain Rd., Lenox; (413) 637-0320.

Hike along the nature trail here and you'll see beaver ponds and lodges, with muskrats sometimes sharing the living quarters. Visit the Trailside Museum and encounter live and stuffed animals, as well as electronic nature games—a fun way for kids to learn about the environment. Fourteen miles of hiking trails cross the area; traverse them on cross-country skis in winter.

⁂ Albert Schweitzer Center
Hurlburt Rd., Great Barrington; (413) 528-3124. Tues.-Sat., 10-4; Sun., 12-4. Donations accepted.

Dr. Albert Schweitzer devoted his remarkable career as a medical missionary, ecologist, and philosopher to preserving and maintaining the quality of life of people, plants, and animals. Set in a 150-year-old farmhouse, the center was founded to honor and sustain Dr. Schweitzer's humanitarian philosophy. Take a walk through the wildlife preserve, and visit the Universal Children's Garden. Here children learn about herbs, beneficial weeds, natural healing, and how to deal gently and nonviolently with nature. Special programs for kids are designed to foster a reverence for life through photography, film, puppetry, music, dance, and environmental awareness. (Contact the center prior to your visit to find out what's happening.) Conclude your visit by ringing the large steeple bell in the barn. This signifies that you, too, pledge to respect all life.

⁂ Jiminy Peak Ski Area
Rte. 7, Hancock; (413) 738-5500.

In winter, this is a downhill ski resort; in summer and fall, you can ride up the chairlift for panoramic views of the Berkshires. Even better, the Alpine slide will zip you down again. An hour or so of this, and your children will be blissfully exhausted. Call for current schedule and rates.

⁂ Norman Rockwell Museum
Rte. 183, Stockbridge; (413) 298-4100. May-Oct., daily, 10-5; Nov.-April, daily, 11-4. Adults, $8; children, $2.

If you're a fan of Rockwell's work, take a look at the originals on display here. During summer, you can also peek at the actual studio where he worked. On Family Days (once a month), special tours and activities are planned, and parents' admission is half-price. Call for information.

🔥 Bartholomew's Cobble

Off Rte. 7A, Ashley Falls; (413) 229-8600. Mid-April–mid-Oct., daily, 9-5. Museum open Wed.-Sun., 9-5.

Let's keep this pretty spot a secret. Junior gardeners will be inspired by the rock garden, with 700 species of plants; the natural history museum has a neat collection of mounted birds, a bobcat, butterflies, arrowheads, and Mohegan Indian artifacts. Also head up to Hurlburt's Hill (the map at the entrance will direct you), a high pasture that's perfect for kite flying. (Fly before May, please, or you'll disturb nesting birds.) Round out your visit with an easy hike along Ledge's Trail or, beside the river, Bailey's Trail. Interpretive programs geared to kids, such as "Life in a Pond," are run several times a year. Call for a schedule.

🔥 Beartown State Forest

Blue Hill Rd., 5 mi. east on Rte. 23, Monterey; (413) 528-0904.

Beartown Mountain is the major feature among a group of wooded peaks. Follow the signs to Laura Tower or the Alcott Trail lookout for scenic views. Hike along the Appalachian Trail, fish for bass, or swim in Benedict Pond. In winter, cross-country ski along 10 miles of marked trails.

RESTAURANTS

🔥 Miss Adams Diner

53 Park St., North Adams; (413) 743-5300. Tues.-Sat., 6:30 A.M.-3 P.M.; Sun., 7-1. Closed Mon.

This downtown landmark is a restored, 1949 Worcester Lunch Car. If you've always wanted to take your kids to a diner but figured they'd balk at the Meatloaf Special, this might be the ticket. There's meatloaf, all right, but there's also good homemade chili, pastrami sandwiches, and, at breakfast, really tasty muffins in 1990s combinations like pineapple-corn and cranberry-pecan. Other treats include malted milkshakes (much better than fast-food shakes) and the Mount Greylock Sundae, a triumph of coffee ice cream, hot fudge, peanut butter chips, blueberries, walnuts, and whipped cream. Wow.

🔥 Dakota Restaurant

1035 South St., Pittsfield; (413) 499-7900. Mon.-Thurs., 4-10; Fri. and Sat., 4-11; Sun., 10-2 (brunch) and 4-9.

This wild-West themed restaurant is a great place to take the kids—even little ones—for dinner. They'll enjoy watching the crustaceans in the lobster tank and selecting their favorite nibbles from the extensive salad bar. Fare includes surf, turf, and cluck (seafood/steak/chicken); the Dakota also offers a children's menu and early-bird specials that are great for families with small fry.

⚓ D & J's American Grill

11 Stockbridge Rd., Rtes. 7 and 23, Great Barrington; (413) 528-3201. Daily, 11:30-9.

Looking for that all-American picnic to take to Tanglewood or the park? This place is famous for pan-fried chicken, no fancy spices, just nice and plain, the way Mom used to make. Add some cole slaw and double-chocolate brownies or apple crisp and you've got the makings of a real feast. There are lots of lighter choices, too, and a casual dining room if you're eating in. Don't let the plain-Jane exterior keep you away; it didn't stop *Gourmet* magazine from requesting a recipe (for the turkey meatloaf).

CAPE COD

More than four million people each year visit Cape Cod and the two tiny sister islands, Nantucket and Martha's Vineyard. It is said that there are more people on this small elbow of sand on a summer day than there are in the entire city of Boston. Why do vacationers continue to flock to the Cape? Why do they endure the legendary Cape Cod bottleneck, waiting sometimes nearly three hours to cross the Sagamore Bridge? Despite the summertime crunch, Cape Cod has an allure that few can resist. Vacationers put up with the traffic and summer crowds because they know what awaits them: miles of sandy, white beaches, wide-open salt marshes and clam flats, scenic harbors, lighthouses, and picturesque, historic sea captains' homes and cedar-shaked beach cottages.

Families enjoy the casual seaside atmosphere, where lobster-in-the-rough and steamers fresh from local shellfish beds are daily fare. For fun, there's hiking, sailing, windsurfing, fishing, swimming, sightseeing, and any amusement your family desires. Think petting zoos, waterslides, video arcades, boat trips, train rides, aquariums, touch pools, museums, and more.

If your kids like lots of action, you won't be disappointed. The bustling resort towns of Hyannis and Provincetown sizzle with energy during the summer months.

If you prefer more peaceful pleasures, they're here, as well, tucked down the back roads of Falmouth, atop one of the striking cliffs in Truro, on a hike along spectacular beaches at Cape Cod National Seashore, or digging for clams in Wellfleet. Nearly everywhere, despite the summer rush, it is possible to get away from the crush to enjoy the Cape's beauty. A local's best advice is to "get lost" (said with a bit of tongue in cheek!); meander the back roads and discover the lovely, hidden spots on the Cape. There, "Old Cape Cod" can still be found, far away from the shopping malls and fast-food eateries. But first you have to get there. Some words of advice:

1. Consider visiting Cape Cod off-season, if you can, during spring or fall. After Labor Day, the crowds diminish but the weather is still balmy—and most attractions stay open through September or October. Also, lodging prices drop dramatically after Labor Day. Personally, we think the Cape and islands are at their best in autumn. Springtime is a bit dicier, weather wise, and many attractions don't open until Memorial Day. Still, if you're looking for a real escape, and if you're not yet tied to school vacation schedules, think about an early visit.

2. Avoid the weekend rush hours; don't try to get to the Cape on Fridays between four and nine, or leave on Sundays between noon and nine (unless sitting in a virtual parking lot is your idea of a fine time).

3. If you find yourself trapped in the infamous Cape Cod congestion, don't despair. In just a few hours you'll be eating some of the best, freshest seafood in the world on some of the most spectacular beaches in the country. Pack car toys for the kids and an ocean-wave relaxation tape to achieve serenity of spirit, and try to make the best of it.

UPPER CAPE
(Includes Sandwich, Falmouth, Bourne)

✄ Heritage Plantation
Rte. 6A at Grove and Pine streets, Sandwich; (508) 888-3300. Mid-May–Oct., daily, 10-5. Adults, $7; 6-18, $3.50.

A mixed bag of Americana spread throughout a beautifully landscaped 76-acre site, Heritage Plantation has something for everyone. It's particularly enjoyable on a warm, sunny day when kids can skip along any of a dozen nature trails past flowerbeds, wood groves, and the shore of Upper Shawme Lake. But it's more than just a horticultural hotspot. A Shaker-designed round barn houses an impressive collection of antique cars, including one the kids can climb on. Other buildings house collections of Native American artifacts, antique military miniatures, firearms, early tools, and folk art. Don't miss the working antique wooden carousel.

≈3 Thornton Burgess Museum
4 Water St., on edge of Shawme Pond, Sandwich; (508) 888-6870. April-Dec., daily, 10-4; Sun., 1-4. Winter hours vary. Story Hour, July and Aug., Tues., Thurs., and Sat., 10:30. Admission by donation.

The word "charming" springs to mind when you discover this place, a favorite of Cape Cod families. The museum is a memorial to Burgess, author of more than 15,000 children's stories. It was established in 1976 to inspire reverence in children for wildlife and the environment—long before such concerns were common. On sunny summer afternoons, join the parents and children who gather under a tree for Story Hour, often "illustrated" with live animals. The small museum houses Burgess memorabilia and an interactive exhibit tied to Cape Cod natural history themes. The Burgess Society sponsors several delightful children's events and activities during the summer. Call for a schedule.

≈3 Green Briar Nature Center and Jam Kitchen
6 Discovery Hill Rd., off Rte. 6A, East Sandwich; (508) 888-6870. April-Dec., daily, 10-4; Sun., 1-4. Admission by donation.

Here's one of those things you'd only consider doing while on vacation: watching jams and jellies being made in an old-fashioned kitchen. This is no factory tour; they use turn-of-the-century cooking methods. Take home some beach-plum jelly. Visit the award-winning wildflower garden, and take the mile-long hike down historic Old Briar Patch trail. (Shorter walks are offered, too.) Before you leave be sure to check out the natural history exhibits, and say hello to Peter Rabbit, who resides here in his bunny hutch.

≈3 Yesteryears Doll Museum
Old Main St., Sandwich; (508) 888-1711. Mid-May–Oct., Mon.-Sat., 10-4. Adults, $3; under 12, $2.

Hello, dollies. If you like dolls, you'll adore this collection of antique dolls, many of them rare finds, along with dollhouses, each elaborately decked out. Got an injured doll around the house? Bring her/him along; this is the best doll hospital around. Between May and October about 200 dolls are treated here, for injuries ranging from broken limbs to torn neck sockets.

≈3 Aptucxet Trading Post Museum
Aptucxet Rd., Bourne; (508) 759-9487. Mid-April–mid-Oct., 10-5; Sun., 2-5. Closed Mon. Adults, $1.50; children, $.50.

Sure it's touristy, but this attraction has some redeeming historical value. Established as a trading post by Pilgrims in 1627, it's billed as the first-known commercial enterprise in English-speaking North America. Today, this replica of a Pilgrim-Dutch trading post is filled with Native American artifacts. The site includes a windmill, a Victorian railroad station (built for the exclusive use of President Grover Cleveland, who owned a summer home in Bourne), herb and wildflower gardens, and picnic areas.

National Marine Fisheries Aquarium

Cor. of Water and Albatross streets, Woods Hole; (508) 548-7684. Mid-June–mid-Sept., daily, 10-4. Off season, Mon.-Fri., 9-4. Free.

This little gem—the oldest research aquarium in the United States—is a great place to get in touch with Cape sea life. Touch tanks house starfish, lobsters, horseshoe crabs, sea turtles, and snails. Watch the harbor seals' feedings at 11 A.M. and 3 P.M.

Water Wizz

Rtes. 6 and 28, Wareham; (508) 295-3255. Memorial Day–mid-June, Sat. and Sun., 10-7; mid-June–Labor Day, daily, 10-7, weather permitting. Adults, $15.75; children under 48 inches tall, $10.

There's lots of wet-and-wild summer fun at Water Wizz water park. Soak up some action on the giant waterslide, the speed slides (with tunnels and dips), and the wild tube ride (a plunge from six stories high). The "Not-So-Lazy-River" ride is great—you start slow and easy, and then—look out! There's also a kiddie play area, game room, picnic area, and snack bar.

Cape Cod Children's Mini-Museum

Falmouth Mall, Falmouth; (508) 457-4667. Mon.-Sat., 10:30-6; Sun., 12-5. Admission, $.50.

Outdoor plans rained out? Kids age one to 10 won't balk at a trip to the Falmouth Mall; an in-mall children's museum offers lots of fun stuff to play with. There are a four-car wooden train, a dress-up area, puppets, a pirate's den, and lots of games and puzzles.

Beaches

Upper Cape beaches include Scusset Beach (Scusset Beach Road, near the Sagamore Rotary in Sandwich), a nice state-run beach on Cape Cod Canal. Town Neck Beach (on the bay side, off Route 6A and Tupper Road, Sandwich) has pretty views and good swimming. It's a favorite spot of local photographers and artists. There's a nice hike along the boardwalk across Mill Creek. Bourne Scenic Park (Route 6, Buzzard's Bay on Cape Cod Canal, Sandwich) has 70 acres of hiking, fishing, swimming, and playgrounds. Take a dip in the unique sea-level pool—it changes with the tide. Other fine beaches include Surf Drive Beach (on Vineyard Sound, off Surf Drive, Falmouth); Old Silver Beach (on Buzzard's Bay, off Bay Shore Drive, North Falmouth); and Menauhant Beach (on Vineyard Sound, off Menauhant Road, East Falmouth).

⌇ Kettle Ponds

If you like gazing at the ocean but would rather dive into something, well, cozier, how about one of Cape Cod's little fishing holes, a kettle pond? Tucked behind the ocean beaches, these ponds were dug out of the landscape by Ice Age glaciers. They're round, deep (in the middle), clear, and warm. In short, they're perfect natural freshwater pools, great for swimming. Locally, check out Long Pond in Harwich (covering more than 700 acres, it's a biggie) and Wakeby and Mashpee ponds, both in Mashpee. Pack a picnic and enjoy.

⌇ Hiking

One of the best places to hike on the entire Cape is Beebe Woods, off Depot Road in Falmouth Center. The 400-acre property offers an abundance of trails, for novices to experts. Intricate stone fences remind you that you're in New England.

⌇ Bicycling

The Shining Sea Bikeway is a three-mile trail running from Falmouth Center to Woods Hole along the shoreline. Stop, take a break, and watch the activity at busy marinas along the way. Pick up the path on Locust Street in Falmouth; you'll end up at the Steamship Authority dock in Woods Hole.

▶ RESTAURANTS

⌇ The Lobster Trap

290 Shore Rd., Bourne; (508) 759-7600. Daily, in season, 11:30-8:30. Spring and fall, Sat. and Sun. only.

So, you've just hit the Cape and can't wait another nanosecond for a taste of fresh seafood? This is the place. Located right off the Bourne Bridge (take an immediate right as you exit the bridge), it's ultracasual, and on the water (well, on the river). More important, the food is great and the prices are low. Try the Bourne scallops, lobster, fried clams, or, a good bet for kids, the expertly made lobster rolls, which are heavy on the lobster meat, light on the mayo. Already, the wretched ride is but a memory....

⌇ The Wharf

Grand Ave., Falmouth Heights; (508) 548-2772. April-Dec., daily,
11:30-10 or -11.

This is no family restaurant, it's more of a beachfront hangout. Part of
a ramshackle structure that includes a dairy bar, T-shirt shop, and casino,
The Wharf has lots to look at, making it the perfect place for kids. (We'd
still avoid the peak dinner hour on Friday and Saturday night; it's just too
smoky and noisy.) Inside, it's like a T.G.I Friday's run amok—absolutely
stuffed with junk like mooseheads, anchors, and buoys. Outside, there's
the gorgeous sweep of Vineyard Sound and, off aways, Martha's Vineyard.
The best views, naturally, are from the deck. And the eats are great;
blackboard specials usually feature fresh fish (often, caught by the restaurant's owner) priced to move, and steak, chicken, pasta, and prime rib.

⌇ Hearth 'N Kettle

874 Main St., Falmouth; (508) 548-6111. (Other locations in Hyannis,
South Yarmouth, Orleans, Centerville, and Plymouth.) Daily, 7 A.M.–10 P.M.
(Sat. and Sun. in season, 7-11.)

This local chain offers friendly family dining at great prices; nothing
fancy, but reliably good. The Falmouth outpost was the first in the chain
and has survived on the Cape for more than 20 years, as trendier places
have come and gone. You can get anything from a hearty breakfast to
grilled tuna steak, served by pleasant waitpeople in colonial costumes.
More reasons to give the H 'n K a try: lots of low-fat options, a good kid's
menu (the cod nuggets 'n fries win rave reviews), and early-bird specials
served 'til 6 P.M.

◤ MID-CAPE

(Includes Hyannis, Barnstable, Yarmouth, Dennis)

⌇ Cape Cod and Hyannis Railroad

252 Main St., Hyannis; (508) 771-3788. June-Oct., Tues.-Sun., departures
at 10, 12:30, and 3. Adults, $10.50; children, $6.50.

Board a refurbished 1920s parlor car and take a scenic tour of undiscovered Cape Cod. You'll see Cape Cod Bay, historic villages, salt marsh,
cranberry bogs, and more, with stops at Sandwich and the Cape Cod Canal. The trip takes one and three-quarter hours, departing from the station
in downtown Hyannis. If you're planning a grown-up's night out, note
the railroad also offers a three-hour dinner trip. Call for reservations.

⅔ Cape Cod Potato Chip Tour

Breed's Hill in Independence Park (near Cape Cod Mall), Hyannis; (508) 775-7253. Mon.-Fri., 10-4. Free.

Looking for an unusual rainy day activity? Head to the potato chip factory, and watch them hand-cook these tasty chips. Tours are self-guided. Even if you've sworn off chips forever, you won't be able to resist a sample.

⅔ Cape Cod Melody Tent

West Main St., Hyannis; (508) 775-9100. Children's performances, Wed., 11 A.M. Tickets, $4-$5.

Put a little culture into your Cape escape with a show at the Melody Tent. Productions feature all the kid's classics, like *Goldilocks and the Three Bears, Rumplestiltskin,* and *Beauty and the Beast.*

⅔ Aqua Circus

Rte. 29, West Yarmouth; (508) 775-8883. July and Aug., daily, 9:30-6:30; mid-Feb.–June and Sept.–late-Nov., daily, 9:30-5. Shows at 11, 1, 2:30, and 4. Adults, $7.50; under 10, $4.50.

Many a road-weary family, trapped in traffic along Route 28, has sought refuge at the Aqua Circus marine aquarium and zoo. Features include sea lion and dolphin shows, pony rides, and a petting zoo. You'll encounter monkeys, llamas, parrots, a shell exhibit—enough, in short, to chase away the worst case of kiddie car crabbiness.

⅔ Crab Creek

Public dock, North Dennis Rd., Yarmouth.

This is considered the best spot on the Cape for blue crabbing. No fancy equipment needed, just some leftover, cooked chicken (for bait) and some string. Crash-course in crabbing: standing on the dock, tie some string around a piece of chicken. Lower it into the water, and wait for some action.

⅔ Josiah Dennis Manse and Old West Schoolhouse

Nobscuset Rd. and Whig St., Dennis; (508) 385-2232. July and Aug., Tues. and Thurs., 2-4 P.M. Donations appreciated.

This site features a 1770 schoolhouse with marine artifacts and a Children's Room. See spinning and weaving demonstrations in the attic workroom.

⅔ Bicycling—Cape Cod Rail Trail

Trail begins in South Dennis off Rte. 134, across from Hall Oil Co. Bike rentals available.

Formerly the railroad right-of-way, this 14-mile tarred trail runs from Dennis to Eastham, where you connect with the National Seashore bike path. Take your swimsuits; you'll end up at Coast Guard Beach. You'll share the path with fellow cyclists, walkers, and horseback riders, through woods and bogs, around lakes and ocean shores.

❦ Cape Playhouse

Rte. 6A, East Dennis; (508) 385-3838. July and Aug. Children's performances Fri., 9:30 and 11:30 A.M. Tickets, $5. Reservations not accepted.

This 1927 theater has hosted such luminaries as Humphrey Bogart, Bette Davis, and Henry Fonda on the boards. Grown-ups still get all duded up to visit the Playhouse, but kids can get in on the act(s) on Friday mornings, when traveling theater groups perform shows just for children. It's a great escape on bad-weather days, much more rewarding than a video arcade or shopping mall excursion.

❦ Sea View Playland

Lower County Rd., Dennisport; (508) 398-9084. Late June–Labor Day, daily, 10-10.

This is pure honky-tonk fun. Skeeball, miniature golf, pitch and putt, and an old barn filled with nearly 100 different arcade games. Hey, you're on vacation—if not now, when? You'll find the newest and oldest coin-operated games. Ask anyone in the area for directions to the Barn of Fun; they'll be able to tell you.

❦ Boat Cruises

The mid-Cape area offers just about any kind of ocean adventure you could wish for: island excursions, harbor tours, Cape Cod Canal cruises, and whale-watching trips. Local cruise operators include Hy-Line Harbor Cruises, Ocean St. Dock, Hyannis, (508) 778-2600; and Hyannis Whale Watcher Cruises, Barnstable Harbor, (508) 362-6088.

❦ Beaches

Sandy Neck Beach, on Sandy Neck Rd. (off Rte. 6A) in Barnstable, is considered one of the best public beaches on the Cape. It's easy to hang around here for an entire day, sunning, swimming, and exploring the surrounding dunes and marshlands. For a spectacular view of the unspoiled Cape, take one of the many trails along Sandy Neck. Walk quietly, and you're likely to spot rare birds and wildlife; you can also search for relics in the dunes along the way, and wade in the water along this magnificent stretch of beach. Be sure to return to the main entrance before dusk, where a wonderful surprise awaits: musicians, storytellers, and mimes performing around a campfire. Sea Gull Beach, off South Sea Avenue in Yarmouth, is another winner; on Nantucket Sound, it's calm, sandy, and considered the best beach for swimming in the Yarmouth area. It has a snack bar and picnic area. Teens or preteens in your group? They'll insist on making the scene at popular Craigville Beach. It boasts fine sand, gentle surf, and warm water. (An MTV beach party segment was shot here; enough said.) Resist the temptation to mention Annette Funicello's beach party movies.

RESTAURANTS

⅋ Baxter's Fish 'N Chips

117 Pleasant St. Wharf, Hyannis; (508) 775-4490. April-Oct., Mon.-Sat., 11:30-10; Sun., 1-9; off season, Thurs.-Sun., 11:30-10.

Boat-less in Hyannis? A meal at Baxter's is the next best thing. The outdoor deck of this classic fish house juts out into the harbor amid fishing boats and pleasure cruisers. Sometimes sea planes land alongside the restaurant, causing drinks to slosh. (Kids find this a hoot.) But don't get too distracted, or a seagull will make off with your entree. (Kids don't find this funny at all unless the disappearing dinner was on your plate, not theirs.) The menu features the usual fried seafood plates and fresh fish, grilled or broiled.

⅋ Swan River Seafood Restaurant

5 Lower Country Rd., Dennisport; (508) 394-4466. Daily, lunch and dinner.

Good, fresh seafood and breathtaking views of Nantucket Sound make this one hard to beat. Try the steamers, seafood pasta salad, or Cape-caught boiled lobsters. Not into fish? The menu includes paw as well as claw. There's a kid's menu, too.

⅋ Barby Ann's

120 Airport Rd., Hyannis; (508) 775-9795. Daily, 11:30-10; Sun., 12-10.

Home-style cooking is the draw at this popular family restaurant. Try their famous seafood stew or barbecued ribs, or one of the blackboard specials. The decor is casual but nice and the children's menu has an all-star line-up of chicken fingers, fish 'n' chips, hot dogs, and burgers.

❧ Four Seas Ice Cream

360 S. Main St., Centerville; (508) 775-1394. Late May–mid-Sept., daily, 9 A.M.-10:30 P.M.

After almost 60 years, still arguably the best on the Cape.

OUTER CAPE

(Includes Brewster, Chatham, Wellfleet, Truro, Provincetown)

❧ Trampoline Center

Rte. 28, across from A & W Restaurant, Harwich; (508) 432-8717. Mid-June–Labor Day, daily, 9-11; April school vacation week–mid-June, Sat. and Sun., 9-9 (approx.). For 10 min., per trampoline, $3 (more than one person can jump at a time).

Bounce-o-rama! Jump those sillies out at this place, an outdoor, fenced-in area with 12 trampolines, 6 by 12 feet. Parents can jump with young children, up to age six or seven, if desired. Spotlights keep the place jumping 'til way past bedtime.

❧ New England Fire and History Museum

Rte. 6A, Brewster; (508) 896-5711. Memorial Day–Labor Day, Mon.-Fri., 10-4; Sat. and Sun., 12-4; Labor Day–mid-Oct., Sat. and Sun., 12-4. Adults, $4.50; 5-12, $2.50; 4 and under, free.

This museum contains a fascinating assortment of antique fire engines, one of the largest collections in the country. "They put out fires with buckets of water?" "They had to pull this by hand?" "How fast could the horses get them to the fire?" Children are full of questions as they view this interesting exhibit of 18th- to 20th-century fire engines and related memorabilia. Kids can climb aboard a fire truck, a fire engine, and a fire boat, complete with hoses.

❧ Bassett Wild Animal Farm

620 Tubman Rd., between Rtes. 124 and 137, Brewster; (508) 896-3224. Mid-May–mid-Sept., daily, 10-5. Adults, $5.50; 2-12, $3.75.

Meet a mountain lion, zebu, alpaca, lemurs, and other exotic creatures here. Of course, when you visit it's likely to be an entirely different lineup, as someone new is added every year to keep things interesting for repeat visitors. Kids love the monkeys and also the domestic animals in the petting zoo. There are pony rides and hay rides (each $.75), too.

❧ Cape Cod Museum of Natural History

Rte. 6A, Brewster; (508) 896-3867. May-Oct., Mon.-Sat., 9:30-4:30; Sun., 12:30-4:30. Mid-Oct.–May, closed Mon. Adults, $3.50; 6-14, $1.50.

Play nature detective and discover mysterious species of sea life; put your hand in a secret box and try to figure out what lurks within; test your knowledge of underwater creatures when you take the hands-on discovery quiz. These are among the many interactive displays at this nature museum. Stay awhile and hike one of the nature trails, or watch a movie. The museum runs several creative and fun kids' programs and special events, like Bubble-Blowing Day, Make Your Own Kite Day, field walks, and museum sleep-overs.

Salt Pond Visitor Center

Cape Cod National Seashore headquarters, Eastham; (508) 255-3421. Spring-fall, daily, 9-5; winter, 9-4:30 (in Jan., Sat. and Sun. only.) Call to confirm tour schedule. Free.

Early birds: Take a guided, 8:30 A.M. Beach Walk and learn about the shoreline of Nauset Beach. Night owls: Plan to join an Evening Campfire Walk along the beach. Meet back at the campfire to tell stories and enjoy the aroma of woodsmoke and salt air. More than 40 tours are offered in summer, including beach and inland walks and fishing and shellfishing demonstrations. Children's Hours, held two to three times weekly in summer, feature fun projects like scavenger hunts for kids up to age six. Most activities are free, and they offer a great way to get acquainted with the Cape Cod National Seashore.

Stony Brook Mill and Herring Run

Stony Brook Rd., Brewster.

If you're visiting in springtime (March through June) join local Cape Codders as they watch spawning herring run upstream. The herring swim against the current through a series of ladders that run from Cape Cod Bay to Upper Mill and Lower Mill ponds. A restored 19th-century grist mill shares the property; it grinds corn every Thursday through Saturday from 2 to 5 P.M., July through August.

Nickerson State Park

Off Rte. 6A, Brewster; (508) 896-3867.

This lovely, 1,750-acre park is perfect for hiking and biking (part of the Cape Cod Rail Trail passes through it). Swimming, camping, and fishing in one of four trout-stocked ponds are available for the sports-minded.

Chatham Fish Pier

Shore Rd. and Bar Cliff Ave., Chatham. Daily, after 2.

Bring your camera and watch salty New England fishermen unload their daily catch. You'll stand atop a visitor's balcony and see nets full of haddock, flounder, halibut, cod, and more being pulled in and readied for shipping to local markets and restaurants.

✣ Kate Gould Park

Main St., Chatham Center. July and Aug., Fri. at dusk (around 8 P.M.).

If you're in Chatham and it's Friday night, catch the Chatham Band concert at Kate Gould Park. Bring a blanket and refreshments and join right in. It's a terrific, fun freebie.

✣ The Railroad Museum

Depot Rd., Chatham. Mid-June–mid-Sept., Tues.-Sat., 10-4. Donations accepted.

Attention, fans of *Thomas the Tank Engine*: This historic depot, once the Chatham Company Railroad Station, houses a restored 1910 caboose and numerous model trains. Lots of "railroadiana" (relics and photos) is displayed, much of it more than 100 years old.

✣ Clam digging

This is the home of the world-famous Wellfleet oyster. For a true New England experience, roll up your pants cuffs, grab a bucket, and go clam digging. The shellfish beds here are abundant. Check the local paper for times of low tide, when you can pick steamers, quahogs, mussels, oysters, cherrystones, and scallops from the rich shellfish beds along the shoreline. Shellfish licenses are available at the town shellfish offices near Mayo Beach and at Town Hall. You might ask local enthusiasts for their recommendations of best places to go, as these vary throughout the year.

✣ Highland Light

Off Lighthouse Rd., North Truro.

Sometimes called Cape Cod Light, this is one of the most powerful beacons on the Atlantic Ocean. The lighthouse dates back to 1797 and is the first one seen by seafaring visitors traveling from Europe to Boston. It's a pretty drive to the lighthouse, which sits atop a bluff in a quiet, country setting. There's also a small collection of materials on shipwrecks and other local lore.

✣ Pilgrim Monument and Provincetown Museum

High-Pole Hill on Winslow St., off Bradford, Provincetown; (508) 487-1310. Year-round, daily, 9-5; July and Aug., 9-7. (Winter schedule may vary; call ahead.) Adults, $5; 4-12, $3. Admission includes monument, museum, and Whydah *exhibit.*

This impressive monument—the tallest all-granite structure in the United States—was built to commemorate the landing of the Pilgrims here in 1620. Climb to the top of this 252-foot tower for a commanding view. (It's a stamina-testing 116 stairs and 60 ramps.) On a clear day, you'll see Boston skyscrapers as you look across the bay and, to the southeast, the Atlantic Ocean. Even if you choose not to climb the monument, you'll get a nice overview of Provincetown from this site.

Located at the base of the Pilgrim Monument, the Provincetown Museum houses some unique items of interest to adults and children. You'll see model ships (the *Mayflower* exhibit is especially good), marine and whaling artifacts, and a collection of toys and children's books from the 17th and 18th centuries. Currently, the treasures of the pirate ship *Whydah,* which was shipwrecked off the coast of Wellfleet in 1717, are the featured exhibition. Watch restorers at work on these relics during your tour of the museum.

⚞ Provincetown Heritage Museum

356 Commercial St., Provincetown; (508) 487-0666. Mid-June–Columbus Day, daily, 10-6. Adults, $2; under 12, free.

Provincetown's past is celebrated at this little museum, offering a mix of art, Victorian memorabilia, fishing, and—the centerpiece—a half-scale model of the fishing schooner *Rose Dorothea.*

⚞ MacMillan Wharf

Commercial St., Provincetown.

This busy wharf on Provincetown Harbor is the perfect spot to park your car and watch the fishing boats and yachts come and go.(Leave your car here and explore the rest of the town on foot.) This is also the place you'll find charter fishing boats, harbor cruise excursion boats, and whale-watching tours. Cruise companies include Portuguese Princess Whale Watch, (800) 442-3188 or (508) 487-2651; Provincetown Whale Watch Inc., (800) 992-9333 or (508) 487-1582; and Dolphin Fleet, (800) 826-9300 or (508) 255-3857.

⚞ Horse and Carriage Rides

In front of Town Hall, Provincetown; (508) 487-6584. Rates vary according to size of party. A 10- to 12-minute ride for two adults and two children costs $17.

Tired of walking? See Provincetown in style, via horse-drawn carriage. Rambling Rose Carriage Rides offers tours ranging in length from 10 minutes to approximately 20 minutes. The longer rides take you along the back streets of town. The company also offers pony rides at Bayberry Hollow Farm; call for information.

⅊ Cape Cod National Seashore

The Cape Cod National Seashore is more than a beach; it's a unique national park (run by the National Park Service) that encompasses private residential and commercial land. Private businesses and residents are subject to strict building regulations and restrictions as part of an effort to protect the 400-mile coastline of the Cape's outer arm. The government owns about 27,000 of the 44,000 acres of land within the boundaries of the National Seashore. Six towns have boundaries within it: Chatham, Orleans, Eastham, Wellfleet, Truro, and Provincetown. Now for the fun part: the Seashore offers a wonderful variety of self-guided tours, bike trails, and ranger-guided activities, and they extend over six spectacular beaches.

⅊ Province Lands and Salt Pond Visitor's Centers

Salt Pond Visitor's Centers, off Rte. 6, Eastham; (508) 255-3421. Province Lands Visitor's Center, Race Point Rd. off Rte. 6, Provincetown; (508) 487-1256. Summer, open daily, 9-6. Spring and fall, daily, 9-4:30.

Visit either of these two National Seashore Visitor's Centers and pick up information, maps, and a schedule of activities and programs. The centers offer exhibits and introductory audiovisual programs on the area. Nature films are shown on summer evenings in the amphitheaters.

⅊ Beaches

Of the six National Seashore beaches, Race Point Beach, off Route 6 in Provincetown, is tops for families. It's a protected beach and is also a prime spot for watching the sun set. Coast Guard Beach, on Doane Road in Eastham, and nearby Nauset Light Beach (Cable Road, Eastham), are pretty, but the surf is rough. The former is good for boogie-boarding, the latter is known as the surfer's beach, having the highest waves of the National Seashore beaches. Herring Cove Beach, on Province Lands Road, in Provincetown, is another option; the left-hand side draws a gay and lesbian crowd, while the right attracts a mix of singles and families. Other National Seashore beaches are Marconi Beach, in Wellfleet, and Head of the Meadow Beach in Truro, which is not recommended because of seaweed.

On Cape Cod Bay, in Truro, Corn Hill Beach is great for families, offering superb shelling.

∼ Beachcombing

Even when Cape beaches are deserted, they're teeming with life. When the tide is out, see for yourself. Look for horseshoe crabs, starfish, sea urchins, sand dollars, periwinkles, and shellfish (wearing a pair of reef shoes isn't a bad idea, since it's fun to dig in the sand with your toes). The best beaches for beachcombing are the ocean beaches from Chatham to Provincetown, although there's plenty to see along the beaches of Cape Cod Bay, Nantucket Sound, and Vineyard Sound.

∼ Bicycling

The following bike trails are within the Cape Cod National Seashore. Trail maps are available at the Visitor's Information Centers in Eastham and Provincetown. Bike rentals are available at Arnold's, 329 Commercial St., in Provincetown, (508) 487-0844.

∼ Nauset Trail

Salt Pond Road Visitor's Center, off Rte. 6, Eastham.

This 1.6-mile paved bike trail offers views of the cedar banks, Nauset Marsh, old Nauset Coast Guard Station, and other points of interest. The trail ends at Coast Guard Beach.

∼ Head of the Meadow Trail

High Head Rd., Truro.

This two-mile marshland bike trail begins on High Head Road in Truro and heads toward Head of the Meadow Beach (you can also pick it up at the beach parking lot). Venture off the trail to the spring where the Pilgrims took their first drink of fresh water in America (follow signs to Pilgrim Lake and Pilgrim Spring Trail).

∼ Province Lands Trail

Herring Cove Beach, Provincetown.

This eight-mile paved bike trail crosses forests, ponds, bogs, and some of the most spectacular sand dunes along the Atlantic coast. Segments include a 5.25-mile loop trail; Herring Cove Beach spur (1 mile); Race Point Beach spur (.50 mile); Bennett Pond spur (.25 mile); and Race Point Road spur (.25 mile).

∼ Hiking

Self-guided nature walks and ranger-guided tours and activities are offered throughout the year. You don't have to be an expert trail blazer—

many are short but interesting nature walks suitable for beginners and children. Particularly enjoyable are some of the National Park Service hikes, such as the Seashore Surprise (parents and kids learn about the sea through scavenger hunts, stories, and games along the way); the Sunset Beach Walk, featuring stories around a campfire at sunset; and Cape Cod Whales and Historic Beach Apparatus Drill (divers demonstrate the methods once used to rescue shipwrecked mariners). Call the Province Lands Visitor's Center for times and starting points; (508) 487-1256.

RESTAURANTS

⌇ The Lobster Claw
Rte. 6A, Orleans; (508) 255-1800. April–mid-Nov., daily, 12-9.

This sprawling, rustic eatery is a real visit to Crustacean Land; the gift shop has more than 250 lobster-themed knickknacks, the menu is shaped like a lobster claw...you get the idea. It's extremely popular. We recommend it for families with a caveat: dine early, especially on weekend nights. You'll avoid long waits and get an incentive: free chowder, beverage, and ice cream with dinner between 4 and 5:30. That's a good deal, and the prices are pretty reasonable to begin with. Lobsters, mussels, and steamers are good buys, as are fish dinners, and the food isn't bad at all. There's a kid's menu, too. This is a good option when you want a step up from an eat-in-the-rough place.

⌇ The Mayflower Cafe
300 Commercial St., Provincetown; (508) 487-0121. First Sun. in April–third Sun. in Oct., 11:30-9:30.

Need a break from seafood? This wonderful family-run place has served P-town natives and tourists for 65 years. The Italian and Portuguese specialties are delicious, and the waitresses fuss over you (well, over your adorable children) like doting aunties. Kale soup and pork chops *vinho dahlos* are house specialties, and for the kids, you can't go wrong with spaghetti and meatballs or pizza. (Children's portions are available.) Prices are remarkably low. Decor is plain-Jane, but what the Mayflower lacks in looks it makes up for in friendliness.

⌇ Bayside Lobster Hutt
Commercial St., Wellfleet. Memorial Day–Columbus Day, daily, 4:30-9 P.M.

Inside this old oyster shack you'll find some of the best seafood on the Cape. Eat in the rough and enjoy lobster, steamers, fried oysters, broiled flounder, or whatever else is fresh that day. Yes, there are cheeseburgers and hot dogs—sort of an unofficial kids' menu—but why not split up the generous Fisherman's Platter instead? Veggie lovers can opt for corn on the cob and a trip to the salad bar.

THE ISLANDS

Martha's Vineyard and Nantucket, accessible only by air or sea, are vacation playgrounds for thousands of travelers each year. Both islands offer miles of splendid beaches, tall, white sand dunes, nature trails, picturesque harbors, sleepy fishing villages, and bustling main streets lined with trendy boutiques and fine restaurants. And yet each island has a unique personality and charm of its own.

Martha's Vineyard, located just seven miles off Cape Cod, is the largest island in New England—20 miles long and 10 miles wide.

The Vineyard, as it's commonly known, is full of surprises; its textures, rhythms, and amenities are as diverse as the people who visit it. Of course, one is never far from the sea, so the preferred pasttimes are swimming, sunbathing, surfing, sailing and exploring. Surrounding the sea are forests and salt marshes, meadows and cliffs, hills and plains. Much of the action—shopping, restaurants, attractions—centers in the towns of Edgartown and Vineyard Haven (also known as Tisbury). Oak Bluffs is famous for the "Flying Horses" antique carousel and charming gingerbread cottages in the center of town.

You'll find as much or as little to do as you want on this island, from bustling Edgartown to the rustic harbor village of Menemsha, where the current generation of fishermen still hauls in the daily catch. Menemsha Public Beach is superb.

Nantucket, meaning "far-away land," is 30 miles off the coast and offers a 100-year flashback in time. You'll step off the ferry to enter a perfectly preserved 19th-century village of cobblestone streets and red-brick mansions. Elegant sea captains' homes, reminiscent of a time when Nantucket was one of the great whaling centers of the world, now house fine restaurants, boutiques, and country inns. Pack up a picnic lunch and venture beyond the village to the shoreline, where cedar-shingled homes hug the coast. Swim in the surrounding island waters—the calm Nantucket Sound to the north, the mighty Atlantic to the south.

Travelers who plan ahead (book your accommodations as far in advance as possible) and avoid summer traffic congestion (consider leaving your car behind) can find the vacation they want in the islands. Most return revitalized, refreshed by the clear salt air that has the therapeutic power to wash away 20th-century stress.

Hy-Line Cruises, (508) 778-2600, and the Steamship Authority, (508) 540-2022, provide regular ferry service to the islands from Hyannis and Woods Hole. Nantucket is 2 hours and 30 minutes from Hyannis and 3 hours from Woods Hole. Martha's Vineyard is 45 minutes from Woods Hole and 1 hour and 45 minutes from Hyannis. Call for schedules.

MARTHA'S VINEYARD

❄ The Flying Horses
Circuit Ave., Oak Bluffs; (508) 693-9481. Easter Sun.–mid-June, Sat. and Sun., 10-6; mid-June–Columbus Day, daily, 10-10. Per ride, $1; 10 rides, $8.

Doing the island thing with little ones? This may be the highlight of their visit. Grab the rings as you whirl around this antique carousel— nab the brass one and you win a free ride. The challenge is as exciting as the ride for most children. A short walk from the ferry dock in Oak Bluffs, the Flying Horses is said to be the oldest operating carousel in the country.

❄ Felix Neck Wildlife Sanctuary
Edgartown Rd., Edgartown; (508) 627-4850. Grounds open year-round, daily, dawn-4; visitor's center, daily, 9-4. Adults, $3; children, $2.

A wonderful place to commune with island wildlife, this property offers four miles of self-guided nature trails plus a nature center with native waterfowl and nesting ospreys.

❄ Cedar Tree Neck Wildlife Sanctuary
Off Indian Hill Rd., West Tisbury; (508) 693-5207.

Walk off the effects of those ice cream cones from Mad Martha's with a day of hiking. This 300-acre preserve has 250 acres of North Shore head-lands, with woods, ponds, brooks, and dunes and several scenic view trails.

❄ The Lobster Hatchery
Shirley Ave., Oak Bluffs; (508) 693-0060. June-Sept., Mon.-Fri., 9-12 and 1-3. Free.

A trip to New England wouldn't be complete without a real close look at one of these crustaceans. You'll see baby lobsters and large lobsters and learn all about the lobster life cycle. (Did you know it takes seven years for a lobster to grow to one-pound size in our waters?) And just wait 'til the next time you try to boil one....

⅔ Gay Head Cliffs
Moshup Trail, Gay Head.

Formed by glaciers, these multicolored cliffs are a national landmark. They rise 150 feet above the shore, affording spectacular views. There's a small parking lot at the top of the cliffs and a trail that leads to Gay Head Clay Cliffs Beach.

⅔ Beaches

There are some great sandy beaches on the Vineyard, including Bend-in-the-Road Beach on Nantucket Sound, Edgartown; Joseph A. Sylvia State Beach, off Beach Road between Oak Bluffs and Edgartown; Menemsha Public Beach, at the mouth of the harbor on Vineyard Sound (try to forget that the movie *Jaws* was filmed in Menemsha); and Owen Park Beach in Vineyard Haven, a calm public beach that's right next to a park and great for kids.

► RESTAURANTS

⅔ Giordano's Restaurant
107 Circuit Ave., Oak Bluffs; (508) 693-0184. June-Sept., daily, 11:30-10:30.

Bless this place—it's one of the few Vineyard restaurants where you can go in, plop down, and relax, kids in tow. None of that Geez-I-hope-they-can-behave-themselves-in-this-place tension. Giordano's is cheerful and generally inexpensive, and the menu is a happy mix of pasta, pizza, fried seafood, and Italian specialties. Almost everything is made from scratch, including the sauces. Try spaghetti with white littleneck clam sauce, or chicken parmesan (the most popular dish here), or shrimp cacciatore. A children's menu is offered, but prices are on the high side, so if yours are light eaters you might do well with a side of meatballs and some shared spaghetti.

⅔ Black Dog Tavern
On the beach in Vineyard Haven; (508) 693-9223. Mid-June–Oct., daily, 11:30-10:30.

You've seen the T-shirts—everywhere—so you might as well try this local landmark yourself. Sit on the open porch overlooking Vineyard Haven Harbor and feast on fresh seafood.

⅔ The Aquinnah
Gay Head Cliffs; (508) 645-9654. Mid-June–Oct., Mon.-Thurs., 8-5; Fri.-Sun., 8 A.M.–sunset.

More great views at this casual restaurant, high atop Gay Head Cliffs overlooking the Atlantic. It's open for breakfast, lunch, and dinner; naturally, you'll sit outside.

NANTUCKET

⚓ Whaling Museum

Broad St., head of Steamboat Wharf; (508) 228-1736. Summer, daily, 10-5; spring and fall, 11-3. Adults, $4.50; 5-14, $1.50.

Learn what it was like during Nantucket's great whaling era as you study the museum's collections of maritime artifacts. Learn all about whales, every kid's favorite giant sea mammal; see how they were caught and, well, processed. More fun are a whaleboat, scrimshaw, and the skeleton of a 43-foot finback whale.

⚓ Gail's Tours

(508) 257-6557. Tours at 10, 1, and 3 daily, in season.

If you really want to get to know the island, Gail Nickerson is the one to see. She's been giving tours for ages, knows everyone, and will give you a lively ride. She loves kids and often brings her daughter along. Tours last about 1 hour and 30 minutes.

⚓ Maria Mitchell Aquarium

28 Washington St.; (508) 228-5387 or 228-0898. Mid-June–Aug., Tues.-Sat., 10-4. Admission, $1.

This aquarium and the Hinchman House (see listing) honor Nantucket astronomer Maria Mitchell. See marine life collected from around the island here, including during a recent visit seven types of crabs, 15 kinds of fish, eels, and baby sharks. Some specimens can be taken out to touch; aquarium staffers will tell you all about them. You can even add to the collection here—join a marine life collecting trip (run twice a week), and you'll go out with nets and buckets to look for examples of local sea life. Your specimens may join the other inhabitants of the aquarium. The charge is $7 for adults, and $4 for kids age six to 14. Call for times.

⚓ Nantucket Lifesaving Museum

Polpis Rd., Nantucket Center; (508) 228-1885. Mid-June–mid-Oct., 9:30-4:30. Adults, $2; under 12, $1.

Step into this authentic recreation of Nantucket's Surfside Station, built in 1874, and see lifesaving boats and displays of rescue equipment. Check out the exhibit of treasures from the sunken ship *Andrea Doria*.

🥨 Old Mill

At intersection of Prospect, West York, and South Mill streets; (508) 228-1894. May–mid-June, daily, 11-3; mid-June–Sept., 10-5; Sept. and Oct., 11-3. Adults, $3; 14 and under, $2.

Built in 1746, this is one of the last operating wind-powered mills in the country. It's preserved by the Nantucket Historical Association and is the sole survivor of four mills on the island. Watch the impressive-looking wooden gears turn the millstone, grinding the corn, and take home a freshly ground bag of cornmeal. In summer, join the children's living history program: kids run the old windmill and help the miller make cornmeal. Then the group heads to the island's oldest house to bake cornbread. The program runs once a month, twice daily on Wednesdays; from 9 to 11 A.M., and again from 2 to 4 P.M. Reservations are required.

🥨 Hinchman House

7 Milk St.; (508) 228-0898. Early-June–Aug., Tues.-Sat., 10-4. Adults, $3; children, $1.

This building houses a unique natural history museum, featuring a collection of living reptiles and mounted birds and fauna from the island. There are also native wildflower and plant displays; exhibits focus on environmental issues of Nantucket. Tours are self-guided. Call for the schedule of bird and nature walks.

🥨 Beaches

Children's Beach, on the North Shore (and close to town), is aptly named—it may well end up your family's favorite. Due to its Nantucket Sound location, the water is calm. Facilities include a playground, park, concessions, and rest rooms. Other good choices include Dionis Beach (with sand dunes) and Jetties Beach (with sailboat rentals), both on the North Shore; the local favorite, Surfside Beach (which has good body surfing), and Madaket Beach (which has great sunsets), both on the South Shore; and 'Sconset Beach (with good people watching), on the East Shore.

◤ RESTAURANTS

🥨 The Hearth at the Harbor House

5 South Beach St.; (508) 228-1500. Summer, daily, 5-9 P.M.; after Columbus Day, Tues.-Sun.; after Jan. 1, Wed.-Sun. Sunset special: 5-6:30 P.M.

This appealing restaurant is in the 1860s Harbor House Inn, with high ceilings, exposed beams, and beautiful woodwork. They call it "civilized family dining," so if that describes your bunch, go for it. We like the Sunset Special. A special fixed-price menu is offered, with four entree choices, appetizer, and dessert, along with a special menu for the under-12 set. Two children's dinners are free with each adult special. Has this concept caught on? You bet your lightship basket it has, so reservations are a must. Seafood, beef, and chicken are the bill of fare.

⌘ The Downey Flake
At Children's Beach; (508) 228-4533. April-Oct., 6 A.M.–2:30 P.M.

For melt-in-your-mouth pastries or a great breakfast, walk to this simple island eatery. Kids love the pancakes, stacked high and topped with fresh, locally made cranberry or blueberry syrup, and the homemade vanilla yogurt, topped with granola and served with a bowl of fresh fruit. Drop in at the counter for ready-to-go sandwiches and pastries on your way to the beach.

⌘ Claudette's Box Lunch
On the Square at Siasconset; (508) 257-6622. May and June, daily, 9-4; July and Aug., 9-9; Sept. and Oct., 9-4.

Need a box lunch for the beach? Want a special picnic, without the hassle? This is the place. Try their famous lemon cake—the recipe was requested by *Gourmet* magazine.

New Hampshire

PORTSMOUTH

There aren't many better places for a family to spend a day or two than in Portsmouth, New Hampshire. This gem of a city, New Hampshire's only seaport, is tucked away between the Maine and Massachusetts borders and often gets bypassed by hurried tourists.

In Portsmouth, being a visitor is just plain easier than in most other popular New England towns. While the city offers a list of activities to keep even the busiest of families happy, it also manages to maintain an unpretentious relaxed atmosphere.

Don't rush through this town on your way to Maine. Plan to spend at least a day visiting its unique museums (including a great hands-on museum just for children), strolling lovely Prescott Park, cruising to the Isles of Shoals, or zipping down Geronimo at nearby Water Country. Be sure to stop by the town fish pier, where, if your timing is right, you'll see the fish boats hauling in the daily catches.

⁂ Strawbery Banke

Marcy St. (opposite Prescott Park and the Portsmouth waterfront); (603) 433-1100. May-Oct., daily, 10-5. Adults, $10; 6-17, $7; families, $25.

When the first settlers landed in Portsmouth they found wild strawberries growing along the banks of the Piscataqua River and so named this seaport Strawbery Banke. During the next 150 years, the site became a thriving waterfront town and later an immigrant neighborhood known as Puddle Dock.

Today, salvaged from demolition and restored, this area is a unique living history museum. You'll see 30 of the 35 original historic buildings, all in various stages of restoration. A number of archaeological and restoration exhibits show how we piece together facts about the past. Part of the fun is seeing restoration projects still going on, in various stages of readiness.

Some of the houses are furnished to reflect time periods ranging from the 17th to the 20th centuries; others contain exhibits and craft shops. You're likely to see gardeners at work on the grounds, boat builders, barrel makers, archaeologists, carpenters, quilt makers, weavers, and more.

Older children (six and older) can get firsthand knowledge of what it might have been like to live in an earlier time by signing up for daily workshops. During the 45-minute sessions, they might make a basket, patch a piece of quilt, spin yarn, or perform other 19th-century tasks. The museum also hosts a number of special programs and activities throughout the year, ranging from New England Gardening Day in June to Fall Festival in October.

⚛ Port of Portsmouth Maritime Museum and Albacore Park

Market Street Extension; (603) 436-3680. Columbus Day–April, Thurs.-Mon., 9:30-3:30; May–Columbus Day, daily, 9:30-5. Adults, $4; 7-17, $2; families (two parents and up to three children), $10.

When you sit at the controls of a real submarine it's easy to pretend you're in charge. At the Portsmouth Maritime Museum you get the chance to climb aboard the U.S.S. *Albacore* and go below to its tiny engine room, captain's quarters, radio room, and dining area. A short film describes the history of the 1,200-ton submarine, and a tour guide leads you through it. The 10-acre park includes a Visitor's Center, small museum, and gift shop.

⚛ Children's Museum of Portsmouth

280 Marcy St.; (603) 436-3853. Sept.-June, Tues.-Sat., 10-5; Sun., 1-5; July and Aug., daily, 10-5. Admission, $3.50; under 1, free.

Where else can your children don rain slickers and fishing hats, jump aboard a lobster boat, and pull up a trap full of plastic flounders, lobsters, haddock, bass, and shrimp? And where else can they take their "catch" over to the fish market, where their playmates become make-believe customers? This cozy, historic-home-turned-museum is a child's paradise. When they're done fishing, children can head up to the rocket ship. They'll take turns at the controls, while a video screen before them helps them imagine their journey through space. There's lots to do and see here—dozens of hands-on exhibits and many daily-scheduled art activities. There are many children who probably never even get past the big yellow submarine on the first floor. This three-story play structure contains tunnels, platforms, peek holes, slides, and poles. Relax in the convenient adjacent sitting area—they're bound to come out sooner or later.

⚛ Prescott Park

Marcy St. on Portsmouth waterfront; (603) 436-2848.

When it's time to relax (or the kids need to let off a little steam), walk over to Prescott Park. This lovely waterfront expanse is full of flower

gardens and fountains and has room to roam. Snack pushcarts are here
if you need replenishing, and often you'll see a variety of arts and crafts
exhibits throughout the park. If you can, be here for the family art and
music festivals held during the summer. Sit on the lawn and listen to
outdoor concerts or watch dance programs. It's great family entertainment
in a hard-to-beat setting.

⅋ Water Country

*Rte. 1 (3 mi. south of downtown Portsmouth); (603) 436-3556. Memorial
Day–mid-June, weekends, 10:30-6; mid-June–July 1, daily, 10:30-6;
July–late-Aug., daily, 9:30-7; late Aug.–Labor Day, daily, 10:30-6.
Adults, $17.99; under 4 ft., $10.99. Admission does not include tube rental.*

On a hot summer day this place is a real treat. Tube down a quarter-
mile "river" through waterfalls and caves, speed down the dips on the
double dive-boggin slide, bank around the curbs on the triple giant slides,
or swallow your stomach down Double Geronimo, the fastest waterslide in
New England. If that sounds a bit too active, there are simple pools to
soak in and lots of lawn chairs. For younger kids (under four feet tall)
there are three large kiddie areas, including the Octopus Lagoon with
minisize waterslides, wading pool, whirlpool, and playground equipment.
But it's the older kids and daredevil parents who get the most for the
money here, challenging the well-named Raging Rapids, the Polaroid
Shooter and Screamer, and the Plunge.

⅋ Boat Cruises

There's no better place to view the coastline, harbors, and islands
than from a boat. The Isles of Shoals Steamship Company, (800) 441-
4620 offers a variety of cruises, including fall foliage and naturalist tours,
whale-watching expeditions, and a special lighthouse cruise that takes you
to five lighthouses in the area. The Steamship Company also offers a special excursion to Star Island (part of the Isles of Shoals) on which you'll be
able to explore the island and learn its interesting history.

Portsmouth Harbor Cruises, 63 Ceres Street, (603) 436-8084, offers a
1-hour-and-30-minute cruise aboard the small (49 passengers) wooden M/
V *Heritage*. Because of its size, the *Heritage* is able to travel to areas not
accessible in a larger boat. You'll get an intimate look at the seacoast area,
including its picturesque inland rivers and the Great Bay.

⅋ Isles of Shoals

Discovered in 1614 by Captain John Smith, the nine shoal islands are
natural havens for birds, wildflowers, and animals. You'll see several species of gulls on the islands, the most common being the herring gull. The

largest is the black-backed gull, with a wing span of five feet. Harbor seals raise their young on one of the islands, and whales have been observed a few hundred yards off shore. Four of the islands are in New Hampshire and five belong to Maine. Sign up for one of the harbor boat cruises to get there.

🐎 Horse & Carriage Rides

Market Square; (603) 427-0044. May-Oct., daily; Nov.-April, weekends. 20 minute ride, $20; 30 minute ride, $25; 40 minute ride, $30. Prices are per carriage ride; carriages fit up to 4 adults or 2 adults and 3 children.

What kid doesn't like a horse-and-buggy ride? Mom and dad will enjoy it, too, in these quaint historical horse-drawn open carriages that tour Portsmouth in style. This is particularly special during the Christmas holidays when the downtown area is decked out in its old-fashioned finery, and the sleigh bells add the perfect touch.

🐎 Bow Street Theatre

125 Bow St.

Both the Portsmouth Academy of Performing Arts, (603) 433-7272, and the Seacoast Repertory Company of P.A.P.A., (603) 433-4472, perform at this intimate, comfortable theater. There's lots of quality, live theater going on here year-round, including a top-notch Saturday and Sunday children's series. Some past favorites have included *Rumpelstiltskin, Aladdin, The Wizard of Oz,* and *Beauty and the Beast.* Call for details.

🐎 Urban Forestry Center

45 Elwyn Rd.; (603) 431-6774. Year-round, daily 'til dusk. Free.

This center is a peaceful nature escape just outside the city, where you can walk Brook Trail alongside native wildflowers and herb and perennial gardens. Try your skill at identifying local trees—many are noted along the trail.

RESTAURANTS

🐎 The Stockpot

53 Bow Street; (603) 431-1851. Daily, 11-11:30.

The Stockpot began in 1982 as a soup-and-stew hangout for local artists. Today it draws a more diverse crowd that comes for its good, relatively cheap food and waterfront location. Housed in a remodeled 19th-century brewery, it offers nice views of Portsmouth Harbor and freshly made, simply prepared food including lots of great homemade soups, salads, and sandwiches. It also offers a nice selection of dinner preparations running the gamut from meatloaf and mashed potatoes to stuffed scallops and shrimp stir fry.

⭐ Poco Diablo's
37 Bow St.; (603) 431-5510. Daily, 11-11.

This always-crowded eatery in Portsmouth is especially appealing on warm, pleasant evenings when you can snag a table on the outside deck, munch on a platterful of Nachos Grande, and watch the boats come in and out of the harbor. Inside, you'll miss the view, but the fare is equally good. Tacos, enchiladas, burritos, and other standards are great tasting, and the servings are plentiful.

NEW HAMPSHIRE SEACOAST

This small, condensed region of New Hampshire encompasses only 18 miles of shoreline and centers on the busy resort area of Hampton Beach. Nearly 150,000 sunbathers crowd this long stretch of beach on sunny summer days. The hardy ones swim in the cold waters of the Atlantic (averaging only 55 degrees in July); the rest soak up the sun's rays and the area's frolicking, carnival atmosphere. This is the Daytona Beach of the Northeast, full of noisy fun and enough activities to fill your days and nights.

If you're in need of a bit more solitude, don't despair. Visit the seaside town of Rye, where you can picnic at Odiorne Point State Park and take a quiet oceanside nature walk. Stroll the cobblestone streets of quaint downtown Exeter, or pick fruit at a nearby orchard. If you venture just a few miles from Hampton Beach in either direction, you're back in storybook New England.

⭐ Hampton Beach
Ocean Blvd; (603) 926-8717. Year-round. Free.

Your teenagers—and near teens—will love this place. There are three miles of white, sandy beach surrounded by restaurants, boutiques, game rooms, arcades, souvenir shops, waterslides, and hot dog, pizza, candy, fried dough, and ice cream stands. Don't bother driving around town; you'll spend too much time stuck in traffic. Hop the town trolley car (on which you'll hear about the day's list of area activities), or walk the boardwalk on Ocean Boulevard. On Monday nights, there are talent shows; Wednesday nights, fireworks; Friday nights, sing-alongs; and there are free band concerts nightly. At last count there were five arcades, including the granddaddy of them all, the 40-year-old Hampton Beach Casino's Funarama Arcade. Of course, the beach settles down after Labor Day, which is when the locals are to be found enjoying its special beauty on sunny fall days.

Hampton Beach Casino
Ocean Blvd., Hampton Beach; (603) 926-4541.

This is where just about everything cool happens at Hampton Beach—at least according to the kids. Wall-to-wall baseball hats, T-shirts, and Reeboks crowd the seven-acre playground that includes shops, food (like cotton candy, hot dogs, slushes, fried dough, clams, sausages, and lots more), minigolf, arcades, kiddie rides, waterslides, a teen club—you get the idea. Noisy, elbow-to-elbow 20th-century fun.

Odiorne Point State Park
Rte. 1A, Rye; (603) 436-1118, (603) 436-8043. Year-round.

Located just a few minutes from Hampton Beach in Rye is this lovely oceanside park, the largest undeveloped stretch of shore on New Hampshire's coast. The area is expansive, offering great views and lots to do. Be sure to wear a pair of shoes that you don't mind getting wet. Odiorne is one of the best places around to go tidepooling. As you hop rocks and peer into the pools, you'll likely find an abundant array of marine creatures, including sea urchins, snails, starfish, lobsters, shrimp, and more. (It's okay to pick them up, even to put them in a bucket for viewing—but everything needs to be put back before leaving.)

There are wading areas, picnic tables, grills, and a playground in this 230-acre preserve. There are also a number of trails (lots of people bring their mountain bikes) that take you along the rocky coastline or inland through the salt marshes, ponds, and woodlands. The recently opened Science Center is a must-see, too.

Seacoast Science Center
Odiorne State Park, Rte. 1, Rye; (603) 436-8043. Year-round, Tues.-Sun., 10-5; May-Sept., also open Mon., 12-5. Free.

Get your hands on a starfish, snails, sea urchins, and more at this pretty marine center that sits atop a bluff overlooking the ocean. The best strategy here is to stop at the Science Center first to see and learn all about the creatures that inhabit the nearby ocean waters. Then go exploring the hundreds of tidepools outside for a look at some of the same critters. The center houses a number of aquariums and marine exhibits that interpret the seven habitats found at the park, including a tidepool touch tank, a 1,000-gallon Gulf of Maine tank, and a "Look Under" tank. Local school kids act as volunteer guides during the summer and are eager to answer any questions.

Rye Harbor Cruises/Whale Watches

On the seacoast, you spend a lot of time looking at the ocean; you'll get a different perspective of the region from the water. New Hampshire Seacoast Cruises, Rye Harbor State Marina, Rte. 1A, Rye Harbor, (603) 964-5545, will take you and your family on a two-hour tour of all nine Isles of Shoals. It also offers a six-hour whale-watch excursion, led by research biologists.

The Atlantic Fishing Fleet, Rte. 1A, Rye Harbor State Marina, (603) 964-5220, offers sunset cruises on its 80-foot M/V *Atlantic Queen II*. The Tuesday and Friday evening whale watches offer a close-up view of these great ocean giants. On the narrated trips, you're also likely to spot dolphins, seals, and an array of seabirds.

Wallis Sands

Rte. 1A, Rye; (603) 436-9404. Memorial Day–Labor Day.

This white, sandy beach is 800 feet long, 150 feet wide, and a popular summertime swimming spot. There are refreshments, rest rooms, and changing facilities. From the rocky bluff at the north end of Wallis Sands you can see Seal Rocks, frequently during the colder months covered with seals sunning themselves. On the horizon you'll be able to see the Isles of Shoals, nine tiny islands off the coast.

Fort Constitution and Fort Stark

Fort Stark, Rte. 1B (take Wild Rose Ln. to the fort), Newcastle; (603) 436-6607. Memorial Day–Labor Day. Free. Fort Constitution, Rte 1B (follow signs to Coast Guard Station), Newcastle. Weekends only. Free.

These two sites in Newcastle provide a peek at early military installations and offer great views of the Atlantic coastline.

Fort Stark is a 10-acre former U.S. coastal harbor defense facility, where you'll get a historical look at the state's fortification system and a spectacular view of the Atlantic Ocean, Little Harbor, Ordione Point State Park, and the Isles of Shoals. Be careful as you walk through the site: there are lots of rough ground and slippery rocks.

On December 13, 1744, Paul Revere rode from Boston with a message that the fort at Rhode Island had been dismantled and troops were coming to take over Fort Constitution (then named Fort William and

Mary). The fort was damaged in the raid, which was an important link in the chain of events leading to the Revolution. Today you can walk the site and enjoy the coastal views.

≈ Kingston State Park
Off Rte. 125, Kingston; (603) 452-9621.

Swim in the fresh waters of Great Pond and have a picnic in this 44-acre state park; it's just outside Exeter.

≈ Applecrest Farm Orchards
Rte. 88, Hampton Falls; (603) 926-3721. Year-round. Call ahead for seasonal hours.

A visit to Applecrest is more than just a stop at an apple farm; it's also a nice family outing. One of the oldest and largest apple orchards in the seacoast area, Applecrest also offers pick-your-own strawberries, raspberries, and blueberries. There are special activities and festivals throughout the year and cross-country skiing in winter.

≈ Raspberry Farm
Rte. 84, Hampton Falls; (603) 926-6604. July-Oct; daily, 9-sunset.

If you've ever picked wild blackberries or raspberries, you'll appreciate this farm even more. The bushes are trained on a trellis, so you can pick while standing. Set on a nearly 200-year-old site, this farm grows more than 10 different varieties of blackberries and raspberries. You'll have more than six miles of rows to pick from, and all containers are furnished.

≈ Emery Farm
Rte. 4, Durham; (603) 742-8495. Mid.-May–Dec.; daily, 9-6.

There are more than 12 acres of pick-your-own fruit on this family farm, established in 1655 in Durham. A small animal petting farm and an old-fashioned country store are also on the grounds.

≈ Little Bay Buffalo Company
Langley Road, Durham; (603) 868-2632. Mon.-Sun., 9-sunset.

Home, home on the range...can this be right? Yes, native New Englanders don't have to head west to catch a glimpse of the mighty American bison. Come see the unexpected at this farm. There are tours and a small shop (anyone care for a bison burger?), but just a stop by for a close-up look at these hefty beasts can be enough.

American Independence Museum

225 Water Street, Exeter; (603) 772-2622. Year-round, Tues. and Sat., 12-3. Adults, $4; children, $2.

This 1721 house was once the governor's mansion. Now, you'll see a small display of Revolutionary War artifacts, furnishings, and documents. Of note are the Purple Heart stitched by Martha Washington and an original Dunlap Broadside copy of the Declaration of Independence. This place probably won't receive the same reception from your kids as a visit to an action-packed arcade, but it's a quick lesson in history. Besides, there's a great homemade-chocolate specialty store in town.

Exeter Park Concerts

Swasey Parkway, Exeter; (603) 778-0595.

Bring a blanket and some lawn chairs, sit under the stars, and listen to music for all tastes. Summer concerts are held in the early evenings (about 6:30-7) during the week. You're likely to hear anything from brass bands to comedy quartets. Call for a schedule of performers. During inclement weather, concerts are moved indoors to Exeter Town Hall.

Seabrook Science and Nature Center

Seabrook Station, just off Rte. 1, Seabrook; (800) 338-7482. Year-round, Mon.-Sat., 10-4. (Closed national and New Hampshire holidays.) Free.

Okay, this is a nuclear plant. That said, let's go on. The science center set up here contains a number of informative, hands-on exhibits and sensitively presented educational programs about energy and the environment. There are more than 30 exhibits and displays. You'll take an imaginary journey nearly 260 feet below sea level to Seabrook's cooling tunnels. Kids can test their "Energy I.Q." with the center's computer quizzes and their "Pedal Power" at the bicycle-powered generator. There are aquariums and a touch pool for a look at regional marine life, and a short nature trail through surrounding salt marshes and woodlands.

A visit here is sure to be a springboard for a good family discussion on energy and the future.

Hilltop Fun Center

Rte. 108, Somersworth; (603) 742-8068. April-Oct., Sun.-Thurs., 10-9; Fri.-Sat., 10-10.

You'll find all the favorite, noisy, of-no-redeeming-educational-value, just-plain-fun activities under one roof at the Hilltop. This is one of the largest amusement centers in the region, complete with miniature golf, go-carts, batting cages, driving range, bumper boats, arcade, kiddie rides and more. Don't worry, you've already taken them to the art gallery and science center, right?

RESTAURANTS

✺ Captain Newick's
431 Dover Point Rd. (exit 6W off Spaulding Tpke.), Durham; (603) 742-3205. Mon.-Thurs. and Sun., 11-8; Fri. and Sat., 11-9.

A great family place, especially if you have a taste for fresh fried seafood or lobster in the rough. This always-crowded, quick-service place serves hefty portions at fair prices. You'll sit at long picnic tables, probably eat most of your food with your fingers, and take home a doggie bag of leftovers.

✺ Loaf & Ladle
9 Water St., Exeter; (603) 778-8955. Mon.-Wed., 8-8; Thurs.-Sat., 8-9; Sun., 11-9.

Help yourself, cafeteria style, to an assortment of homemade breads, soups, chilis, and salads. Grab your plate and head outdoors to the deck overlooking the tumbling river. This is hearty, healthy fare, with great breads, vegetables, soups, and salads. At dinner, the chef prepares a couple of special entrees to choose from (like creamy alfredo fettucine with fresh veggies or lemon-baked herbal chicken).

MERRIMACK VALLEY

More than half the population of New Hampshire lives in the Merrimack Valley region, and most visitors see it only in passing, on their way north to the most popular tourist destinations. Nashua, Salem, Manchester, and Concord are probably not on the top of your "places to go" list, but the cities offer an abundance of fun-filled family activities and still maintain much of their small-town charm. You'll find a host of interesting museums, from the Children's Metamorphosis Museum in Londonderry to the larger Christa McAuliffe Planetarium in Concord. And just outside the city centers you'll find rolling, peaceful countryside, clear rivers and lakes, and some very scenic state parks.

Next time you're driving by, get off the highway for more than a stop at a fast-food chain. Spend the afternoon at the Canobie Lake Amusement

Park, take a refreshing swim at Silver Lake or a journey into space at the planetarium. Ride a rowboat in Bear Brooks State Park, or canoe down the Merrimack River. You'll return to the car refreshed, and the kids will be tuckered out for the rest of the journey. Or you might just decide to stick around the area awhile to discover its other hidden gems.

Canobie Lake Park

Exit 2 off I-93, Salem; (603) 893-3506. Memorial Day–Labor Day, daily, noon-10; mid-April–Memorial Day, weekends, noon-10. Adults, $14 (includes all rides and shows), under 42 inches, $9; under 2 years, free.

This is a kids' delight. It has all their favorite amusement rides, boats, and games, plus an arcade, a haunted house, live puppet shows, a Sensaround theater, and music revues. There's a large kiddie area with lots of rides and a great roller coaster for the teens. Bring your bathing suit; there's a swimming pool and a wild log flume ride. You can also take a boat cruise around the lake or a train ride around the park. The park features a wide variety of entertainment, as well, including fireworks, live shows, and specialty acts.

On your way home, head north a few miles and take a look at America's Stonehenge.

America's Stonehenge

Mystery Hill (off Rte. 111), North Salem; (603) 893-8300. June–Labor Day, daily, 10-5; May and Labor Day–Oct., weekends, 10-4. Adults, $6.50; 13-18, $4; 6-12, $2.50.

Some claim this series of unusual rock formations is the 4,000-year-old astronomical complex built by Celts who came here from the Iberian peninsula. It most likely is the oldest manmade construction in the United States. Formerly known as Mystery Hill, it has presented an intriguing puzzle to archaeologists and historians. It was, and still can be, used to determine specific lunar and solar events of the year. There are a few trails here for the kids to run on while you ponder this controversial site and take in the view.

Busch Clydesdale Hamlet

Anheuser-Busch Brewery, Rte. 3, Merrimack; (603) 883-6131. May-Nov., daily, 9:30-3:30; Dec.-April, closed Mon. and Tues. Free.

You can get a close-up look at the famous Clydesdale horses on this free tour through the stables. Also on display are wagons, harnesses, and other riding equipment.

⅋ Children's Metamorphosis Museum

217 Rockingham Rd., Londonderry; (603) 425-2560. Tues.-Sat., 9:30-5; Fri., 9:30-8; Sun., 1-5. Adults, $3.50; under 1, free.

Curiosity the Caterpillar, this museum's mascot, is waiting to show children around. Best for children age two to eight, the Metamorphosis features a variety of fun-filled learning rooms.

In the World Cultures Room, you're surrounded by giant maps and will learn about people from around the world. You can try on regional clothing and costumes and enjoy playing traditional games and listening to music. In the Emergency Room, kids take pulses, listen to heartbeats, give shots, and use a wheelchair and crutches. At the Construction Site, future architects, builders, and engineers can work the bulldozer, design with blocks, and use tools at the workbench. Other exhibits include the Sticky Room (full of Velcro boards and Legos), Five Senses Room (touch it first and then see if you can quess what's hiding in the box), Grocery Room, Nature and Science Area, puppet theater, and an arts and crafts activity area. A great place for kids.

⅋ Amoskeag Fishways

Amoskeag Dam, Fletcher St. (exit 6 off I-293), Manchester; (603) 626-FISH. May and June, daily. Free.

What a treat, to see several species of ocean fish return to spawn in the Merrimack River. An underwater viewing window gives you a fish-eye view of what's going on. You'll learn about fish migration through a number of dioramas and displays.

⅋ Science Enrichment Encounters–Discovery Center

324 Commercial St., Manchester; (603) 669-0400. Late June–Aug., Mon.-Fri., 10-3; Sat. and Sun., 12-5. Per person, $2; per family, $8.

Don't miss this family-focused Science Center. Throughout the summer the Science Enrichment Encounter organization offers daily workshops and activities for children. Stop by the Discovery Center and learn how to build your own rocket. Or how about spending a few hours together making a bongo drum or a paper tube kazoo, making pennies shiny, or constructing a weather wheel, or an air rocket. Every day is a new project. Stop by.

⅋ Scouting Museum and Library

Camp Carpenter, Bodwell Rd., Manchester; (603) 669-8919. July and Aug., daily, 10-4; Sept.-June, Sat. only, 10-4. Free.

If you have avid little Brownies or Cub Scouts in your troop, they might enjoy a visit to this museum. There are lots of scouting artifacts and memorabilia that trace scouting through the years. There's also a small picnic area.

‡ Christa McAuliffe Planetarium

3 Institute Dr. (off I-93), Concord; (603) 271-2842. Tues.-Sun., call for show times. Adults, $5; 3-17, $3. Shows extra.

This museum was named after one of the Challenger teacher-astronauts, who was a Concord native. It is a pleasing mix of small hands-on exhibits and razzle-dazzle video presentations. Call ahead to be sure to get reservations for the shows; these sell out quickly and you're likely to be disappointed if you go without reservations. Once you enter the theater, you'll sit back for a self-guided tour of the universe and an up-close look at the moon, planets, stars, comets, and more. You'll press buttons and answer questions along the way, as you plot your journey through space. Everyone is likely to learn lots—and have fun.

‡ State House Center

107 N. Main St., Concord; (603) 271-2154. Mon.-Fri., 8-4:30. Free.

The hub of activities in downtown Concord is the State House Plaza, where New Hampshire's most famous sons (including Daniel Webster and Franklin Pierce) are immortalized in bronze. The gold-domed capitol building can be seen from afar, and its picturesque grounds are always inviting. New Hampshire's state legislature is the fourth largest deliberative body in the world, and a tour of the State House is well worth the time.

Inside, visit the Hall of Flags and view a variety of displays and interesting dioramas that depict New Hampshire historical events. You'll find just about the friendliest set of guides and staff people you'll meet anywhere. Come with questions; they love to answer them, and to show you around. Tours are given daily, and if the legislature is in session, you can catch a glimpse of state government in action.

‡ Museum of New Hampshire History

30 Park St., Concord; (603) 225-3381. Mon.-Fri., 9-4:30; Sat. and Sun., 12-4:30. Free.

The American Association of Museums described the museum as "the single most important body of material, culture and decorative arts in the state of New Hampshire." Okay, that's great for museum or history buffs, but what about the rest of us? Keep the tiny tots home, but school-age kids should find this collection of historic treasures, including the old Concord Coach, Revolutionary flags, early New Hampshire furniture, and 19th-century paintings of the White Mountains quite interesting—a lot more so than learning about it from a history book.

ᘔ Audubon Society of New Hampshire Headquarters

3 Silk Farm Rd., Concord; (603) 224-9909. Mon.-Sat., 9-5; Sun., 1-5. Free.

What are those small black-and-white birds we see all the time? What kind of woodpeckers peck in New Hampshire? How far do shore birds go? What birds will we see in the mountains? Stop by the Audubon Society state headquarters to learn all about our native feathered friends. There are a number of exhibits, a nature store, and trails to explore. The society also hosts a variety of special programs throughout the year. Write or call for its brochure.

ᘔ Society for the Preservation of New Hampshire Forests Conservation Center

54 Portsmouth St., Concord; (603) 224-9945. Mon.-Fri., 9-4:30. Free.

With conservation high on everyone's list, a visit to this society's headquarters is an interesting learning experience. There are a number of displays that will show how to conserve energy and natural resources. You'll enjoy a visit to the passive solar energy building on the premises, and a walk on one of the nearby nature trails.

ᘔ Canoeing the Merrimack River

Merrimack River Watershed Council, 54 Portsmouth St., Concord; (603) 224-8322.

It's a lazy, hazy summer afternoon and a canoe ride down a lazy, calm river would be just great; how about a free canoe ride on the Merrimack River? Perfect. Call or stop by.

ᘔ American Stage Festival

Rte. 13 North, Milford; (603) 673-7515.

This is New Hampshire's largest professional theater group, and it offers an abundance of great concerts, stage plays, readings, and children's theater. Call for a complete schedule of events and dates.

ᘔ Silver Lake State Park

Rte. 122, Hollis; (603) 465-2342.

This is a popular family picnic area and beach in the Merrimack Valley region. The sandy, 1,000-foot beach is great for toddlers. Older swimmers will enjoy racing to the raft and diving off it. The park has a bathhouse, rest rooms, and concession stand. Picnic tables and barbecue grills are nestled in the pine groves surrounding the beach.

ᘔ Bear Brook State Park

Rte. 28, Allentown; (603) 485-9874. Mid-May–Columbus Day.

This 9,000-acre park offers a playground, picnic area, nice swimming beach, and rental boats. You'll also find the Museum of Family Camping located at the park. The museum houses exhibits, memorabilia, and documents on family camping dating back to the early days. This is a good spot to spend the day outdoors.

Pawtuckaway State Park

Off Rte. 156, Nottingham; (603) 895-3031. Mid-May–Columbus Day.

This is a great spot, with lots of room to roam and lots of things to do. Besides a swimming beach there are picnic areas, boats, and a number of trails to explore. This is a popular place for area campers, too.

Sleigh Rides at Charming Fare Farms

774 High St., Candia; (603) 483-2307. Oct.-March, daily, 1-midnight. Adults, $6; children under 12, $4.

A lovely place to take a horse-drawn sleigh ride through snow-covered fields and woods. Be sure to call ahead and check on availability; the sleigh only goes out when it has a full load.

RESTAURANTS

Thursdays

6-8 Pleasant St., Concord; (603) 224-2626. Lunch and dinner.

The emphasis here is on healthy, fresh preparations, without forfeiting taste. It's a small, well-known and well-liked casual eatery, serving up great-tasting fish and chicken dishes. There are lots of vegetarian offerings, too.

Green Ridge Turkey Farm

235 Daniel Webster Hwy., Nashua; (603) 888-7020. Lunch and dinner.

Going to Green Ridge is like going to Grandma's house for Sunday dinner. This popular family restaurant is located off the major highway in Nashua. Smaller portions of turkey, mashed potatoes (real ones) and gravy, and all the traditional trimmings are available for children.

LAKES REGION

This region in central New Hampshire is dominated by Lake Winnipesaukee, the state's largest lake, encompassing 72 square miles and more than 280 miles of shoreline. The picturesque lake is surrounded by three mountain ranges and speckled with 274 islands. Claiming to be home to the country's oldest summer resort (Wolfeboro), it also lays claim to having New Hampshire's "most popular vacation spot" (Weirs Beach), although the tourist folk in Hampton Beach and the White Mountain Region might have something to say about that. But a look at the level of activity and number of visitors on any summer weekend makes the claim hard to dispute.

On the western side of the lake you'll find busy Weirs Beach, often crowded but full of amusements. For a slower pace, visit nearby Lakes Waukewan and Winnisquam, or Lake Squam, the setting for the movie *On Golden Pond.*

Especially popular in the summer, this area by no means closes down the rest of the year. With the crowds gone, this is a great spot to spend a warm autumn day admiring fall foliage, and winter brings cross-country and downhill skiing at the Gunstock ski area.

M/S *Mount Washington* Cruises
Weirs Beach Dock, Weirs Beach; (603) 366-2628. Mid-May–mid-Oct., daily. Adults, $10–$12; 5-12, $5–$6.

For a good view of the lake and its islands, take a cruise ship from the Weirs Beach pier. You can choose from a 3-hour tour aboard the 1,200-passenger M/S *Washington* or a 1-hour-and-30-minute cruise aboard the smaller *Doris E.* and *Sophie C.* Call for departure times.

Weirs Beach Water Slide
Rte. 3, Weirs Beach; (603) 366-5161. Memorial Day–mid-June, weekends; mid-June–Labor Day, daily. Rates vary with your height and the season.

There are waterslides here for all levels of bravery, from the 70-foot-long Tunnel Twister to the high-acceleration Sling Shot ("reserved for the slider seeking the ultimate sliding experience"). Or, try Super Slide, billed as the longest and highest water slide in New England. Daredevils will love the Pipeline Express; it drops you down into a black hole and around underground curves, then blasts you up into daylight and down the flume. Whew! This attraction is best enjoyed by older children.

Surf Coaster
Rte 11B, Weirs Beach; (603) 366-4991. Memorial Day–mid-June, weekends; mid-June–Labor Day, daily, 10-8. Adults and children above 4 ft. tall, $15; children 4 ft. and under, $12; under 3 years, free.

If you're tired of sand in your shoes but still want to cool off in the surf, a visit to Surf Coaster is in order. This attraction boasts a giant wave pool (nearly a half-acre in size), four water slides, two miniature golf courses, and a Kiddie Play Park. There are lounge chairs and picnic tables from which to enjoy the views of the mountains and lakes.

☙ Endicott Rock Beach

Rte. 3, Weirs Beach; (603) 524-5046. Year-round. Lifeguards on duty July–Labor Day, 8:30-5.

This small, sandy beach, located next to the Weirs Beach Water Slide, is one of the few public beaches in the area. (Despite its size, Lake Winnipesaukee has few public access points; most of the lodging places have their own private beaches for guests' use.) There are lifeguards on duty at a roped-off swimming area, and picnic tables and swings.

☙ Winnipesaukee Railroad

Weirs Beach Dock, Weirs Beach; (603) 528-2330. Memorial Day–mid-June and Labor Day–Columbus Day, weekends; June–Labor Day, daily. Trains run every hour, 11-5. One-hour ride: adults, $6.50; 4-12, $4.50. Two-hour ride: adults, $7.50; 4-12, $5.50. Long ride: adults, $7; 5-12, $4.

Travel along the shores of Lake Winnipesaukee in this locomotive. The train can be picked up from Weirs Beach or Meredith. The one-hour round trip to Meredith is perfect for younger ones with short attention spans. There are lots of other longer excursions offered, too, including fall foliage tours and Santa Claus specials. Call for details.

☙ Funspot Amusement Center

Rte. 3 (one mile north of Weirs Beach; (603) 536-4377. Year-round, 10-10; July–Labor Day, 24 hours a day. Admission free.

A rainy day is the perfect excuse to visit Funspot, although kids need no excuse at all. This is home to more than 500 electronic games. You'll find all the latest machines, along with 20 lanes of bowling (ten pin and candlepin), minigolf, and a driving range. The preschoolers in your group will love the Aqua Blasta splash guns and Kiddie Bumper cars. You'll go through a lot of quarters here.

☙ Science Center of New Hampshire

Rte. 113, Holderness; (603) 968-7194. May-Oct., daily, 9:30-4:30. Adults, $6; 5-12, $3.

Live, native bear, deer, raccoons, owls, eagles, reptiles, bobcats and other animals roam this 200-acre sanctuary, contained by natural enclosures. You'll discover the wonders of nature, learning about plant and animal life through a number of unique indoor and outdoor displays and interactive exhibits. Children will push buttons, solve puzzles, skip along the nature trail lined with exhibits, and have fun learning all about nature. In the summer, attend "Up Close Animals," a live animal demonstration held twice each day.

⚛ New Hampshire Farm Museum
Rte. 16, Milton; (603) 652-7840. June–Labor Day, Tues.-Sat., 10-4; Sun., noon-4; Labor Day–mid-Oct., Sat. and Sun., noon-4. Adults, $4; 12 and under, $1.

Ever wonder what it was like in the old days, growing crops for your food, weaving your clothes on a loom, churning your butter, pumping your water from a well? You'll find out here. Children get a chance to see and touch a large collection of old farm tools and equipment as they tour the New Hampshire Farm Museum. You'll see a blacksmith shop, cobbler shop, old house and tavern, herb garden, country store, and two large barns full of all sorts of antique harvesting, planting, and woodworking tools. Often children are invited to work the equipment—making butter in an old churn, working an antique loom, or cleaning clothes in the old wash basin. Special family events are held each weekend throughout the summer.

⚛ Castle in the Clouds
Rte. 171, Moultonborough; (800) 729-2468. May–mid-June, weekends; mid-June–mid-Oct., daily, 9-5. Adults, $10; under 10, free.

Thomas Plant, an eccentric millionaire, wanted to own a piece of land "from the mountains to the water." This 5,000-acre site in the middle of the Ossipee Mountain Range is testimonial to his desires. There are guided tours of Plant's spacious retirement home, but the real attraction is outside—there are beautiful views everywhere and lots of ways to enjoy them. Talk the short path (off the driveway entrance) to either the Fall of Song or Bridal Veil waterfalls. Hitch a ride on a tractor-train up to the house, which sits on the estate's highest point. Here you are truly in the clouds, with a fabulous view of mountains, woods, and lakes.

Guided trail rides on horseback are offered, covering some of the more than 85 miles of bridle paths on the property. The shorter half-hour or hour tours are perfect for younger children. If you have more time, have a picnic at Shannon Pond. There are tables, grills, and paddle boats to rent. Castle in the Clouds is especially beautiful in the fall, when the mountainside is ablaze with color.

⚛ Polar Caves
Rte. 25, Plymouth; (603) 536-1888. Mid-May–Oct., daily, 9-5. Adults, $7.75; 6-12, $4.

Get your first taste of spelunking as you sink through narrow passageways and climb rocky inclines. You'll explore the area where giant boulders were deposited many years ago by glaciers, forming a maze of caves. Kids who love a challenging climb and don't mind getting their knees dirty will enjoy finding hidden Smuggler's Cave, squirming through Lemon Squeeze, and screaming in dark Fat Man's Misery. You can back out along the way; there are detours to get you by the most challenging caves. A picnic area, museum shop, cafeteria, and ice cream bar are also on the grounds.

⅋ Squam Lake Tours

The serene, picturesque setting of Squam Lake was the site of the classic movie *On Golden Pond.* The best way to see the lake's pristine beauty is with one of the boat tours. In fact, the lake is not easily seen from the roadside—you need to get on the lake to appreciate it.

The Original Golden Pond Tour departs from The Manor, Route 3 at Shepard Hill Road in Holderness: (603) 968-3348. Captain Pierre Havre takes folks to the actual locations from the movie, and entertains with friendly, flowing narration.

Squam Lake Tours is located on Route 3 a half-mile south of the center of Holderness: (603) 968-7577. Captain Joe Nassar boards passengers on his 28-foot pontoon boat for a tour of the lake and lovely Church Island.

⅋ Ellacoya State Park

Rte. 11, Gilford; (603) 293-7821.

This is a small beach, 600 feet long, on the southwest shore of Lake Winnipesaukee. There are rewarding views of the Ossipee and Sandwich mountains from the shoreline.

⅋ Centre Harbor Children's Museum and Shop

Rte. 25, Centre Harbor; (603) 253-TOYS. June–Labor Day, daily, 9:30-6; Labor Day–May, Tues.-Sat., 9:30-5; Sun., 11:30-5. Adults, $5; under 2, free.

When you're tired of sun-drenched lake activities or it's raining in the Lakes Region, head for Centre Harbor for some indoor fun at this small, hands-on kid's museum. "This is a place for parents and kids to share together," explains the proprietor. Together you'll make giant bubbles in the Bubble Room, build castles and cities in the Lincoln Log Room, dress up in the Make Believe Room, and discover some scientific laws in the Ball and Chain Room. All in all, it's eight rooms of hands-on fun.

⊰ᔆ Stonedam Island Natural Area

Lake Winnipesaukee, Meredith; (603) 279-3246.

Ready to get away from it all? Load a day pack with some goodies and a can of bug repellent, and catch the Stonedam Island boat from Weirs Beach. Now, relax. This is a 112-acre unspoiled island in Lake Winnipesaukee, with two and a half miles of nature trails.

⊰ᔆ Mount Major

It's a steep climb to the summit but worth every grunt and groan along the way. The trail begins at a marked parking area on Rte. 11, about five miles north of Alton Bay, and climbs one and a half miles to the Mount Major summit. It'll take one and a half to two hours to reach the top. From here, you'll see commanding views over the mountain ranges and across Lake Winnipesaukee. You're likely to see groups of people along the way, including many small children. There are many alternate paths; choose any way, they all lead to the top.

⊰ᔆ White's Miniature Horse Petting Farm

Off Pittsfield Rd., Pittsfield; (603) 435-8258. May-Sept., daily (unless rain), 10-5. Adults, $3; 2-12, $2.

This very low-key, small family farm features a hands-on, huggable visit with these cute miniature horses. There's a handful of other friendly farm animals clamoring around for attention, too. Small tots get a kick (figuratively, of course) out of this place.

⊰ᔆ Gunstock Ski Area

Rte. 11A, Gilford; (603) 293-4341. Adult lift tickets, $31; junior, $20; 6 and under, free. SKIwee program (including lunch), $45; nursery and day care, $5-$7/hr.; $25/day. Rates listed are for weekends and holidays; special packages available.

This area offers more skiing than you think at first glance. Tucked away in the Lakes Region, the area has trails for all levels of expertise, with 39 trails and seven lifts. It's a good, solid intermediate area, with a special user-friendly section for beginners and children and a handful of black diamonds thrown in.

The staff shows a commitment to family and children's services. The Buckaroos Children's Center is located at the heart of Gunstock's base complex so parents can drop in frequently throughout the day, if they wish. The nursery and day-care programs include arts and crafts, outdoor play, and social activities. Children three to 12 years can join the SKIwee course. The full-day program includes lunch, supervised playtime for younger ones, and snacks. Add $7.50 to the rate if rental equipment is necessary. Children six and under ski free anytime.

RESTAURANTS

Hart's Turkey Farm and Restaurant

Rtes. 3 and 104, Meredith; (603) 279-6212. Mon.-Thurs., 11-8; Fri.-Sun., 11-9.

Every day is Thanksgiving at this turkey-farm-turned-restaurant. On a busy day, Hart's serves more than a ton of turkey. It has all the trimmings, too, like mashed potatoes, cranberries, and squash pie. The children's menu includes the "Tiny Tot Turkey Plate"—a real feast.

Yankee Smokehouse

Rtes. 16 and 25, West Ossipee; (603) 539-RIBS. Daily, 11:30-9.

The Yankee Smokehouse proudly proclaims it will "sell no swine before its time," and it does not disappoint. This is real barbecue, with lots of smoky taste and messy fingers. You'll eat at picnic-style tables, among the Smokehouse's vast collection of pig paraphernalia. All the meat is smoked slowly over hardwood coals in an open pit out back, on the premises. The top seller is the Smokehouse Sampler for two—chicken, ribs, beef, and pork, with fries, beans, cole slaw, corn on the cob, and garlic toast.

Franken Sundae

Rte. 3, Meredith; (603) 279-5531. Memorial Day–June, weekends only; July-Sept., daily, 11:30-10:30.

Build a "monster" ice cream sundae, take it to one of the lakeside tables, and dig in. What a great way to enjoy a lazy, hot afternoon.

SUNAPEE AREA

"I don't like to talk too much about Sunapee. It's the best-kept secret in New England, and I'd like to keep it that way." "You won't find boardwalks lined with T-shirt shops and fast-food stands here. It's a relaxing, beautiful place to vacation, void of the typical tourist traps." These are among the comments you're apt to hear from Sunapee locals and visitors.

Indeed, nestled high in the mountains of western New Hampshire, the Lake Sunapee area extends a quiet, slow welcome to its visitors. You'll find nothing pretentious or fancy here. Despite natural beauty and bountiful oportunities for sports and activities, the Lake Sunapee area is fairly non-commercial, retaining much of its rural charm. Aware of its increasing appeal, its citizens have adopted the motto "Preserve the Best of the Past." They're doing a good job.

That's not to say you'll spend your entire time here sitting under a giant white pine, skipping stones on Lake Sunapee (unless, of course, you want to). There are plenty of activities: aerial rides, band concerts, boat cruises, hiking, water and snow skiing, apple picking, horseback riding, science and art museums, forts, and playhouses are all in the area, as is the Craftsmen's Fair (see under Annual Events). This is the oldest craft fair in the nation, with lots of hands-on activities and crafts for children.

☃ Mount Sunapee State Park

Rte. 103, Newbury; (603) 763-2356. Beach open Memorial Day–mid-June, weekends, 9:30-8; mid-June–Labor Day, daily, 9:30-8.

If it's a nice day, start it with a visit to this state park located on the southern shores of Lake Sunapee. The whole family will enjoy the sandy park beach. The swimmers in your family will have fun racing to the raft; toddlers are safe along the calm, shallow banks. There are picnic areas in the park, a playground, and a small concession stand at the beach.

☃ Sunapee Harbor

Off Rte. 11

Sit at the edge of the lake and watch the boats come and go, or picnic on the lawn that stretches from the lake to the road. Nobody hurries here. During the day you can rent boats and waterskiing equipment from a nearby marina. (Sailboat, canoe, and motor rentals are also available, a few miles north of the harbor.) Don't miss the free outdoor band concerts held here every Wednesday evening during the summer. Bring a blanket—the kids can dance and play on the lawn while you listen to the music float across the lake.

☃ M/V *Mount Sunapee*

Sunapee Harbor (off Rtes. 91 and 89); (603) 763-4030. Mid-May–mid-June, Sat. and Sun., 2:30; mid-June–Labor Day, daily, 10 and 2:30; mid-Sept.–mid-Oct., Sat.-Sun., 2:30. Adults, $9; 5-12, $5.

"Who wants to take the wheel?" Captain Hargbol yells. By the end of the boat ride, nearly every child has taken the helm and played out the fantasy of "sea captain." This one-and-a-half-hour cruise, departing from Sunapee Harbor, takes you around the lake, past beaches, lighthouses, and summer homes. Captain Hargbol gives a lively narration on history,

points of interest, and lore. It's a relaxing way to see this crystal clear
mountain lake.

⅔ Mount Sunapee Chairlift Ride

*Rte. 102, Newbury; (603) 763-5626. June–Labor Day, Wed.-Sun., noon-
7; Memorial Day–mid-June and Labor Day–Columbus Day, weekends, 9-5.
Adults, $5:50; 6-12, $2.50.*

The triple chairlift will whisk you up to the summit of Mount
Sunapee, where you'll be rewarded with panoramic views of the mountains and lakes. There are plenty of trails for hiking and lots of perfect
spots for a picnic.

⅔ Ruggles Mine

*On Isingglass Mountain (off Rte. 4), Grafton; (603) 448-6911. Mid-
May–mid-June, weekends, 9-5; late-June–mid-Oct., daily, 9-5. Adults, $9;
4-11, $4.*

Hammer and pound and chisel away as you look for precious metals
and stones. Prospecting in Ruggles Mine is a real adventure, no matter
what your age. The mine is big, and it's full of caves and tunnels, high
ledges, and water pools. You're allowed to pick away at the walls and take
whatever you extract. The kids are sure to leave with a heavy load of "precious" souvenirs. In fact, more than 150 types of minerals have been found
in the cave. You can rent hammers, chisels, picks, flashlights, and carry-
ing sacks, or bring your own. Consider packing a lunch; the scenic view
of mountains and valleys makes this a nice setting.

⅔ Fort No. 4

*Rte. 11, Charlestown; (603) 826-5700. Late-May–Columbus Day, daily
except Tues., 10-4. Adults, $6; 6-11, $4.*

This living history museum is a reproduction of the original fortified
settlement at No. 4, Charlestown, New Hampshire, during the French-
Indian War era. The 20-acre site on the Connecticut River includes a
stockade surrounding 14 buildings: a watch tower you can climb into,
a blacksmith shop, cabins, and barns. As you walk through the village,
you'll see costumed guides demonstrating a variety of early crafts, such as
musketball molding and candle dipping.

⅔ Shaker Village

*Shaker Road, Canterbury; (603) 783-9511. May-Oct., Mon.-Sat., 10-5;
Sun., 12-5; April, Nov., and Dec., weekends only. Adults, $7.50; 6-15,
$3.75.*

As you walk through this historic communal village, you'll get a glimpse of what life was like for the Canterbury Shakers. Watch artisans make a broom, spin yarn, or weave a rug in the self-sufficient tradition of Shaker life. Skilled craftspeople use other traditional Shaker skills to make baskets, tinware, herbal sachets, and ladderback chairs. There are six buildings on the spacious grounds, and walking tours are given by knowledgeable guides who interpret 200 years of Shaker history.

⁂ Mount Kearsage Indian Museum
Warner; (603) 456-2600. May-Oct., Mon.-Sat., 10-5; Sun., 1-5. Nov.-Dec., weekends only. Adults, $5; 6-12, $3.

Indian lore comes alive at this interesting New England museum. Walk along the paths in Medicine Woods, where you'll learn about medicinal plants and how they were used by the Indians. Imagine yourself living the life of an Eastern Woodlands Indian, as you sit in the outside teepees. Or put on one of the wolf robes, the kind the Indians used to wear on their buffalo hunts. The museum displays artifacts and exhibits covering the lives and lore of the Eastern Woodlands, Southwest, and Plains Indians. A fun place for kids and adults alike.

⁂ Barn Playhouse
Main St., New London; (603) 526-4631. July and Aug.

The summer stock theater here in New London is a great way to introduce your family to the stage; the Playhouse does a warm job of welcoming children. Catch the magical Monday series throughout July and August. All programs are held in a refurbished barn. Call ahead for program information and schedules.

⁂ Gould Hill Orchards
Gould Hill Rd. (off Rte. 103), Hopkinton Village; (603) 746-3811. Aug.-May.

If you're in the Sunapee area in the fall (and what a nice place to be), take a side trip to the Gould Hill Orchards for apple picking and fresh cider. The farm's scenic mountain setting is a good place to view fall foliage.

⁂ Winslow State Park
Exit 10 off I-89, toward Wilmot; (603) 526-6168.

Take the auto road from the park entrance up to Mount Kearsage (2,937 feet), and you'll find a peaceful picnic area with a great mountain view. From here you can take a short hiking trail to the summit. This is an extra special spot at twilight, when the sunset you'll be privy to is likely to be wonderful.

⁂ Wadleigh State Park
Sutton; (603) 927-4727.

The 52-acre beach and picnic area on the south shore of Kezar Lake makes this park a special spot for families. It's rarely crowded.

⁂ Pillsbury State Park
Rte. 31, Washington; (603) 863-2860.

With 5,000 acres, Pillsbury is a great place for fishing, hiking, and camping. There are nine picturesque woodland ponds and several hiking trails in the park. Walk to Balance Rock, a large glacial erratic in such a teetering position that it's said one can actually move it by hand.

⁂ Cross-Country Skiing

Young or old, big or little, novice or expert, if you're thinking of cross-country skiing, you'll find what you're looking for in the Sunapee area. Head for the Norsk Touring Center, Rte. 11, New London; (603) 526-4685. It has 17 trails in a pretty location, and lots of amenities right on site: lodging, restaurant, and ski shop. The Eastman Cross-Country Center in Grantham, (603) 863-6772, offers lots of area for the novice on 40 kilometers of trails.

⁂ Mount Sunapee Ski Area
Sunapee National Park; (603) 763-5626. Adult lift tickets, $32; 7-12, $22; 6 and under, free; SKIwee, ages 5-12, $50/day (lunch included); $30/ half-day. Rates listed are for weekends and holidays; special rates and packages are available.

This small, friendly area has plenty of skiing to offer, with 37 trails serviced by seven lifts. If you're looking for a place away from the crowds, consider Mount Sunapee Ski Area. This is a great place either to learn how to ski or to perfect your skills. The majority of the trails are for intermediate skiers, with a special area for beginners and a handful of black diamond runs. The pace is relaxed, the scenery inspiring.

The Duckling Nursery, located at the ski area, will take care of your youngsters while you ski. The nursery is free midweek, on a first come, first served basis. Reservations are suggested for weekends and holidays, when you pay by the hour. The Little Indians program will give your three- and four-year-olds a nice welcome to the sport of skiing. Class size is small, with a small child/teacher ratio, and the emphasis is on fun. The nationally recognized SKIwee program is offered for children five to 12.

King Ridge Ski Area

King Ridge Rd. (exit 11 off I-91), New London; (603) 526-6066. Adult lift ticket, $25; SKIwee, $35/day. Prices listed are for weekends and holidays; special rates and packages are available.

You're likely to meet the Mad Hatter or the White Rabbit as you traverse the gently sloping trails at King Ridge. This is a low-key, small resort that caters to families. Most of the 20 trails are for beginners—12 in all, including Cheshire Cat, the Big Tea Party and Alice's Return. If you haven't guessed by now, the trails are all named after Lewis Carroll's most memorable characters, and the atmosphere throughout the area is casual and fun.

Besides Alice and her friends, King Ridge features two nurseries for children age four months through six years. Nursery care is offered to nonskiing kids. SKIwee programs are offered for children five to 12.

Pat's Peak

Rte. 114, Henniker; (603) 428-3245. Adult lift ticket: $28; 6-14, $20; nursery, $15/day; a variety of kid's learn-to-ski programs range $35-$45/ day. Rates listed are for weekends and holidays; special rates and packages are available.

For 30 years families have been going to southern New Hampshire's Pat's Peak ski area. The modest area has 19 trails and seven lifts and is a local favorite with families and area school groups. On selected evenings Pat's Peak offers night skiing, and you'll share the trails with lots of hot-dogging preteens and teens. It's a good place to learn the sport; most of the terrain is gentle and three isolated areas are just for beginners. Look for specials throughout the year; Pat's Peak hosts a number of family-friendly events, including an early-season free learn-to-ski week, family day, and a number of other themed celebrations.

RESTAURANTS

Pizzas and Cream of New London

Colonial Plaza, New London; (603) 526-2875. Daily, 11:30-11.

This family-style restaurant is popular with summer visitors. The top-selling item is the deep-dish pizza. You can also get children's portions of spaghetti, lasagna, and other Italian specialities. Add home-made ice cream for dessert.

⚛ Peter Christian's Tavern
186 Main St., New London; (603) 526-4042. Daily, 11-10; weekends 11-11.

This 19th-century tavern-style eatery serves up hearty soups and stews and hefty sandwiches. Its relaxed, casual nonsmoking atmosphere is a favorite with families. You'll find lots of menu options, from full dinners to lighter soup-and-sandwich fare.

LINCOLN AND FRANCONIA AREA

This picturesque mountain area on the western flanks of the White Mountain National Forest is a pine-scented, four-season playground. Summer is the most popular season, when the valleys are full of flowers and the streams run with cool, clear mountain water. Each summer, thousands come to see the natural beauty of the White Mountain National Forest, to visit the Franconia Notch State Park gorges, flumes, and waterfalls, and to drive the scenic Kancamagus Highway, lined with mountain and valley vistas. Outdoor activities abound—take a hike to tumbling falls, swim in pristine mountain lakes and pools, canoe or kayak the Swift River, or take an aerial ride to the 4,200-foot summit of Cannon Mountain. The children can explore caves, zip down waterslides and roller coasters, visit haunted houses and petting zoos, and learn about nature, music, and history at a variety of local museums. In the winter months, there are ice skating, sleigh rides, and cross-country and downhill skiing.

⚛ Lost River Reservation
Rte. 112, North Woodstock; (603) 745-8031. Mid-May–Oct., weather permitting: May, June, Sept., and Oct., 9-5; July and Aug., 9-6. Adults, $6.50; 6-12, $3.50.

Your children will be dirty, tired, and happy when they leave this place. You'll become explorers and navigators as you climb your way up and down ladders, belly-slide under rock ledges, and slither through caves. You can also take the easy way around—on the boardwalk—and simply enjoy the fine scenery. (But really, what fun is that?) The three quarters of a mile trip of an hour or so follows the river as it appears and disappears through giant glacier boulders. You'll learn about the geological and ecological history of the river along the way. Be sure to wear comfortable shoes and outdoor clothing. A snack bar and picnic area are on the grounds.

৺ Clark's Trading Post

Rte. 3, Lincoln; (603) 745-8913. Memorial Day–mid June and mid-Sept.–mid-Oct., weekends, 10-6; late-June–Labor Day, daily, 10-6. Adults, $6; 6-11, $4; 3-5, $1.

From an adult's point of view, Clark's Trading Post is a hodge-podge of amusements, its best being the performance of a family of trained black bears. But the kids will skip along in amused bliss, laughing at the slanted floors in Tuttle's Haunted House and the flying pianos in Merlin's Mystical Mansion. They will even enjoy the antics of "Wolfman," who jeers at them as they ride aboard the White Mountain Central Railroad. There are a snack bar, an ice cream parlor, and picnic grounds.

৺ The Whale's Tale and Amusement Park

Rte. 3, Lincoln; (603) 745-8810. Memorial Day–mid-June, weekends, 11-5; late-June–Labor Day, daily, 10-6. Adults, $14; 6-12, $12; under 36 inches, free.

Combine carnival rides and waterslides and you come up with a sure kid pleaser. At the amusement park you'll find rides for your teenage thrill seekers, as well as slower, tamer rides for the younger set. The kids will love bouncing in the sea of balls and getting wet on the water boats. When you're ready to cool off, walk over to the adjoining water park. Brave souls can streak down the Blue Lightning and Serpentine slides. For a more relaxing pace, you'll want to soak in the wave pool or tube down Lazy River. Younger children will love Whale Harbor, a special pool just for them. There are snack bars, changing facilities, and locker rentals.

৺ Hobo Railroad

Rte. 3, Lincoln; (603) 745-2135. Memorial Day–Halloween. Trains leave at 11, 1, 3, 5, and 7 in summer; as needed in spring and fall. Adults, $7.50; 6-11, $4.50.

For some outstanding mountain views (and a fun way to have lunch), consider taking the 14-mile trip along the Pemigewasset River aboard the Hobo Picnic Train. Your picnic lunch comes packed hobo style—wrapped in a bandana and tied to the end of a stick. (If you can't make lunch, there are other rides throughout the day and evening.) Your children will probably not let you get away without a ride on Diamond Eddie's Ferris wheel. This giant wheel takes you for a gentle 10-minute ride as you sit on benches in enclosed compartments. It's a fun way to get an aerial view of the mountain range, after the train ride.

⅋ Loon Mountain Park and Skyride

Rte. 112 (Kancamagus Hwy.), Lincoln; (603) 745-8111. Memorial Day–mid-Oct., daily; mid-Oct.–late-Nov., weekends. Adults, $8; 6-16, $3.

The beauty of the New Hampshire mountain ranges, forests, and lakes is spectacular from the mountain summits. In the Lincoln area, ride the Loon Mountain Gondola to the top of Loon Mountain, where you'll see a panoramic view of many White Mountain peaks. The enclosed gondola ride takes about 10 minutes. On top, there's a four-story observation tower, cafeteria, and lots to explore: glacial caves, nature trails, and ongoing programs. At the base area, you'll find mountain bike and in-line skate rentals, horseback riding, archery, and a lodging and food area.

⅋ Children's Theatre

Mill at Loon Mountain, Rte. 112 (Kancamagus Hwy), Lincoln; (603) 745-6032. July and Aug., Wed., 11 and 1. Adults, $3.50; 12 and under, $3.75.

Special theater performances for children are held at this pretty setting in the mountains. Sponsored by the North Country Center for the Arts, performances take place each Wednesday through July and August.

⅋ Franconia Notch State Park

Travel for eight miles through a spectacular mountain pass—the Franconia Notch Parkway—and through the 6,440-acre state park. The Notch Parkway is located between the high peaks of the Kinsman and Franconia mountain ranges. As you travel through the notch, from the Flume at the south end to Echo Lake at the north, you'll see wonderful vistas, waterfalls, mountain lakes, and natural attractions. Visit the Flume, then stop for a peek at the Basin. This beautiful waterfall has a granite pothole of 20 feet in diameter at its base. Below the Basin, look for the Old Man's Foot rock formation. Show the kids Boise Rock, where Thomas Boise, a teamster from Woodstock, New Hampshire, sought shelter during a blizzard in the early 1800s. Killing his horse, Boise skinned it and wrapped himself in its hide. Searchers cut away the frozen hide and found him alive the next day.

Just north of Boise Rock, you'll see Profile Lake, headquarters of the Old Man's Washbowl. Look up; hovering above Profile Lake is the Old Man of the Mountains. This natural rock formation was formed nearly 200 million years ago. The Old Man is made of five separate granite ledges arranged to form a man's profile. At the northern side of the Notch Parkway, you'll find beautiful Echo Lake, the perfect spot to stop for a swim or a picnic.

⌇ The Flume
Rte. 3, Franconia Notch; (603) 745-8391. mid-May–Oct. (weather permitting), daily, 9-4:30. Adults, $6; 6-12, $3.

One of the most popular attractions in the area, this natural 800-foot chasm is a must-stop along the way. The rushing waters of the Pemigewasset River carved this wonder thousands of years ago, leaving walls that rise as high as 70 feet. If you don't mind sharing space with the inevitable summer crowds, you'll enjoy the cool, misty mountain air and marvel at the surrounding natural beauty. You'll walk boardwalks and hiking trails across covered bridges to waterfalls, cascades, river basins, and pools.

⌇ Cannon Aerial Tramway
Rte. 3, Franconia Notch; (603) 823-5563. Year-round, every weekend, weather permitting; Memorial Day–mid-Oct., daily, 9-4:30, and 'til 7 in July and Aug. Adults, $8; 6-12, $4.

In Franconia Notch, the Cannon Aerial Tramway whisks you to the summit of 4,200-foot Cannon Mountain; on a clear day, you'll be able to see into Maine, Vermont, and Canada. The ride takes six minutes. Plan to spend some time at the top. Consider packing snacks or lunch (or buy something at the summit cafeteria) to enjoy along one of the summit trails. The Rim Trail is perfect for families. You'll be treated to some great mountain views, and you'll find plenty of picnic spots along the way. At the end of the trail is an observation deck for more viewing. It'll take only about 20 minutes to walk, not counting time out for picnics and viewing. Saturday nights are extra special, when you can partake of the barbecue at the top of the mountain.

⌇ New England Ski Museum
Base of Cannon Mountain, Franconia Notch; (603) 823-7177. Memorial Day–Columbus Day and Dec. 26–mid-April, daily (closed Wed.), noon-5. Free.

Older children who have been bitten by the ski bug might enjoy a visit here. The exhibit that traces the evolution of ski equipment is particularly interesting—we've come a long way. The museum also features changing ski-related exhibits and displays and archival film footage on video that outlines the history of New England skiing.

❧ Robert Frost Place

Ridge Road, Franconia; (603) 823-5510. Spring, weekends, 1-5; summer and fall, daily, 1-5 (closed Tues.). Adults, $3; 6-12, $1.50.

The Frost farm homestead is an unpretentious, quiet tribute to the renowned poet. You'll find a small museum and an interpretive nature trail highlighting some of Frost's poems.

❧ Crossroads of America Museum

Main St., Bethlehem; (603) 869-3919. June-foliage season, daily, 9-6. Adults, $3; 6-12, $2.50.

This quiet, small museum has a good collection of model trains and railroads, old toys, planes, trucks, and ships. Children will especially like the five working railroads and villages that are set up here.

❧ Swimming

On hot days, head for Echo Lake (Route 3, Franconia Notch), a pristine, spring-fed lake at the base of Cannon Mountain. The white, sandy beach, cool mountain waters, and picturesque background make a hard-to-beat combination. There are changing and bathhouse facilities.

Other great cooling-off spots include the Lady's Bathtub, near the Riverfront Condos entrance, on Route 112 in Lincoln; Russell Pond in Woodstock; and Franconia Notch State Park.

❧ Fishing

For some of the best fly fishing, head for Profile Lake in Franconia Notch State Park. This small, clear body of water is the headwater of the Pemigewasset River. The lake, well known for its brook trout, is open for fly fishing only. In Franconia, grab a rock, or wade the Gale River for freshwater fish. You'll also want to try your luck at Coffin Pond on Route 18. This is a favorite local fishing hole. Stop by Pro-Bait and Tackle on Harvard Street in Franconia for equipment, bait, and good advice on fishing spots; (603) 823-8419.

❧ Horseback Riding

Horseback rides through meadows and forests, offering beautiful views of Mount Lafayette, Mount Mooslauke, and the Franconia Range, are available at the Franconia Inn, Route 116, Franconia, (603) 823-5542. You'll ride with a guide on trails through the 117-acre estate in the Easton Valley. Children must be at least 54 inches tall to reach the stirrups properly.

Trail riding is also available at Loon Mountain Park, Route 112,

Lincoln, (603) 745-8111; and at Waterville Valley Resort, Route 49, Waterville, (603) 236-4666.

⅗ Snowmobiling

Lincoln and Woodstock are located on the Corridor Trail 11, one of New Hampshire's major north-south corridors. All the trails in the area are maintained and groomed by White Mountain Snowmobile Club members. Access to the trail system is from the parking lot at the Hobo Railroad on Route 122 in Lincoln.

⅗ Cross-Country Skiing

If you like to be on your own, skinny skiing through the country-side, check out the Echo Lake area. Cross-country skiing along Echo Lake is a visual treat. You'll see Cannon Mountain in the background and a glimpse of the Old Man in the Mountains. Or there are lots of cross-country opportunities in Franconia Notch State Park, where you can follow the bike paths.

The Loon Mountain Cross Country Center, on the Kancamagus Highway in Lincoln, (603) 745-8111, maintains more than 30 kilometers of groomed trails that run along the Pemigewasset River and traverse the mountains. There are lots of gentle trails for beginners and children. Information on trails, lessons, and rentals is available at the headquarters in the base lodge at Loon. There's also a skating rink with skate rentals available.

Waterville Valley, on Route 49, (603) 236-4666—selected as "one of the top cross-country ski resorts in North America"—offers a vast trail network laid out over 7,000 scenic acres. There's a variety of terrain; 70 kilometers of trails are groomed, 35 kilometers provide wilderness ski access. At the Cross Country Ski Center, in Town Square, you'll find services and amenities including refreshments, ski rentals, lessons, and special programs and activities.

Other cross-country ski opportunities can be found at the Franconia Touring Center, (603) 823-5542, which offers 50 kilometers of groomed trails.

⅗ Waterville Valley Ski Area

Rte. 49 (Waterville Valley Access Rd.); (603) 236-8311. Lift tickets: adults, $39; teen or student (age 13 to college undergrad), $34; juniors (6-12), $24. SKIwee, $50/day. Rates listed are for weekends and holidays; discounts and special packages are available.

Waterville knows how to treat families. Come for the day and ski the 53 trails serviced by 13 lifts. But it won't be enough—and you'll want to stay to browse the Town Square, ice skate in the indoor arena, soak in a hot tub, or enjoy the twilight sleigh ride. Despite its amenities, this resort manages to maintain a cozy, New England village atmosphere.

Waterville Valley offers a professionally run nursery for infants six weeks and up, located at the ski area. This friendly facility includes an infant's game room equipped with cribs, playpens, high chairs, and plenty of toys. Depending on your child's age and your preferences, a typical day may include reading, arts and crafts, lunch, and indoor and outdoor play. It's available by the hour, in half-day, full-day, or multiple-day packages.

If your children are old enough, however—that's three years and up at Waterville—enroll them in one of the children's learn-to-ski programs. "We believe in the all-smiles, no-tears approach to learning here," says Joseph Jung, director of the Waterville Valley Ski School. Waterville Valley has a special children's ski area, complete with its own kinderlift. Petite SKIwee (ages 3 to 5), SKIwee (ages 6 to 8), and Grand SKIwee (ages 9 to 12) half-day and full-day programs are offered. A teenage group ski lesson is also available. There's a lot of flexibility in choosing programs. It's best to talk over the options with one of the staff members ahead of time (advance reservations are always recommended) so you can choose the best package for you and your children—and get the most for your money.

Remember, this resort does get crowded on the weekends. Your best bet? Play hookey and head up midweek.

❄ Loon Mountain Ski Area

Kancamagus Hwy., Lincoln; (603) 745-8111. Lift tickets: adults, $38; 6-12, $26; Honeybear (4-5), $50/day; Bearcubs (6-8) and Mountain Explorers (9-12), $60/day; nursery, $35/day; Honey Bear Nursery Plus, $45/day. Rates listed are for weekends and holidays; discounts and special packages are available.

Loon is a popular Northeast ski resort, offering 41 trails for skiers of every level. Loon's trails ski long. Even a beginner can ride to the top of the mountain and take a gradual, easy run down to the base.

This place does get crowded, however. Some tips to get more skiing for your dollars include to get your lift tickets the night before, get to the mountain early, avoid the gondola during peak usage (from 10:30 to 11:30 and from 1 to 2:30), and head to the less-crowded West Basin double chairs.

The SKIwee program is offered for skiers age 4 to 8, of all abilities. The Honeybear Program, for kids between 4 and 5, is offered half or full day. Bearcubs, age 6 to 8, is a full-day program. Older kids, from 9 to 12, can sign up for the all-day Mountain Explorers Program.

The Honeybear Nursery offers supervised care for children ages 6 weeks through 6 years. The Honeybear Nursery Plus program (for "willing, potty-trained three-year-olds") is an introduction to skiing through group ski games and snow-related play.

≋ Cannon
Franconia Notch State Park, Franconia; (603) 823-8521. Lift tickets: adults, $35; 12 and under, $25. SKIwee (4-12), $45/day ($54 with rental equipment); day care (minimum age 1 year), $21/day; infant care, $5/hr.

Cannon has thousands of ardent followers and loyal return skiers. It's earned a reputation as a "skier's mountain," and you won't find a lot of frills and developments here. Predominately known for its challenging ski runs and the spectacular views from its 4,200-foot summit, Cannon has made several changes recently to lure families. This small, manageable ski area now has the Peabody Slopes, offering a variety of intermediate and beginner trails. You'll find 31 trails in all, and six lifts. And its views—the glistening Echo Lake below and the national forest around—are visual treats.

Cannon offers a SKIwee program for children, and a day-care center (for children one year and older) is located on the lower level of the Peabody Lodge (Parkway Exit 3). Infant care is also available by the hour.

◗ RESTAURANTS

≋ Jigger Johnson's
On the Green, Plymouth; (603) 536-4FUN. Mon.-Sat., 11-10; Sun., 4-10.

Named after the New Hampshire folk hero and logger Jigger Johnson, this place works hard at not taking itself too seriously. Full of memorabilia and bad jokes, posters and souvenirs, it's casual, fun, and the food is surprisingly good. There's a big menu—pizza, burgers, nachos, sandwiches, salads, and a full section of dinner entrees. There's a fun kid's menu with all the favorites, and the chocolate milk comes with cherries.

≋ The Common Man
Main Street, Ashland; (603) 968-7030. Lunch, Tues.-Sat.,11:30-2; dinner, daily, 5:30-9.

Rustic charm abounds in this restaurant. The old mixes with the new and you'll get a feast for your eyes as well as your palate. Neon clocks mix with lobster traps, Shaker baskets, and white tablecloths. Upstairs you'll find a relaxing lounge with comfy chairs, books, board games, and puzzles. Families can elect to eat in this casual area or wait for a table in the dining room. Either way, the food is good old American fare—steaks, baked potatoes, salad. There's a handful of nicely prepared fish and poultry dishes, too.

CONWAY AND JACKSON AREA

If your family has a love of the great outdoors, you'll revel in the natural beauty and abundance of activities available at the rugged mountain village of Jackson. This is the home of the Appalachian Mountain Club and center for hiking, mountain climbing, and cross-country skiing. The beauty of this area is best seen on a hike into the White Mountain National Forest, a picnic on the shores of a mountain lake, or a horse-drawn sleigh ride through a covered bridge and past the white-steepled church in the village center. There's fishing, swimming, hiking, canoeing, rafting, kayaking, golf, tennis…and more. And in the winter there's some of the best cross-country and downhill skiing in New England. Drive a few miles south to North Conway and you're in a different world of factory outlets and discount shopping. (Watch out for the traffic jams through town, especially at the end of the day.)

Amid the natural beauty of the mountains, you'll find an abundance of commercial attractions to delight children. Your family can visit Cinderella at her castle, ride a gondola to the top of a mountain, and zip down it on a waterslide. It's a wonderfully diverse and popular area for family vacationing.

❦ Heritage, New Hampshire

Rte. 16, Glen; (603) 383-9776. Mid-May–mid-June, daily, 9-5; mid-June–Labor Day, daily, 9-6. Adults, $7.50; 4-12, $4.50.

This museum puts you in the middle of history-in-the-making as you journey through time, from 1634 to the 20th century. You'll be carried across the ocean aboard the ship *Reliance.* From there you'll walk through history, as special effects and audiovisual techniques do a good job of putting you right in the middle of the action. The kids' imaginations will run wild, and you'll learn about early American history along the way.

❦ Story Land

Rte. 16, Glen; (603) 383-4293. Father's Day–Labor Day, daily, 9-6; Labor Day–Columbus Day, weekends, 10-5. Admission, $14; under 4, free.

Look, it's Cinderella and Little Bo Peep, with her sheep. Youngsters will squeal with delight as they meet their favorite story-book characters.

Take a ride on a pirate's ship, set sail on a swan boat, or travel around the track in a miniature Model T. You can also take a voyage to the moon or a rolling journey on the Polar Coaster. Cool off on Bamboo Chutes, a water flume ride. There are other amusement rides, a castle, live animals, and daily shows. Good for little ones.

⅋ Attitash Alpine Slide, Cannonball Express, and Aquaboggin

Rte. 302, Bartlett; (603) 374-2368. Memorial Day–mid-June, weekends only, 10-5; mid-June–Labor Day, daily, 10-6; Labor Day–Columbus Day, weekends, 10-5. Adults, $6, single ride; 5-12, $5, single ride; under 4, free.

Combine a scenic ski lift ride with an exhilarating trip down an alpine slide. The three-quarter-mile slide takes you through woods and meadows—at your own pace. You control your own sled, going as fast or as slow as you like. Little ones can hop on with you. On hot days you can cool off with a trip down the waterslides, the Cannonball Express or Aquaboggin.

⅋ Conway Scenic Railroad

Rte. 16, Conway; (603) 356-5251. Mid-April–mid-May, weekends; mid-May–Columbus Day, daily; Columbus Day–late-Dec., weekends. Adults, $7.50; 4-12, $5. Trains depart at 11, 1, 2:30, and 4.

Several trains depart daily from the old Victorian railroad station in North Conway. The hour-long ride is a peaceful trip through the scenic New Hampshire countryside. Also offered are longer excursions and gourmet dining in Chocurua, the deluxe dining car.

⅋ Community Center Playground

Main St., North Conway

This is where all the kids hang out. The outdoor playground is full of monkey bars, tunnels, slides, swings, and jungle gyms, and it's right next to the Conway Railroad Station in the center of North Conway Village. You can't miss it; just follow the sounds of children at play.

⅋ Eastern Slope Playhouse

Main St., North Conway; (603) 356-5776. Tues.-Sat., 8.

For a special evening, consider attending a performance of the Mount Washington Valley Theatre Company, held throughout the summer at the Eastern Slope Playhouse. The renowned summer theater performs first-rate productions of Broadway musicals. A nice, upbeat, toe-tapping night out with older children. Call starting mid-June for schedule, reservations, and ticket prices.

☙ Arts Jubilee

Box 647, North Conway; (603) 356-9393. Performances held at Settler Green, intersection of Rtes. 16 and 302, North Conway.

You're likely to see anything under the Arts Jubilee tent in North Conway: magicians, dragons, and acrobats; folk dancing and ballet; barbershop quartets, jazz reviews, and classical orchestras; knee-slapping country music and bagpipes. This ongoing arts festival is well known for its weekly summer family entertainment series (monthly events are held the rest of the year) and free evening concerts. Call or write for a schedule of events.

☙ Grand Manor Antique Car Museum

Rtes. 16 and 302, Glen; (603) 356-9366. Mid-June–Labor Day, daily, 9:30-5; rest of year, weekends, 9:30-5. Adults, $5; 6-12, $3.

Auto buffs will enjoy this museum filled with 40 mint antique and classic models from 1908 to 1963. Take a close-up look at the car Bonnie and Clyde drove in the infamous movie. There are lots of cars of the "rich and famous" and old movie cars. A vintage movie theater and radio shows enhance the setting. Enjoy a ride in the paddleboats or a picnic on the grounds.

☙ Wildcat Mountain Gondola

Rte. 16, Jackson; (603) 466-3326. Mid-May–July 4, weekends, 10-4; July 4–Columbus Day, daily, 10-4. Adults, $8; 6-12, $4.

Enjoy the views atop the 4,100-foot summit at Wildcat Mountain without having to walk up or to ski down it. Take a 25-minute (round-trip) sky ride to enjoy the fabulous views of the White Mountain National Forest and beyond. A great place for a picnic, if you have the time. Picnic areas, snacks, and nature trails are at the summit.

☙ Echo Lake State Park

Rte. 302 (just off Rte. 16), North Conway; (603) 356-2672. June–Labor Day.

This small park is the perfect spot to stop for a refreshing swim or a relaxing day outing. The clear, spring-fed lake has a good swimming area for children. There are trails to take you around the lake and to ledges above, depending on your time and inclination. There are picnic tables, grills, and boats for rent. This is a very popular hot-summer-day spot.

ᨱ Swimming

There are plenty of places to pull off the road for a refreshing dip in the pristine mountain rivers and falls. On hot summer days, you'll see lots of people sunning on the rocks and swimming in the clear waters of the Saco and Swift rivers, accessed from the Kancamagus Highway (Route 112) and Route 302. If you want to avoid crowds, prowl around a bit. You'll find many good swimming holes a bit off the highway that are easily accessible.

ᨱ Canoeing

Rte. 302, Center Conway; (603) 447-2177. Also Main St., North Conway; (603) 447-3801.

The Saco River is well known for its excellent canoeing. You need not be experienced. Stop by the Saco Bound offices in North Conway, where you'll get all the equipment and instruction you need. You can go for a few hours or make a day (or more) of it. The scenery is wonderful, the waters are calm and shallow in summer, and there are lots of great places along the way to stop for a picnic and swim. In the spring, when the waters are swifter, you might consider an exhilarating kayaking or whitewater rafting trip.

Be sure to plan several weeks ahead for weekend rentals; these are very popular activities in this area. Write Saco Bound for a free brochure, at Box 119, Center Conway, New Hampshire 03813.

ᨱ Gold-Panning

The locals swear there's gold in them thar rivers (Saco and Swift), but the rangers are quick to add that while many have found gold, no one's struck it rich, yet. Pack a couple of shallow pans and try your luck. It's a fun way to spend a few hours on the river. And who knows?

ᨱ Horse Logic Hay and Sleigh Rides

Rte. 116, Jackson; (603) 383-9876.

There's something special for kids—and grown-ups alike—about a sleigh ride through freshly fallen snow around a picturesque New England village. Relax in a wagon or sleigh pulled by horses as they prance around Jackson Village. Take the kids (of course, they'll love it), or get a babysitter and reserve it for a quiet night out.

ᨱ Hiking

Many who come into this area find they want to go farther, into the woods and mountains. Your first stop should be a visit to the Pinkham

Notch Camp at the base of Mount Washington. This is the hub of White
Mountain hiking activity, and it serves as the northern New England
headquarters for the Appalachian Mountain Club. Everyone is welcome to
use its facilities and services. The AMC is a nonprofit organization offering a wide variety of recreation and conservation activities. Besides expeditions, these include research, back-country management, trail and shelter construction and maintenance, mountain search and rescue, book pub-
lishing, and outdoor recreation.

At Pinkham Notch you'll see mountain climbers and backpackers,
downhill and cross-country skiers, novices and experts all gathering about,
planning the day's activities. You'll want to talk to the people on staff
here for updated information on trail conditions and recommendations for
families, and to pick up trail maps. You might even want to stop for a
hearty meal at the center's dining room. The Saco Ranger Station at the
junction of Route 112 and Route 16 is another good spot to stop for hiking information. The folks here are always friendly and helpful.

There are thousands of miles of hiking trails in the White Mountain
area and many are appropriate for the inexperienced hiking family. (Most,
however, do not accommodate wheelchairs or strollers; put baby in a backpack.) Here's a selection of family-friendly hikes in the area:

➳ Glen Ellis Falls

Off Route 16, .8 mile south of the Pinkham Notch Camp, is a very
easy walk to Glen Ellis Falls. The trail passes under the highway through
a tunnel and reaches the falls in .3 miles. The main fall is 70 feet high,
with many pools and smaller falls below.

➳ Winneweta Falls

This trail leaves Route 16 three miles north of Jackson. You'll cross
the Ellis River (watch out in the spring when the water is high) and follow the Miles Brook until you get to Winneweta Falls. A refreshingly wet
hot-day hike, this is about 1 mile long and takes about 40 minutes.

➳ Mountain Pond Trail

This trail begins .6 mile up the road that leaves Maine 113 at a spot
.2 mile north of the Congregational Church in Chatham. You'll walk
through a birch and fir forest to the pristine Mountain Pond. From here,
take the northerly route around the pond and head back (you'll want to
stop first for a dip in the pond or a picnic along its shores). If you continue
south past the AMC cabin, you'll be in for a much longer hike, about
three hours. Otherwise, it's a short, easy hike to the pond and back.

☸ Sawyer Pond Trail

This trail leaves the Kancamagus Highway 2 miles east of the
Sabbaday Falls Picnic Area. You'll head north and cross the Swift River,
pass between Coreens Cliff and Owls Cliff, and cross Sawyer Brook. Here,
Sawyer Pond will come into view. The pond is clear and inviting—a great
place for a swim after your hike. There's a nice sandy area for sunning and
picnicking. You can continue on the trail (you'll cross a couple more
streams) and end up on the Sawyer River Road, from which you'll need
transportation back to your starting point. (AMC runs a shuttle service;
arrange for it before you start out.) It will take about three hours to go the
entire 6 miles. A better option for families with young children might be
just to head back the way you came, once you reach the pond. This will
take about two-and-a-half hours on an easy 4- to 5-mile trail.

☸ Sabbaday Falls Trail

This is a pleasant, easy walk to a picturesque series of cascades. The
trail begins off the Kancamagus Highway (about 15 miles west of Route
16) and has a number of descriptive signs along the way pointing out
wildlife and rock formations. It'll take about a half-hour to go the .4 mile.

☸ Black Cap Mountain

Drive to the top of Hurricane Mountain Road. There's an easy hike
from here to Black Cap Mountain, at which you'll be rewarded with great
views of the national forest, mountain peaks, and Maine to your east.
Watch for the migrating hawks that are often seen here. The trail will
take about an hour, for 1.2 miles.

☸ Black Mountain Trail

The trail begins as a toll road leaving Carter Notch Road, 1 mile
north of the junction of Routes 16A and 16B. You'll walk along woody
slopes and rocky outcrops to the summit of Black Mountain. The small
spur trail heading east leads to fabulous mountain vistas with fine views of
Mount Washington, Wildcat Mountain, and Carter Notch. The trail is
less than 2 miles long and will take about one and a half hours.

☸ Cathedral Ledge

For several years this area has been honored with the presence of a
pair of nesting Peregrine falcons, seen on Cathedral Ledge. When the
falcons are in town, cars are not allowed to drive to the ledge (hikers only).
But if you're here when they're not, take the short, winding road, off
Route 16, just north of North Conway. The view from Cathedral Ledge is

fantastic—the entire valley stretches below you, with the Saco River running through the middle.

⅋ Ice Skating

There are three rinks open to the public in this area. Watch for signs in Conway Village, Jackson Village, and North Conway Village.

⅋ Cross-Country Skiing

The Jackson, New Hampshire, area has been rated as one of the four best places in the world for cross-country skiing. The Jackson Ski Touring Foundation, (603) 383-9355, maintains more than 90 miles of trails throughout the area, beginning in the village of Jackson and running into the White Mountain National Forest. The trails are well maintained and marked for all abilities.

Many of the trails of the Appalachian Mountain Club, Pinkham Notch, (603) 466-2727, are perfect for cross-country skiers. (Some of the trails described in the preceding hiking section are also good for beginner ski tourers.)

The Intervale Nordic Center, North Conway (603) 356-5541, offers lessons and ski rentals plus 40 kilometers of scenic trails. There's a pleasant dining area on the grounds.

You'll also notice a number of cross-country skiers and snowshoers right in the middle of Jackson as they traverse the town golf course.

⅋ Mount Cranmore Ski Resort

Off Rte. 16, North Conway; (603) 356-5544. Lift tickets: adults, $33; SKIwee, $45/day; nursery, $25/day.

Conveniently located in North Conway, Mount Cranmore has old-time appeal, nothing too flashy or fancy. Skiing is easygoing and gentle on 28 trails. Take one of five lifts, or for something different, ride the unique skimobile to the 1,665-foot summit.

The nursery, open to children of walking age to 6 years, offers a structured program of activities that includes arts and crafts, games, and outdoor play. As soon as youngsters are willing and able (about 2.5 to 3 years), the staff takes them out for ski lessons. Kids 4 to 12 can join the SKIwee Program. The daily program runs from 10 to 3 and includes a morning ski lesson and an afternoon mileage program. They take to the trails with an instructor for some real skiing.

⅋ Attitash Ski Resort

Rte. 302, Bartlett; (603) 374-2368. Lift tickets: adults, $35; children's daily ski programs, 1-3, $45/day; 4-8, $30/day; 9-16, $60/day; nursery, $25/day.

A nice intermediate area, Attitash offers 20 trails: 5 expert, 10 intermediate and 5 novice. It gets crowded on the weekends, but the area tries to avoid congestion by limiting lift tickets. Best to get tickets ahead of time (many area lodgings sell them to guests), to avoid disappointment. Always make reservations for the nursery or children's programs. The on-site nursery is available for children from 1 to 6 years old. Children's ski programs are available for 6 to 12 year olds.

Wildcat Mountain

Rte. 16, Jackson; (603) 466-3326. Lift tickets: adults, $35; Kitten Club, $25/day; SKIwee, $40/day.

Wildcat's 2,100-foot drop and its 4,100-foot elevation make it an exciting ski area for the more experienced skier. The trails here run steep and narrow. But there are concessions to beginners: a handful of easier trails, lessons, and nursery and SKIwee programs.

The Kitten Club Childcare Center offers day care for children starting at 18 months. The center has a large area for toddlers to play and climb in, an arts and crafts space, and a separate room for napping. A SKIwee program is offered for children ages 5 to 12.

Black Mountain

Rte. 16B, Jackson; (603) 383-4490. Lift tickets: adults, $25; Youth Program, $42/day, $26/half-day; nursery, $14/day.

Billed as the "Great American Family Ski Place," Black Mountain offers gentle, sheltered slopes and a slow, relaxed atmosphere that are welcoming for family skiers. There are 20 trails here, with snowmaking on 95 percent of the mountain.

The Youth Proficiency Program is a structured program for children 5 to 12.

RESTAURANTS

Elvio's

Main St., North Conway Village; (603) 356-3307.

If you're in the mood for pizza, head to Elvio's. Locals argue that it's the best pizza in the world. Three different types are offered: the regular, round thin-crust pizza baked in a stone deck oven; a rectangular, thick-crust, Sicilian pan-cooked pizza; and white pizza, a round pie made without tomato sauce but with mozzarella and ricotta cheeses, olive oil, garlic and spices. Dine in or take out.

ᮣ Grammy MacIntosh Village Cafe

151 Main St., Conway Village; (603) 447-5050. Mon.-Thurs., 7 A.M.–
9 P.M.; Fri. and Sat., 7-10.

Homespun comfort and homebaked goodies await diners at
Grammy's. You'll walk upstairs to the second-floor dining room and
immediately smell them. If you're out for breakfast, this is definitely the
place to go. Potato pancakes, homemade muffins, buttermilk pancakes,
waffles (with ice cream!) and specially made jams and jellies will start
your day right. Burgers, salads, sandwiches, and, of course, homemade
soups are served for lunch. Everything's fresh.

ᮣ Studebaker's

Rte. 16, North Conway; (603) 356-5011.

The kids will love this '50s theme restaurant even if they don't recog-
nize the rock-and-roll tunes blasting from the jukebox. This is a fun,
casual place with great burgers and fries and malted milkshakes. Or how
about a Coney Island hot dog and a root beer float?

MOUNT WASHINGTON AREA

Majestic Mount Washington, the highest peak in the Northeast, looks
down upon an area rich in beauty and abundant with activities. The
Presidential Range, a string of mountain peaks named after U.S. presidents, and the surrounding national forest offer miles of fine hiking trails,
cascades, waterfalls, and mountain lakes. Chug along in a steam-powered
railroad car or take the slow, climbing auto road to the top of Mount
Washington. The view, of mountain peaks and valleys below, is spectacular; the air is chilly, so dress warmly.

Families who ski will enjoy the relaxing Bretton Woods ski area for
cross-country and downhill skiing. Young children will enjoy a visit with
Santa, and the entire family can get a taste of the Old West at Six Gun
City in nearby Jefferson.

ᮣ Santa's Village

Rte. 2, Jefferson; (603) 586-4445. Late-June–Labor Day, daily, 9:30-7; Labor
Day–Columbus Day, weekends, 9:30-5. Admission, $12; 3 and under, free.

Santa is never out of season with young children. If you can tolerate
the "When is Christmas?" questions that will inevitably follow, stop in to
see Santa and his elves. Besides a visit with the host of honor, children

will enjoy splashing down the log flume, riding on the enchanted train, and circling on the old-fashioned carousel. There are music and bird shows, and Santa's Skyway Sleigh, a monorail ride that encompasses part of the park.

Six Gun City

Rte. 2, Jefferson; (603) 586-4592. Mid-June–Labor Day, daily, 9-6; Labor Day–Columbus Day, weekends, 9-5. Admission, $9.25; under 4, free.

This is a kid's fantasy come true—a visit to the Old West when cowboys ruled the land, sheriffs caught outlaws, and horses were the mode of transportation. Children will love to become deputies, helping the sheriff go after law-breaking outlaws, or to take a ride on a pony or burro. The live cowboy skits and Frontier Show are fun family entertainment. Throughout Six Gun City, you'll see more than 100 horse-drawn vehicles and many Old West antiques. And there are plenty of rides, bumper boats, and a miniature golf course. Be sure to bring your bathing suit for a trip down the Tomahawk Run Waterslide.

Mount Washington Auto Road

Rte. 16, Gorham; (603) 466-3988. Mid-May–Columbus Day (weather permitting), daily, 8-4:30. Car and driver, $14; each additional adult, $5; 5-12, $3.

This winding, steep, eight-mile toll road offers some of the most scenic views in the Northeast. The 45-minute trip to the summit—at 6,288 feet it's the highest mountain in New England—takes you through mountain forests 'til you reach the top, where on clear days views stretch across six states. There's an observatory and a small museum with displays of the rare, arctic flowers often found in this cold environment. Be sure to dress warmly—it's chilly up here. If you prefer not to drive yourself, there are guided tour vans that will take you up, or you can catch a ride on the Cog Railway.

Mount Washington Cog Railway

Rte. 302, Bartlett; (603) 846-5404. May-Oct. Round trip, $32; 6-12, $22; under 6, free.

This ride up the mountain railway to the summit of Mount Washington is not unlike being on a slow roller coaster. The steam-powered train, dating back to 1869, hits inclines that reach a 35 percent grade, making this the second steepest railway track in the world. The round trip takes about three hours. Get a window seat, if you can, to enjoy the lovely mountain panoramas. Consider taking the early morning train when fares are reduced, and dress warmly.

⅋ Crawford Notch
Rte. 302, Bartlett; (603) 374-2272.

One of the most scenic places in the area is this mountain park on the Saco River, surrounded by the White Mountain National Forest. Dip your toes in the clear waters of the Saco River and listen to the nearby Silver and Flume cascades. There are lots of hiking trails nearby.

⅋ Hiking

Don't miss the chance to hike one of the many trails in the Mount Washington area—the best way to enjoy its natural beauty. Stop by one of the Appalachian Mountain Club camps or huts scattered throughout the area for trail maps, recommendations, and up-to-date trail conditions. (The closest one in this area is just south of Bretton Woods at the Crawford Notch Camp on Route 302.) The following trails are short, easy hikes appropriate for families:

⅋ Alpine Garden Trail

Tie a short hike into your trip up or down the Mount Washington Auto Road. This trail leaves the road at the Alpine Gardens Junction at about the 6-mile mark. A pretty hike, it's best from late June to early July when the dainty alpine flowers are in bloom. It'll take about an hour to cover the 1.5 miles.

⅋ Jackson-Webster Trail

There are a few steep spots along the way, which makes this trail best for families with older children (seven years and older). The trail, marked in blue, leaves the east side of Route 302 just south of the Crawford Depot. (You'll see a side trail, Elephant's Head, veering to the right. Take this short side trip to the top of the ledge overlooking Crawford Notch for some fine views.) The main trail runs above Elephant Head Brook, crosses Little Mossy Brook, and rises, rather steeply, to Flume Cascade Brook. It's about 45 minutes and .9 mile to this point. Head back now, or continue on the Webster branch (to the right) to a beautiful cascade and pool. That'll be enough for most families.

⅋ Sylvan Way

This is a great trail for families, particularly in the fall when foliage is spectacular. Pick it up at the Link at Memorial Bridge on Route 2, .7 miles from the Appalachian parking area in Randolph. You'll pass falls and cross brooks on this easy 2.5-mile trip. It should take about an hour and a half.

Jefferson Notch

A trip through Jefferson Notch is not recommended for the weak, but it's worth the effort. The narrow, steep road is one of the highest in New Hampshire, reaching almost 3,000 feet. From U.S. 2, 3 miles east of Jefferson Highlands, you'll turn south on the road heading from Labyan to the Mount Washington Cog Railway Station. You'll be rewarded with great mountain and valley panoramas, and a fine view of Jefferson Notch.

Dixville Notch

When the summer crowds start to feel oppressive, you can escape. Head north through Conway and Jackson up Route 16, past Berlin and Gorham. You'll notice the pace slowing and the traffic thinning. Keep going to Dixville Notch, set high in the White Mountains—the vistas are breathtaking, the air crisp and clean, and the atmosphere slow and easy. You'll find great fishing, hiking, cross-country and downhill skiing, and unsurpassed wilderness views.

As you weave your way through the Notch, you'll climb high, round a bend—and stretched before you, you'll see The Balsams, one of the world's poshest resorts—a castle in the middle of nowhere. For a real treat, consider a brief stay or one of their week-long summer programs. It's an experience you won't soon forget. (In fact, 80 percent of The Balsams' summer guests are repeat customers.) The resort has 15,000 acres, a private lake, hiking trails, cross-country and downhill skiing, two golf courses, and one of the best restaurants in New England.

If you think "Dixville Notch" sounds familiar, you're right. It's here, in the tiny Ballot Room at the Balsams Resort, that the first ballots are cast in every U.S. presidential election. The distinction has made this tiny town famous for decades.

Cross-Country Skiing

There are many trails in the Appalachian Mountain Club network open to cross-country skiers. Stop by the AMC headquarters in Pinkham Notch (603) 356-5541 for information on conditions and for detailed trail maps.

Nordic skiers will also enjoy the well-maintained course at Bretton Woods Ski Area, Route 302, Bretton Woods; (603) 278-5000. The trails are generally old logging roads or rail beds that head through forests, over bridges, and down picturesque lanes. There are lots of nice views of Crawford Notch and the Ammonoosuc Ravine along the way. You can warm up and replenish at the Ski Touring Center at the base of the ski resort.

⅋ Bretton Woods Resort

Rte. 302, Bretton Woods; (603) 278-5000. Lift tickets: adults, $30; Hobbit Ski School, $45/day; nursery, $3.75/hour. Rates listed are for weekends and holidays; special discounts and packages available.

The slow and easy atmosphere here makes this perfect for families, or for anyone looking for a relaxed ski getaway. You'll be skiing Mount Rosebrook, which has a 1,500-foot vertical drop mostly felt in long, relaxed runs. There's not much of a challenge at this area, which has only a handful of for-experienced-skiers-only runs, including a short, fast trip down the headwall on Short & Sweet or Upper Express. Just about everything a skiing family needs, however, is here: lessons, restaurants, and a nursery. And people tell us that the area gets twice as much snow as the other ski resorts in the vicinity, a phenomenon that locals call the "Bretton Wood flurries."

Kids, age four to 12, can sign up for the fun-filled all-day Hobbit Ski School. They're awarded badges as they progress through the program.

RESTAURANTS

⅋ Fabyans Station

Rte. 302 (next to the Cog Railway Road), Bretton Woods; (603) 846-2222. Open lunch and dinner.

Housed in a restored railroad depot, this restaurant offers a selection of appetizers, salads, burgers, and sandwiches. Dinner entrees feature swordfish, pork pie, chicken, ribs, and beef dishes. Ask for half-portions for children, or split the order. It will be plenty.

⅋ Darby's Restaurant

Rte. 302, Lodge at Bretton Woods; (603) 278-1500.

This family-oriented restaurant in the lodge at Bretton Woods Resort offers great views of the Presidential Mountain Range. In winter, you'll be warmed by two open fireplaces. The menu offers veal, chicken, steaks, and seafood. Make reservations for weekend dinners; it gets crowded.

⅋ Wilfred's

117 Main St., Gorham; (603) 466-2380. Daily, 7 A.M.–9:30 P.M.

The down-home cooking here starts with a warm, crusty slice of homemade bread and a large bowl of salad to share with those at the table. Next, thick slices of baked turkey, stuffing, potatoes and gravy, and cranberry sauce. Finish it all off with Indian pudding and vanilla ice cream. This is what Wilfred's does best and what it's known for.

MONADNOCK REGION

White-steepled churches set in village centers, old-fashioned country stores, covered bridges, and rolling hills all set in quiet meandering valleys and farmlands welcome you to rural New Hampshire. You'll want to stroll Main Street in the town of Peterborough, the model for Thornton Wilder's *Our Town,* or Main Street in Keene, the widest paved Main Street in the world. And if you like a parade, this is the place—the Monadnock Region may well hold the most parades per capita in the country. Stay more than a day or two in the summer, and you'll likely see one. This is small-town U.S.A.

The area surrounding Keene is New Hampshire countryside at its best. You won't find neon lights, flashy hotels, or amusement parks, here. This is the place to come for lazy summer drives (be sure to drive Route 10 from Keene to West Swanzey—you'll see six covered bridges along the way), hikes in the woods, swimming in rivers, casting in lakes, and sleigh rides in the snow.

☙ Monadnock Children's Museum

147 Washington St., Keene; (603) 357-5161. Tues.-Fri., 10-5; Sat., 10-4; Sun.,1-4. Adults, $2.50; 1 and under, free.

This hands-on museum for children of all ages is housed in a reno-vated 1850s colonial home that's chock full of learning fun. There's a little bit of everything here to please all interests and to help fulfill the insatiable curiosity of children. In the Crystal Room, budding scientists will perform tests to identify crystals. Children will learn about other cultures in the World Room, and about sea life from the variety of fresh- and saltwater fish tanks. During the sumer, there are special Clubhouse mornings (call ahead for current schedule) when children are admitted to the museum simply by bringing something to add to the museum's tree house area. The tree house is filled with collections of unusual objects that children have donated.

☙ Little Nature Center

59 Boyce St., Weare; (603) 529-7180. By appointment only, usually several weeks in advance. Adults, $2; 4-16, $1.

This long-standing private museum is open to the public and boasts an extensive collection of Indian artifacts, shells, fossils, and insects. Chil-dren will beam with wonder at the mounted birds and fluorescent miner-als and will enjoy the many hands-on activities. A lovely nature hike is also available. Call ahead to make arrangements.

☙ Friendly Farm

Rte. 101, Dublin (a half-mile west of Dublin Lake); (603) 563-8444.
May–Columbus Day, daily, 10-5; Labor Day–mid-Oct., weekends, 10-5.
Adults, $4; 1-12, $3.

Children will enjoy a visit to this farm where they can pet and feed
their favorite animals. At the hen house, you're likely to see eggs hatching
and you can hold and cuddle baby chicks. Brilliantly plumed peacocks
strut their stuff alongside a pen housing baby bunnies; take a look at the
observation beehive, too. The natural setting is pleasant. You can bring a
packed lunch to enjoy in the picnic area.

☙ New England Marionette Theatre

24-26 Main St., Peterborough; (603) 924-4022.

Treat yourself to an unusual night of entertainment that the folks
here bill as "an opera on a string," with two-foot-high puppets worked by
a talented corps of puppeteers. The theater is located in a restored Baptist
Church and has plush red velvet seats and fine acoustics. Call for a schedule of performances and rates.

☙ Mount Monadnock State Park

Rte. 124, Jaffrey; (603) 532-8623. Year-round.

Getting to the top of Mount Monadnock is a popular pursuit. First
scaled by settlers in 1725, Grand Monadnock is the single most climbed
mountain in North America. If you have the energy (sure you have!) for
the two-mile trek up to the 3,165-foot summit, you'll be rewarded with
lovely views of Boston to the east and Mount Washington to the north. It
will take about three hours to complete the round-trip hike (plus time for
viewing and picnicking). If that sounds too ambitious for your group,
there are more than 30 miles of other trails to choose from at the park.

You'll also want to stop in the Ecocenter, where you'll find exhibits and
programs on nature and ecology as well as information on the various hikes.

☙ Sleigh Rides

Take a winter sleigh ride through snow-covered country lanes, rolling
fields, and pine-scented forests. James Anthony Farm, Dudley Brook Road
in Weare, (603) 529-1123, offers winter rides at the charming, 175-year-
old farm. At Silver Ranch, Route 124E in Jaffrey, (603) 532-7363, you can
ride in a covered carriage, or hop aboard a wagon for a fun-filled hayride.

☙ Miller State Park

Rte. 101, Peterborough; (603) 924-9963.

While you're in the Peterborough area, consider taking the scenic drive to the summit of Pack Monadnock Mountain. Pick up the road within the park. You'll find walking paths, picnic sites, and a great view at the 2,280-foot summit.

᪣ Greenfield State Park
Rte. 136, Greenfield; (603) 547-3497.
This is a nice family park of more than 350 acres along Otter Lake. The sandy beach is great for swimming, and children will enjoy the small playground. If you'd like to do some rowing or fishing, you can rent small boats. The picnic area includes tables, grills, and a refreshment stand. There are also hiking trails in the park. Pack your trout-fishing gear and head for Hogback or Mud ponds; locals say the fishing is good.

᪣ Clough State Park
Off Rte. 114, Weare; (603) 529-7112.
This is a great place on a hot summer's day. Take a dip in a cool river pool, rent a boat, or explore the park's 150 acres. The beach and picnic areas are usually large enough to accommodate the summer crowds.

᪣ Fox State Forest
Center Rd., Hillsborough; (603) 224-4666.
This state park offers more than 20 miles of trails through more than 1,400 acres of woodlands and forests. Stop by the Visitor's Center on Center Road, just outside of Hillsborough Center, for detailed information on the trails most suitable for families. Bring your bug spray!

᪣ Cross-Country Skiing
Many of the trails in the Greenfield State Park (see entry above) and at Pisgah State Park (off Routes 63 or 119 in Chesterfield or Hinsdale) are good for cross-country skiing. There are also a number of ski touring areas, including B.U. Sargent Camp and Temple Mountain Touring in Peterborough, (603) 525-3311; Tory Pines Resort in Francestown, (603) 588-2000; Hampshire Hills in Milford, (603) 673-7123; Inn at East Hill Farm in Troy, (603) 242-6495; Road's End Farm in Chesterfield, (603) 363-4703; Shattuck Inn Nordic Center in Jaffrey, (603) 532-4300; Windblown Ski Touring in New Ipswich, (603) 878-2869; and Woodbound Inn in Jaffrey, (800) 688-7770.

RESTAURANTS

⅋ Colony Mill Marketplace
222 West St., Keene; (603) 357-4011. Daily, 10-10.

Instead of opting for a fast-food lunch, consider stopping here, where your group can select anything from corn dogs to gourmet salads. Order from one of the take-out eateries, then find a table in the adjacent courtyard. Two good choices are a chicken burrito at Portable Feast and then a chocolate lollipop to go from Ye Goodie Shoppe.

⅋ Nonie's Bakery and Luncheonette
Main St., Peterborough; (603) 924-3451. Mon.-Sat., 4 A.M.–2 P.M.

This is where the townies gather for a hearty breakfast or lunch and for all the local gossip. No one needs a menu—it's bacon and eggs, pancakes, and french toast; sandwiches and burgers for lunch. The blackboard announces the daily specials, things like macaroni and cheese or a long dog and slaw. Good prices, casual setting.

Maine

If the word "Maine" conjures up visions of rocky shores, picturesque villages, and freshly caught lobsters, you won't be disappointed by the actuality. Maine's southern coast is a favorite with vacationing families for those reasons and more. First, it's not difficult to get here. Many visitors to Boston are surprised to learn that Maine is only 55 miles away. Then there are the sandy beaches. That's right—sandy. Although there are 3,500 miles of shoreline in Maine, fewer than 100 miles are sandy beach. Southern Maine has them—long, silvery strands that stretch for miles. When it comes to swimming, some adults find the ice-cold North Atlantic waters a tad too brisk to be pleasurable. If you prefer being on the water to being in it, you'll find plenty of options, here, including a quintessentially Maine lobstering cruise on which you'll help pull up the traps.

Most families try to visit a museum or two while they're here, and rainy weather usually means a pilgrimage to family amusement centers and arcades along Route 1. A better remedy for less-than-sunny weather? Dress for it, then head outdoors so you won't miss the dramatic, foggy beauty that is Maine at its best.

York's Wild Kingdom

Rte. 1, York Beach; (207) 363-4911. Zoo open, Memorial Day–Columbus Day, daily, 10-5 (weekends only in May). Rides open, Memorial Day–Labor Day, daily, 1-10 (weekends only in June and Sept.). Zoo only: adults, $9.75; 10 and under, $7.75; under 2, free. Combination ticket: adults, $13.75; 10 and under, $12.75.

Kids have a terrific time at this combination zoo and amusement park, where they meet lions, tigers, monkeys, llamas, a zebra, and an elephant. There's also a petting area where children can feed the goats and deer. On the amusement side, there are 25 rides, including a Ferris wheel, a merry-go-round, bumper cars, the "Octopus," and the "Jaguar"—the park's most popular ride.

☜ Old York Historical Tour

Lindsey Rd. (Off Rte. 1A), York; (207) 363-4974. Mid.-June–Sept.,
Tues.-Sat., 10-5. Admission for all buildings: adults, $6; 6-16, $2.50.

The Old York Historical Society offers guided tours of seven historic
buildings, dating back to the days when York was a colonial village and
seaport. You'll start at Jefferd's Tavern (1750), where you'll find period
furnishings and a tap room. You're also likely to see a demonstration of
hearth cooking, basket weaving, or candlemaking during your visit.

Children also enjoy touring the Old Gaol Museum, built in 1719 as
the King's Prison for the Province of Maine and used as a prison until
1860. You can wander through the dungeons and cells that once housed
criminals and debtors, and see the "gaoler's" living quarters. An exhibit
room features the Museum of Colonial Relics, a turn-of-the-century display with old dolls, toys and unusual objects. Other sites on the tour include the Elizabeth Perkins House; the Emerson-Wilcox House; the
George A. Marshall Store, a 19th-century general store; the John Hancock
Warehouse; and the Old Schoolhouse, a one-room school built in 1745.

☜ Wiggly Bridge Footpath

Rte. 103, York Harbor.

For a lovely view of the York River that few tourists see, stroll the
footpath that starts at Wiggly Bridge. Walk over the bridge, passing over
an inlet to the York River, and follow the path along the river to Stedman
Wood.

☜ Ogunquit Playhouse

Rte. 1, Ogunquit; (207) 646-5511.

This classic 700-seat summer theater offers a great way for parents to
spend a special evening out with older children. Helen Hayes and Bette
Davis are among the famous performers who have played here. Call ahead
for curtain times and reservations.

☜ Lobstering Cruise

Barnacle Bill's Dock, Perkins Cove, Ogunquit; (207) 646-5227. May-Oct.,
daily except Sun., every half-hour, 9-3:30. Call ahead since schedule is
limited in May and June and Sept. and Oct. Adults, $7; 4-11, $5.

If you've ever wondered what it's like to trap lobsters for a living, this
is your chance to find out. Take a 50-minute trip with Finestkind Cruises
and learn how to bait lobster traps, read lobster buoy markings, and determine whether a lobster is a "chicken." Children are warmly welcomed.

⬬ Marginal Way

This mile-long shoreline footpath is not to be missed. You'll see
spectacular ocean views, tidal pools, wildflowers, rock formations, and, at
high tide, waves crashing against the rocky shore. The benches that have
been placed along the way are perfect when little feet need a rest. The
footpath begins on Shore Road, near the center of Ogunquit, and continues to Perkins Cove.

⬬ Bald Head Cliff

Shore Rd., Ogunquit.

Be sure to stop and take a look at this fascinating rock formation. Just
south of Ogunquit, on Shore Road, you'll see the signs pointing out Bald
Head Cliff. The cliff rises more than 100 feet from the edge of the Atlantic. Surrounded by stretches of sandy beach and rocky outcrops, the cliff is
a striking spectacle.

⬬ Wells Auto Museum

*Rte. 1, Wells; (207) 646-9064. Mid-June–mid-Sept., daily, 10-5; open
weekends only in May and Oct. (through Columbus Day), 10-5. Adults,
$3.50; 6-12, $2.*

More than 80 antique cars are on display here, some dating from the
turn of the century, including gas, steam, and electric models. Kids will
love taking a ride in a Model-T Ford. Arcade games and nickelodeons add
to the fun.

⬬ Wells National Estuarine Sanctuary

*Off Rte. 1 (1.5 miles north of Well's Corner), Wells; (207) 646-1555.
Daily, sunrise-sunset.*

Budding birdwatchers especially will appreciate a visit here. The
Sanctuary is also a good place to commune with nature while enjoying a
picnic. This 1,600-acre site—mostly marshland— includes the Rachel
Carson Wildlife Refuge and Laudholm Farm. The Sanctuary includes
fields, woodlands, tidal rivers, salt marshes, dunes, and beaches, and offers
a protected environment for wildlife. Marked nature trails lead through
the woods and along the marsh.

⬬ Cape Neddick Light

Perhaps one of the most photographed lighthouses on the East Coast,
The Nubble Light (as the locals call it) personifies the style of lighthouse
for which Maine has become famous. Its white cast-iron tower, built in
1879, stands "atop the nubble," just off the shore, striking a beautiful

pose against the rocky shoreline and blue waters of the Atlantic. Take Route 1A to Long Sands Beach; from the north end of the beach, a local road leads east to the tip of Cape Neddick and the lighthouse.

Old Orchard Beach

Rte. 1, Old Orchard Beach.

Kids love the lively, carnival-like atmosphere of this seaside resort. One of the longest beaches on the Atlantic, Old Orchard Beach is lined with boardwalks full of fast food and fun. In fact, it's been called the Coney Island of Maine. The Atlantic waters here are shallow and warm, and the surrounding amusements are a hit with youngsters.

Palace Playland

1 Old Orchard St., Old Orchard Beach; (207) 934-2001. Late-June–Labor Day, Mon.-Fri., noon-10; Sat.-Sun., 11-10. Memorial Day–late-June, weekends.

All a little heart desires for thrills are here: rides—big ones and little ones—and arcade games aplenty, an antique carousel, a waterslide, junk food, and more. Bet you can't pass by without going in. There are fireworks, too, every Thursday night at 10.

Seashore Trolley Museum

Log Cabin Rd. (off Rte. 1), Kennebunkport; (207) 967-2800. Late April– late-Oct., daily, 10-5. Adults, $6; 6-16, $4.

More than 200 antique trolley cars are housed here—the world's largest collection. You'll see a slide show and tour the cars on exhibit, but the real fun here is an old-fashioned trolley ride. You can hop aboard the authentically restored trolley cars from all over the world.

Dock Square

Bustling Kennebunkport is a great place for people watching, especially at picturesque Dock Square. There are lots of shops and galleries here. Our favorite is Kennebunk Book Port. Located in the loft of a warehouse built in 1775, the shop posts a sign that reads "Ice cream, candy, children, bare feet…small dragons…are welcome anytime." Stop for some lunch or a snack at one of the many outdoor restaurants and watch the world go by.

Ocean Drive

A ride along Ocean Drive to Cape Porpoise and Goose Rock Beach is a pleasant way to view Kennebunkport's coastline. Along the way, you'll see two unmarred natural wonders, too—Spouting Rock, a spectacular ocean fountain, and Blowing Cave, a rock formation where the waves roar in dramatically. Look closely so you don't miss them. When you reach Cape Porpoise, park the car and stroll around this quaint fishing village.

⅋ Boat Cruises

There are a number of options for families who want to get out on the water. Whale watching, deep-sea fishing, and cruising trips are available: Cape Arundel Cruises, (207) 967-5912; Indian Fishing and Whale-Watch Cruises, (207) 967-5912; and Discovery Sailing Cruises, (207) 967-2921.

⅋ Scarborough Marsh Nature Center

Rte. 9, Scarborough; (207) 883-5100. Mid-June–Labor Day, daily, 9:30-5:30.

Bring your bug spray and old sneakers—and a pair of binoculars. This 3,100-acre natural area contains a number of salt-marsh nature trails perfect for birdwatching and canoe routes through the inlets. The center offers guided nature walks, hands-on exhibits, and canoe tours. Canoe rental is available at the park. The park puts on lots of special naturalist programs for children throughout the summer. You'll also find slide shows and a nature store.

⅋ Smiling Hill Farm Barnyard

781 County Rd., Rte. 22, Westbrook; (207) 775-4818. May–Labor Day, Mon.-Fri., 9-4; Sat. and Sun., 10-5. Adults, $3; 1-15, $2.

You might as well head directly to the ice cream barn upon arrival, and grab yourself a fresh, farm-made cup of ice cream. Now, everyone can relax and visit the rest of this working dairy farm. Meet the friendly barn animals in the petting area and visit the native wildlife exhibits. There are also pony rides and hayrides.

⅋ Aquaboggin Water Park

Rte. 1, Saco; (207) 282-3112. Mid-June–Labor Day, daily, 10-7. Over 4 ft., $15.95; under 4 ft., $10.95.

If your children love waterslides, and what kid doesn't, this place is sure to please. Attractions include a wave pool, bumper boats, a swimming pool, and a go-cart race track. Gentler souls can tool around the pond on paddle boats.

⅋ Maine Aquarium

Rte. 1 (Exit 5 off I-95), Portland; (207) 284-4512. Year-round, daily, 9-5; June-Sept., 9-9. Adults, $6.50; 5-12, $4.50; 2-4, $2.50.

Giant octopuses, sharks, seals, and penguins all live here along with tidepool animals you can actually touch. The exhibits are fun as well as educational. Don't miss it.

∂ Funtown U.S.A.
Rte. 1, Saco; (207) 284-5139. May and Sept., weekends, 10:30-11; mid-June–Labor Day, daily, 10:30-11. Free admission and parking; you pay for rides and amusements once inside.

Family fun is the name of the game, here, at Maine's largest theme amusement park. The Thunderfalls Log Flume is most popular, and is very tall and very wet. There's also a high-speed roller coaster, tilt-a-whirl, bumper cars, and kiddie rides galore. And what better to go with those tummy-twisting roller coasters than Mexican food, taffy, and cotton candy? Antique car rides for mellower folk.

∂ Cascade Water and Amusement Park
Rte. 1, Saco; (207) 284-6231. May–Labor Day, daily, 10-7. Adults, $14.95; 10 and under, $11.95.

On a hot day, you'll enjoy this park's waterslides, whirlpools, and tube run. Feeling too much sun and somewhat waterlogged? Take some quarters to the arcade and game room.

∂ Beaches
There are several public beaches along Maine's southern coast. Most are well marked; look for signs leading to beaches on the side roads off Route 1. Arrive early to snare a parking space. The best beaches for families with small children—offering gentler surf—are Ferry Beach in Saco, Crescent Beach in Cape Elizabeth, and Long Sands Beach in York Harbor. The surf can be lively at Ogunquit beaches, but toddlers can wade safely at a protected area near the mouth of the Ogunquit River.

◤ RESTAURANTS

∂ Mabel's Lobster Claw
Ocean Ave., Kennebunkport; (207) 967-2562. Lunch and dinner.

Known locally as Mabel's, this restaurant was featured in *Time* magazine for serving the best lobster rolls in the country. Adults can enjoy a glass of wine with their fresh seafood dinner, which might be the stuffed sole (a house specialty) or lobster prepared in one of several ways. Children can choose from the many sandwiches and fish items on the menu. Be sure to try the onion rings: "Fresh, not frozen," says Mabel. After dinner, the family can stroll next door to Mabel's ice cream shop for dessert.

ᨑ Bill Foster's Down East Lobster and Clambake

Rte. 1A, York Harbor; (207) 363-3255. Memorial Day–Labor Day, daily, noon-8. Reservations required.

Just what you'd expect: lobster, steamed clams, and all the trimmings. Steak and chicken are offered if you're not a crustacean fan (or if you've finally has your fill of 'em). Eat in the rough, then join in the old-fashioned sing-along. Little kids will love this; older children will, of course, be mortified, especially if you sing along.

ᨑ 1790 Candy House, Ben & Jerry's Ice Cream Shop

Ocean Ave., Kennebunk; (207) 967-5838. May-Sept., 11-10.

For a special treat, children will love a visit to this candy and ice cream shop. A large assortment of penny candy and chocolate treats awaits those with a sweet tooth. The ice cream shop offers a variety of delicious flavors made by New England favorite Ben & Jerry's. There is a lovely seating area outside where your group can enjoy the goodies.

PORTLAND

Maine's largest city is an intriguing blend of old and new. Wander around the waterfront and you'll see fish-processing plants and warehouses, just around the corner from specialty shops and fancy restaurants. Many stores and eateries are housed in renovated old warehouses, giving a quaint appeal to even the newest. A great way to see it all is to take a tour of historic Portland on a double-decker bus. The three-hour ride is free— catch the bus at the Old Port Exchange (the Visitor's Bureau on Free Street has more information).

This booming little city is rapidly becoming a cultural presence in New England, with museums, concerts, and festivals aplenty. After visiting Portland, you'll see why it keeps cropping up on those lists of "most livable" cities. The same factors make it a great place to visit.

ᨑ Children's Museum of Maine

746 Stevens Ave.; (207) 797-KITE. Year-round, daily, 9:30-4:30. Admission, $2.50; under 1, free.

"Please touch" is the operative slogan here. This terrific museum has so many things to do that your children will have the happy dilemma of deciding where to head first. Perhaps to the "Bubbles" exhibit, where kids can make a giant bubble screen? Or perhaps to the human skeleton, where kids can learn how "dem bones" really work? Children from one to 10 are certain to have a good time here, and you'll delight in watching them explore. Special activities and workshops are scheduled; contact the museum for details.

⌁ Portland Observatory

138 Congress St.; (207) 774-5561. June, Sept., and Oct., Fri.-Sun., 1-5; July and Aug., Wed., Thurs., and Sun., 1-5, and Fri. and Sat., 10-5. Adults; $1.50, 12 and under, $.50.

This 82-foot octagonal signal tower was once the spot where lookouts informed Portland residents of incoming ships. Now you can climb the stairway to the signal deck and enjoy the same panoramic view.

⌁ Southworth Planetarium

96 Falmouth St., Science Bldg., University of Southern Maine; (207) 780-4249. Astronomy shows: Fri. and Sat., 7; Sun., 2. Laser light concerts: Fri. and Sat., 8:30; Sun., 3:30. Children's shows: Sat., 3:30. Rates vary; call for schedule.

Astronomy goes 20th-century tech at this planetarium. The sky dome theater is the perfect setting for high-tech light shows with full-color motion and sound effects. At the conclusion of each show, constellations and other objects currently visible in the sky are shown. There are also general astronomy shows—a good introduction to this dazzling science—and a special program for young children on Saturday afternoons. Call ahead for information and reservations.

⌁ Kinderkonzerts

What does a conductor do? How does the percussionist know when to bang the big drum or crash the cymbals? To introduce children to a variety of musical instruments and how they work, the Portland Symphony Orchestra presents a series of children's concerts from October to May. Held at various sites in Maine and New Hampshire, the concerts are geared toward kids from preschool to grade two. Each program highlights a particular element of music. For information and reservations, call (207) 773-8191.

The PSO also performs Youth Concerts for children in grades three through six. The concerts are given three times a year at the City Hall Auditorium. The programs feature symphonic music, popular music, and special guest artists.

⌁ Peak's Island

Don't miss the popular day excursion to this small island off the coast from Portland. The 720-acre island can be reached by a 15-minute ferry boat ride. When you hop off the ferry, head to the rental shops for bikes—this is the best way to get around the island. The small community boasts only three restaurants, a gift shop, a market, and a library. But you'll find a nice sandy beach near the ferry landing and lots of scenic vistas and fresh salt air. Take a quick look in the Civil War Museum. It's also possible to see where Longfellow's "Wreck of the Hesperus" was inspired by the 1869 wreck of the *Helen Eliza* on the rocks off the island's south shore. Peak's is the closest major island to Portland, and it can get crowded in the summer.

ᨃ Two Lights State Park

It's too cool for swimming but you want to stay outdoors? Head to this state park to stroll the walkway with great ocean views, and with picnic sites along the way. It's located south of the city on the Cape Elizabeth shore.

ᨃ Crescent Beach

A popular beach with Portland locals, Crescent has a 4,000-foot sandy area. You'll find it south of Portland on the Cape Elizabeth shore.

ᨃ Portland Head

Just off Cape Elizabeth's Shore Road you'll find the Portland Head Light, Maine's oldest lighthouse and one of the most frequently photographed. The lighthouse was built in 1791. You'll enjoy the scenic coastal setting.

ᨃ Boat Cruises

The Atlantic Ocean beckons. Why not take a harbor tour, or cruise to an island for a clambake? Or, if you want a real getaway, take the ferry to Nova Scotia. A number of cruise companies offer a variety of options; you'll find them along Commercial Street in the Old Port section of Portland. Some possibilities: House Island Clambake and Cruises, (207) 799-8188; Longfellow Cruise Lines, (207) 774-3578; and Prince of Fundy Cruises, Ltd., (207) 775-5616.

▶ RESTAURANTS

ᨃ Village Cafe

114 Newbury; (207) 772-5320. Mon.-Thurs., 11-10:30; Fri. and Sat., 11-11:30; closed Sun.

This local favorite is tucked away in a warehouse district just off the waterfront. It's worth looking for, especially if you're hankering after good, family-style Italian food. Children's portions are available. The normal portions are huge, but try to save room for dessert—there's a good bakery, Armato's, next door.

⅔ Cap'n Newick's Lobster House

740 Broadway; (207) 799-3090. Tues.-Thurs., 11:30-8; Fri.-Sun., 11:30-9.

This popular family restaurant offers delicious seafood at reasonable prices. The atmosphere is casual, so you don't have to worry if baby uses the drawn butter as a finger bowl or if junior discovers several unusual things to do with a used lobster leg.

MID-COAST

You could spend a lifetime exploring the mid-coastal region of Maine and still you'd leave some hidden gem undiscovered. This area, running from Portland to Belfast, covers some of the prettiest spots in the country, characterized by quaint New England seaside villages, rocky coastlines juxtaposed against sandy beaches, idyllic peninsulas jutting out into the Atlantic, tidal rivers, classic Maine lighthouses, and more. And in each village you'll visit along the way, recreation and adventure abound.

You'll find outlet shopping, in busy Freeport, home to the famous outdoor-goods company L.L. Bean, and also island hopping. Busy harbors have lots of choices for families who wish to try out their sea legs; just walk to any harbor and check out the offerings. You'll find charming, popular harbor villages, like Camden, Boothbay, and Rockport, with galleries, boutiques, and exquisite seaside dining, and others like Brunswick and Bath that are steeped in nautical history. There are numerous museums to visit, trails to hike, and trains to board, and lots of places to learn about the sea. There's even a scorching hot desert.

The down side of all this is the crowds. On a summer weekend, you'd better have a reservation for a bed and a meal waiting when you roll into town.

⅔ Maine Audubon Society

Gilsland Farm (off Rte. 1), Falmouth; (207) 781-2330. Year-round, Mon.-Fri., 9-5; Sat., 9-5; Sun., 12-5. Donations accepted.

This is the home of the Maine Audubon Society and a great place to visit if you're in the area. You'll learn about solar energy through a variety of displays here and, of course, about native birds. Pack a picnic; there are lots of nature trails and places to stop along the way.

✿ Desert of Maine

Desert Rd. (off Rte. 1 and I-95), Freeport; (207) 865-6962. Mid-May–mid-Oct., daily, 9-dusk. Adults, $4.75; 6-12, $2.50.

The desert of Maine? Yep. Give your kids a real lesson in what happens when you don't respect Mother Earth. This spot was once the Tuttle Farm, located on a glacial sand deposit. After years of tree cutting and planting the topsoil eroded, exposing the sand beneath. Today this sand, covering more than 50 acres, forms dunes that tower over the trees and buildings. But at Desert of Maine you'll also see rebirth. Surrounding the desert are lush forests. After a hot walk through the desert (this area sees temperatures that exceed 100 degrees), cool off with a walk on the forest trails, which are abundant with wildflowers. In fall, visitors can see 30 to 50 different kinds of mushrooms along the nature trail. Narrated tram tours give a good overview of the area. There's also a farm and sand museum, and a variety of sand design artists are at work.

✿ North American Wildlife Expo

Rte. 1, Freeport; (207) 865-1449. June–Labor Day, daily, 9-9; Labor Day–Memorial Day, daily, 10-6. Adults, $4; 3-16, $3; families, $12.

The kids will love this display—one of the largest in the region—of North American wildlife. Hundreds of animals are placed in real-life natural settings. Adults and kids alike will enjoy the art displays, where kids can touch the impressive collection of wildlife sculpture.

✿ Winslow Park

Staples Point Rd., South Freeport; (207) 865-4198. Memorial Day–Sept., 8-9. Free.

When you're tired of outlet shopping in Freeport, head to this park for some cheap outdoor fun. Romp in the sand on the beach, rest at the picnic area overlooking the bay, or take a short walk on the nature trail that runs along the park perimeter.

✿ Railway Village

Rte. 27, Boothbay; (207) 633-4727. Mid-June–Columbus Day, daily, 10-5. Adults, $5; 12 and under, $2.

This turn-of-the-century village is sure to delight young visitors. The main attraction is a two-gauge railway with a working steam train that kids can ride. There are old train cars to explore, antique automobiles on display, a player piano, a doll museum, and—every toddler's favorite—sheep and ducks that love to be fed by little hands. Eat in the diner, or bring your own (no leg of lamb or roast duckling, please) and eat at the village's picnic area.

ꊄ Seaquarium

McKown Point, W. Boothbay Harbor; (207) 633-5572. Note: At press time this attraction was not open but was scheduled to reopen in summer 1994. Please confirm ahead of time.

Your child's first encounter with a lobster will probably be rather unpleasant for both parties, the lobster having been trapped and boiled, and the child thinking, "I'm supposed to eat this thing?" A visit to this small but interesting aquarium will provide a more complete picture of native sea life.

A wonderful "touch pool" is filled with sea urchins, starfish, periwinkles, and other inhabitants of the deep. Even more thrilling is a large open shark tank with dogfish—some as long as two feet—that brave children can reach in and pat. Toddlers will love pressing their noses against the "baby tank" filled with tiny, squirming sea creatures. Be sure to pack a picnic; the Seaquarium has a pretty picnic area right on the water.

ꊄ Brunswick Fishway Viewing Area

CMD Dam, off Rte. 201, Brunswick; (207) 725-6623. May and June, Sat. and Sun., 10-2; Wed., 7-9 P.M. Free.

This is a fun place to visit when the fish runs are in progress, usually in early spring. There's a fish ladder, a counting room, and a viewing area.

ꊄ Peary-MacMillan Arctic Museum

Hubbard Hall, Bowdoin Campus, Brunswick; (207) 725-3416. Year-round, Tues.-Sat., 10-5; Sun., 2-5. Donations accepted.

When the snow falls some things just come naturally to kids: snowball fights, snowman making, and building their own version of an igloo. Kids are naturally interested in igloos and Eskimos, and at this museum they can feed that curiosity and learn more about the Eskimo culture. Actually the museum is a tribute to two Bowdoin alumni, Admiral Robert E. Peary and Admiral Donald B. MacMillan, and also contains equipment from and information about their arctic explorations.

ꊄ Maine Maritime Museum

243 Washington St., Bath; (207) 443-1316. Year-round, daily, 9:30-5. Adults, $6; 6-19, $2.50.

Here the imagination and fascination of Maine's maritime past are captured in a very child-friendly manner. Kids can get their hands on the capstan, and into Morse Code and the World Trade Game, all equipment meant to be touched and played with. The museum hosts a number of changing exhibits celebrating the seafaring past, with lots of hands-on components for children. There are boat models and paintings on display as well. Be sure to stop by and talk to the apprentices in the boatbuilding school.

During the summer there are also tours of the historic shipyard, visits to vessels, demonstrations of seafaring techniques, and a lobstering exhibit. Visitors to the area are invited along with locals to enjoy the weekly lobster bakes and special waterfront activities such as concerts, fairs, and parades.

ᣮ Thomas Point Beach

Cooks Corner, off Rte. 24, Brunswick; (207) 725-6009. Memorial Day–Labor Day, 9-sunset.

Ready to kick back and relax? Enough sightseeing for the day? Spend the afternoon at pretty Thomas Point Beach (it's also a campground) on a sandy ocean inlet. There's a pleasant calm beach area plus picnic spots, a playground, and lots of room to stretch out. Take in a deep breath of that fresh, salty ocean air while the kids run and play and splash in the surf.

ᣮ Popham Beach State Park

Rte. 209, Phippsburg; (207) 389-1335.

A favorite of visitors and locals alike, this pretty beach on the Phippsburg peninsula is the perfect spot for a sunny picnic and a refreshing dip in the ocean. The rocky coastline combines with a sandy beach area to make this a perfect place to spend a hot summer Maine day.

ᣮ Bay Chamber Concerts

Rockport Opera House, Camden; (207) 236-2823. Year-round, ticket office open Mon.-Fri., 9-5.

The beautiful Rockport Opera House is the setting for concerts and plays for children, held year-round. The lively presentations stay just within the attention span of the young. Several are scheduled throughout the year; call the ticket office for a listing of presentations and information.

ᣮ Camden Hills State Park

Rte. 1, Camden; (207) 236-3109.

This park spreads across 5,000 acres at the foot of Mount Battie. Be sure to drive the road to Mount Battie's 900-foot summit. While not the tallest mountain in New England, from its summit you'll still get wonderful panoramic views of Penobscot Bay and the surrounding countryside.

⛄ Owl's Head Transportation Museum

*Rte. 73, Owl's Head; (207) 594-4418. April-Oct., 10-5; Nov.-March,
10-4; winter weekends, 11-3. Adults, $4; 6-12, $2.50.*

Cars, trains, planes, boats…transportation vehicles make every kid's
list of favorite things. Adults, too, will enjoy this collection of historic
aircraft, automobiles, and engines. Stop by the restoration workshop,
where work on pre-1940s vehicles is in progress. Often you'll be able to
hop aboard one of the antique autos for a ride. There are also energy exhibits, a small gallery, picnic areas, and nature trails.

⛄ Fort Knox State Park

*Rte. 174, off Rte. 1, Prospect; (207) 469-7719. Nov.-April, 9-5; May-
Oct., 9-sunset.*

Your kids can hide in the secret passageways, climb the underground
stairways, pretend to shoot the giant cannons, and along the way, learn
about 19th-century armies, battles, and life. Fort Knox is a massive granite and brick fortification dating from 1844; it's now a state park. There's
a guided tour each day at 1 P.M. Bring a picnic; there are tables and
charcoal stoves. And bring a flashlight for exploring the underground
passageways.

⛄ Steve Powell Wildlife Management Area

Swan Island; (207) 547-4167. May–Labor Day, daily, 9-sunset.

For a day in the wilderness, take the ferry from Richmond to Swan
Island. This area, run by the Maine Department of Inland Fisheries and
Wildlife, offers an opportunity for some successful wildlife viewing.
Quiet, observant walkers are likely to see deer, eagles, and several types of
native waterfowl. Bring binoculars and bug spray. There's camping on the
island, too. Be sure to call ahead for reservations and ferry arrangements.

⛄ Darling Marine Center

*Cow Barn, Walpole; (207) 563-3146. July and Aug., Wed. and Sun.,
1-4. Free.*

This small museum located in the cow barn (across from the Walpole
Library) houses a number of marine exhibits, a book shop, and a small
hands-on children's corner. The casual, intimate center is staffed by the
Gulf of Maine Foundation members, who are eager to answer all your
nautical questions.

⛄ Belfast Moosehead Lake Railroad

*11 Water St., Belfast; (207) 338-2931. May-Oct. Call for up-to-date
departure listings and rates.*

What a fun way to see the Maine countryside—chug-chugging along in a vintage 1924 Pullman Day Coach. You'll start at the water's edge and travel up the banks of the Passagassawakeag River. Pulling away from the river, you'll go farther inland, in to the forests, across hills and fields. You'll be in the countryside once populated by Native American tribes and later farmed by the earliest settlers. Bring along some hands-on materials for young tots who may become antsy after the novelty of the train ride wears off and the thrill of scenic vistas wanes.

⁓ Belfast City Park

Families hang out in this 15-acre park that includes an outdoor swimming pool, hiking trails, sailing, golf courses, and tennis courts.

▶ RESTAURANTS

⁓ Miss Brunswick Diner
Rte. 1, Brunswick; (207) 729-5848. Daily, 5 A.M.–9 P.M.

This roadside diner serves up quick, hearty food for wallet-pleasing prices. No need to keep the kids quiet—this is casual and friendly and full of small-town gossip and noise. There's a handful of daily blackboard specials. Fresh, fried seafood meals and Miss Brunswick Burritos are top sellers. And in true diner fashion, breakfast is served anytime.

⁓ The Brown Bag
606 Main St., Rockland; (207) 596-6372. Mon.-Wed., 6:30-4; Thurs.-Sat., 6:30-9; Sun., 7-2.

This is a bright, cheery little eatery with great tasting food. If you're around the area for breakfast, don't bother to go anywhere else. The small street facade belies the open, airy inside dining space with exposed brick, pine flooring, and country decor. You can feast on fresh Maine blueberry muffins, cinnamon swirl French toast, homemade sausages, three-cheese omelets, and smoked salmon, capers, and cream cheese bagels. The Brown Bag also serves great soups, salads, and sandwiches.

⁓ Mama & Leenie's Cafe and Bakery
27 Elm St., Camden; (207) 236-6300. Mon.-Sat., 7 A.M.–8 P.M.; Sun., 7-4.

Bet you can't pass this place up. You'll smell the homebaked cooking—fresh breads, simmering soups, and pastries. How about fresh blintzes filled with cheese, fruit, and sour cream or a slice of spinach and bacon quiche? Lunch brings a list of daily blackboard specials that include hearty soups and chowders, salads, and sandwiches. During evening hours, the blackboard announces the the nightly specials, like fresh seafood and cheese pasta, marinated chicken breast with veggies, chili, or an assortment of pizzas.

Shaw's Fish & Lobster Wharf

Shaw's Wharf, off Rte. 32, New Harbor; (207) 677-2200. May–mid-Oct., daily, 11-9.

This is a busy, busy place, and for good reason. You can sup on fresh steamed clams and corn on the cob overlooking picturesque New Harbor. You'll join people waiting to board boats for Monhegan Island, the lobstermen who haul in their catches here, and tourists buying T-shirts and souvenirs. Walk up to the counter and order your meal (lobster and other fish dishes), then enjoy the views and the people watching. Your dinner will be ready in no time.

DOWNEAST, INCLUDING ACADIA

The Downeast region of Maine includes beautiful Acadia National Park and the prestigious resort community of Bar Harbor. Here you'll see striking stretches of coastline where ragged cliffs meet pounding surf. The combination of fresh salt air, fragrant pines, towering cliffs, and sparkling ocean is a sensory feast you're not likely to forget.

There's more to this area than spectacular scenery. Think of it as the ultimate place to play outside: you can hike, bike, camp, swim, paddle, cruise or ski. Even the museums are of the hands-on variety. At the Natural History Museum, for example, you can help assemble a 20-foot whale skeleton. And the local zoo has the largest petting area in the state of Maine.

The village of Bar Harbor, formerly a vacation mecca for wealthy East Coast families, is full of shops, restaurants, and galleries. While many of its mansions were destroyed in the Great Fire of 1947, some still exist and are now in use as inns. It's a fun place to stroll, with its streets at their liveliest during the Art Show and Musical Festival in late June and the Seafood Festival in early July. Enjoy.

Acadia National Park

It's 22 square miles of wildlife, woodland, mountains, lakes, and valleys surrounded by the Atlantic Ocean. You'll call it paradise. The park is part of Mount Desert Island, a chunk of primitive beauty that owes its unique contours to the action of Ice Age glaciers. In 1919, President Woodrow Wilson set aside much of this lovely island as a national park. Acadia is eminently seeable, with more than 57 miles of car-free paths for hiking, bicycling, horseback riding, and, in winter, cross-country skiing. By car, a trip along scenic Ocean Drive follows the island's entire eastern perimeter.

Begin your visit at the Visitor's Center, Route 3, Hulls Cove. Open from May through October (although the park is open year-round), the Visitor's Center offers a free 15-minute film to introduce you to Acadia. Here you'll find information about Acadia's Naturalist Program, which has activities especially for children. The program offers several guided walks, ranging from easy to strenuous. You might want to join in a "Night Prowl" glimpse of the nocturnal animals who share the park. Others might include guided nature walks and photography workshops, all free of charge. Or sign up for "Nature's Way for Children," a program offered two to three times weekly.

Riding a bike is a wonderful way to see the park, with more than 50 miles of car-free paths to traverse. Bicycle rental shops are located in Bar Harbor.

While the ocean surrounds and beckons (especially on a hot summer's day), even the kids might find the waters here a bit too frigid for fun. Better to swim and play in Echo Lake, which has a nice sandy beach and warmer fresh water. Lifeguards are posted, too. Open mid-June through Labor Day, the lake is located along Route 102, Southwest Harbor.

There are lots of places to get on the water as well, from a variety of ocean-bound boat cruises to a pleasant paddle in a canoe. (Canoe rentals are available at the northern end of Long Pond, located within the park.)

Boat Cruises

Park naturalists conduct hourly or half-day cruises aboard privately owned boats out of Bass Harbor, Northeast Harbor, and Bar Harbor. Naturalists will describe geological history and area wildlife. (Bring binoculars so you won't miss anything.) You'll see seabirds and—to the delight of children—you may spot seals and porpoises. A variety of other sightseeing cruises are also available, including seal-watching, whale-watching, and lobstering trips. You may also choose a 12-hour round-trip cruise to Yarmouth, Nova Scotia.

Robert Abbe Museum of Stone Age Antiquities

Sieur de Monts Spring; (207) 288-2179. Mid-May–Oct., daily. May and June, Sept. and Oct., 10-4; July and Aug., 9-5. Adults, $2; 12 and under, $.50.

This tiny museum, located within Acadia National Park at Sieur de Monts Spring, contains decorative and practical items crafted by Maine

Indians. Artifacts include unusual jewelry (fashioned from animal bones), pottery, baskets, and tools made of stone and bone. A museum shop offers Maine Indian crafts, books, and tapes.

⁂ Cadillac Mountain

Ocean Drive follows the eastern perimeter of Mount Desert Island. Follow it from Sieur de Monts Spring, stopping along the way at scenic lookouts including Thunder Hole, until you reach Seal Harbor. There, a park road will take you north to the summit of Cadillac Mountain (1,530 feet), the highest point on the eastern seaboard. From this 360-degree vantage point, you'll see the surrounding ocean, distant mountains, and offshore islands. It's breathtaking.

⁂ Somes Sound

From Northeast Harbor, take Sargent Drive to the fjord at Somes Sound. The fjord was formed when Ice Age glaciers cut through existing mountains. Stunningly beautiful, Somes Sound is the only natural fjord on the East Coast.

⁂ Mount Desert Oceanarium

Clark Point Rd., off Rte. 102, Southwest Harbor; (207) 244-7330. Mid-May–Oct., Mon.-Sat., 9-5. Adults, $4.95; 4-12, $3.75.

Why does the tide go out? Why is the sea salty? What do lobsters eat? If questions like these have come up during your trip to Maine, help is at hand. The Oceanarium's interactive displays offer a lively look at sea life, answering the kinds of questions kids might ask. And there's more. In the lobster room, a lobsterer explains how a lobster eats, reproduces, and gets caught. The See and Touch room has sea urchins, starfish, and sea cucumbers that children can handle. In the Living Room, live specimens of local marine life are displayed in tanks.

⁂ Mount Desert Oceanarium, Lobster Hatchery

1 Harbor Pl., Bar Harbor; (207) 288-2334. May-Oct., Mon.-Sat., 9-5. Adults, $3; 4-12, $2.

There's no better place than this Downeast waterfront location to learn about lobsters. The Lobster Hatchery was opened in 1990 to enhance Maine's lobster landing. At this facility, lobsters are hatched from eggs and raised for their first few tender weeks, then released in the local waters. You'll see thousands of tiny crustaceans in all stages of growth. You'll even get a microscopic view of very tiny lobsters. Friendly staff people are on hand to explain the whole process.

↝ Mount Desert Oceanarium–Bar Harbor

Rte. 3, Bar Harbor; (207) 288-5005. May-Oct., Mon.-Sat., 9-5. Adults, $4.95; 4-12, $3.75.

Located on pretty Thomas Bay, this attraction is an expansion of the Southwest Harbor Oceanarium. You can visit both—this facility offers exhibits not available in the Southwest Harbor Oceanarium.

The kids will enjoy the harbor seal program, where they get a chance to see the seals during feeding times, and the Maine Lobster Museum, where you'll learn everything there is to know about lobsters and lobster fishing.

↝ Acadia Zoological Park

Rte. 3, Trenton; (207) 667-3244. May-Oct., daily, 10-6. Adults, $4.50; 3-12, $3.50.

Heading north on Route 3, over the causeway from Mount Desert Island to the town of Trenton, you'll find this 100-acre nature preserve and petting farm. More than 150 native and exotic animals make their homes here, amid the woodlands, streams, and pastures. Children will delight in the petting area—the largest in Maine.

↝ Island Soaring Glider Rides

Hancock County–Bar Harbor Airport, Rte. 3; (207) 667-SOAR. May-Oct., daily 'til sunset. Rates vary.

You can't miss this place on busy Route 3 heading into Acadia National Park. You'll see the glider planes, you'll be tempted…go ahead, stop in. What a thrill to soar in these one- to two-passenger aircraft! Great for kids of all ages.

↝ Odyssey Park

Rte. 3, Trenton; (207) 667-5841. Mid-June–Labor Day, daily, 10-dusk.

Even in Downeast Maine, there's no escaping modern day amusements. If you need a break from all that natural outdoor recreation and communing with nature, head to Odyssey Park for some cheap thrills. There are bumper boats, go-carts, speed boats, aqua bikes, and kiddie rides.

↝ Craig Brook National Fish Hatchery

Hatchery Road, off Rte. 1, East Orland; (207) 469-2803. May-Sept., daily, 8-8. Free.

This is the oldest salmon hatchery in the country. You'll find exhibits at the Visitor's Center, display pools, and an aquarium. It's also a nice little park, with a beach area, boat launching facilities, and nature trails. Stop by.

⚞ Hancock County Friends of the Arts

Farmstead Barn, Rte. 1, East Sullivan; (207) 422-3615. July performances. Free.

These folks do a good job of entertaining the kids. Throughout July, children can attend a variety of presentations, including art, music, magic, and storytelling programs. For the younger folk (age six and under) presentations are at 9:30 in the morning. Children seven and older are welcome at the 11 A.M. programs.

RESTAURANTS

⚞ Jordan Pond House

Park Loop Rd., Acadia National Park; (207) 276-3316. Late May–Oct., lunch, 11:30-2:30; tea, 2:30-5:30; dinner, 5:30-9.

A trip to Acadia wouldn't be complete without a visit here. Enjoy huge popovers and homemade ice cream on the lawn, with magnificent views all around. Elegant dinners are served in the evenings with classical music accompaniment.

⚞ Beal's Lobster Pier

Clark Point Rd., Southwest Harbor; (207) 244-3202. Mon.-Sat., 11-4; Sun., noon-4.

For more than 50 years, families have enjoyed seafood "in the rough" here, on picnic tables along the pier. Fresh fish, lobsters, shrimp, clams, and crab meat are available at reasonable prices. You'll soak up the atmosphere of a busy fish pier, while feasting on the freshest fish around.

BANGOR AND AUGUSTA

Just off the major interstate (I-95) in Maine, you'll find the two bustling cities Augusta and Bangor, the state's commercial and cultural hubs. While most vacationers closely hug the jagged coastline of Maine, much of the state's business is done inland.

The mighty Kennebec River cuts through the center of capital city Augusta. Here, you can get a close look at Maine's government in action. Actually, the state capitol building dominates this lively city; its towering gold dome can be seen from afar.

Traveling north, you'll discover Bangor, with its big-city-style shopping, restaurants, and lodging, and also Orono, where the University of Maine makes its home. Visitors are welcome to tour the pretty 1,200-acre campus and take advantage of its cultural and sports offerings.

Despite their modern day conveniences, both cities retain historic architecture and respect for their rural pasts. Venture just a short distance from these hubs and you'll find forests, lakes, and streams abundant with outdoor recreational opportunities.

Maine State Museum

Capitol Complex, Rte. 201, Augusta; (207) 289-2301. Year-round, Mon.-Fri., 9-5; Sat., 10-4; Sun., 1-4. Adults, $2; 6-18, $1; $6/family maximum.

Located in the impressive Capitol Complex, this museum offers a thorough look at Maine, past and present. "Made in Maine," the museum's central exhibit, includes a water-powered woodworking mill, a textile factory, and more than 1,000 Maine-made products. The "12,000 Years in Maine" exhibit features more than 2,000 artifacts and specimens dating from the last Ice Age to the 19th century. Kids will enjoy peeking at "This Land Called Maine," including five nature scenes that show many of the plants and animals found in the state. Other exhibits show Maine's agriculture, fishing, granite quarrying, lumbering, and shipbuilding activities.

State Capitol Tours

Capitol Complex, Rte. 201, Augusta; (207) 289-2301. Year-round, Mon.-Fri., 8-5. Free.

The impressive Maine State Capitol Building can be seen rising above the mighty oak and elm trees that surround it from just about any point in Augusta. Constructed of native granite in 1829, the building's front facade, with its towering arcade, is a fine example of the work of noted American architect Charles Bulfinch. You'll enjoy a walk through the rotunda, where you'll see a large display of Maine battle flags. Also, for a first-hand look at government in action, visit the Legislative Chambers and the Office of the Governor.

Fort Western Museum

City Center Plaza, Augusta; (207) 626-2385. Year-round, Mon.-Fri., 8-4:30. Old Fort Western, mid-June–Labor Day, Mon.-Fri., 10-5; Sat.-Sun., 1-5; weekends only through Columbus Day, 1-4. Adults, $3.50; 12 and under, $2.

Show me a kid who doesn't like a fort. And there's no better way to learn about early American fortification and history than with a close-up look at the real thing. Fort Western, on the eastern bank of the Kennebec River, was built in 1754 for protection from the Indians. The fort's original main house, once the barracks and the store, is still standing. You'll also see reproduction blockhouses and watchboxes. In the adjacent City Hall, visit the Museum Services building with exhibits depicting military, settlement, trade, and family themes.

Wingate Planetarium

Wingate Hall, University of Maine Campus, off Rte. 2, Orono; (207) 581-1341. Call for current shows and prices.

The moon, the planets, the Milky Way, flashing comets, and falling stars...the nighttime sky has always held mystery and fascination for people of all ages. You can learn more about starry nights and space exploration at this small university planetarium. Shows on varied topics in astronomy, space exploration, and other sciences are offered year-round, but you'll need to call ahead for information on programs, schedule, and prices.

Waterville-Winslow Two Cent Bridge

Front St., Waterville. Year-round. Free.

What will you give me to pass? This is one of the few remaining orginal toll footbridges in the United States. The toll-taker's house is on the Waterville side, but you'll be able to walk across free.

RESTAURANTS

Sequino's

735 Main St., Bangor; (207) 942-1240. Mon.-Fri., 11:30-10; Sat.-Sun., 4:30-10.

You can't miss this rather large, pretty white house with bright red awnings. Sequino's fits the bill whether you're in the mood for pizza and beer or a fancier Italian specialty dinner. And families are always welcome. The restaurant rambles with lots of connecting rooms, all tastefully decorated with colorful wallpapering and tables set with red and white linens. The menu is extensive, offering 10 veal specialties, no less than 15 fish dishes, and a handful of steak and chicken preparations, in addition to the traditional pastas and parmigianas. Or just order a large pizza and some Chianti.

❃ The Square Cafe

13 Railroad Square, Waterville; (207) 873-5900. Mon., 5-10; Tues.-Fri., 11-10; Sat.-Sun., noon-10.

Parents and kids alike will love this place. It's a combination eatery and cinema—but you can eat here and not go to the show (or vice versa). Actually, the food is inspired; this friendly, tiny cafe is full of color, character, and surprises. The emphasis is on healthy preparations. Start with one of the appetizers, like the pesto bread rounds with melted cheese and sun-dried tomatoes. Then pick from a number of dinner dishes (all written on the blackboard). Offerings might include Thai shrimp or chicken curry, chili pie, tacos, and burritos. Save room. The Square Cafe is known for its great, homemade desserts.

WESTERN LAKES AND MOUNTAINS

As spectacular as is Maine's rugged coastline, there's more to the state than this, as those who've traveled its western lakes and mountain region can attest. This inland area encompasses the Sebago and Long lakes area, the beautiful Grafton and Evans notch regions of the White Mountain National Forest, and, farther north, the outdoor-recreation-rich Rangeley Lake and Carrabassett Valley.

Sebago Lake, the second largest in Maine, covers 46 square miles and offers plenty of vacation facilities and recreational opportunities, including swimming, boating, fishing, floatplane rides, and more.

Traveling north, you'll find the classic New England town of Bethel (Hallmark once used the town for a Christmas card commercial). The town boasts a host of fine restaurants and country inns and also Sunday River, one of Maine's top ski resorts. Surrounded by the Mahoosuc Mountain Range and Grafton State Park, the region has also grown very popular with hikers and outdoor enthusiasts.

The Rangeley Lakes area has long been a mecca for vacationers, with a wide range of hotels, lodges, restaurants, and shops. Swim and picnic at lovely Rangeley State Park, attend the town cookouts in the square, play golf, or hike the numerous trails.

If you're a skiing family, no doubt you've heard of downhill giant Sugarloaf USA, near the Carrabassett River Valley. When your legs need a break from skiing, take an adventurous ride on a dog sled. Or come here in the summer, for golf, tennis, mountain biking, trail riding, canoeing, hiking, and more.

≈ Grafton Notch State Park
Rte. 16, North of Newry; (207) 389-1335.

Located 14 miles north of Bethel, Grafton Notch is a great place to commune with nature and is one of Maine's best spots for picnicking, hiking, and swimming. Be sure to visit Screw Anger Falls; its rocky ledges are fun to climb, and the falls make a perfect backdrop for a picnic. Other points of interest: the Moose Cave nature walk and Mother Walker Falls.

≈ White Mountain National Forest
Rte. 2, Bethel; (207) 824-2134.

The Evans Notch Ranger District of the White Mountain National Forest is located here. Evans Notch is one of the five districts in the forest, which has lands in both Maine and New Hampshire. The U.S. Forest Service maintains a number of hiking trails that connect with the Appalachian Trail. Pick up trail maps at the Visitor's Center. Take a short loop hike or make a day of it, enjoying magnificent mountain scenery.

≈ Artist's Covered Bridge
Rte. 5, 2 miles beyond Sunday River Ski Resort Access Road, Newry.

This frequently photographed 1872 bridge marks a great family swimming hole. Have a picnic on the rocky ledges beneath the bridge, downstream.

(Special Note: This is private property, so please use discretion.)

≈ Washburn-Norlands Living History Center
Norlands Rd., off Rte. 4, Livermore; (207) 897-2236. Year-round for overnight learning vacations. General tours: July and August, daily, 10-4. Adults, $4.50; 5-18, $2.

This is the very best way to learn. When you check into this living history center, you are assigned an identity—and from then on you live it. You'll remain in costume. You'll probably be sleeping on corn husk mattresses. No showers, no bathrooms (why, that's how they used to live!), in fact Washburn-Norlands gives only two concessions to modern-day conveniences: window screens in the summer and toilet paper all year. You'll love every second and be amazed at how much everyone in the family learns. This place is repeatedly written about as the best of the best in family/learning vacations.

Of course, the ideal way to experience Washburn-Norlands is to stay here for several days. But in July and August the center also conducts brief (two-hour) tours. You'll find an 1853 one-room school house and

Maine's only living history farm. On 445 acres and complete with barns, horses, oxen, cows, sheep, pigs, and poultry, the farm operates year-round. The kids will enjoy lending a hand outdoors and you can also visit the library and Victorian home of the Washburn family, one of the country's greatest political dynasties. Bet you'll want to return for one of the vacation programs.

ᛥ *Songo River Queen II*
Rte. 302, Naples; (207) 693-6861. July–Labor Day, daily; June and Sept., weekends.

Take a lazy riverboat ride on Long Lake and down Songo River on this 92-foot sternwheel river boat. It's very relaxing and scenic. In the summer, several trips are made each day (call for rates and schedule). In June and September one trip is offered each weekend day at 9:45 A.M.

ᛥ **Willowbrook at Newfield**
Off Rte. 11, Newfield; (207) 793-2784. Mid-May–Sept., daily, 10-5. Adults, $6.50; 6-18, $3.25.

History comes alive here, and the kids will enjoy looking at the toys, nurseries, schoolhouse, carriages, bicycles, and other artifacts of days gone by. The beautiful 1894 Armitage-Herschell Carousel is eye-catching for all—24 horses and four chariots fully restored and animated. You'll also see an early stagecoach, old-fashioned country store, and in a nod to the present, restaurant, gift store, and ice cream parlor.

ᛥ **Fish and Wildlife Visitor's Center**
308 Shaker Rd., Gray; (207) 657-4977. April-Nov., daily, 10-4. Adults, $2.50; 5-12, $1.50.

Learn about native wildlife at this game farm. You are free to roam the farm and look at the displays of native animals, birds, and wildlife educational exhibits. There also are trout pools and picnic areas.

ᛥ **Perham's**
Rtes. 26 and 219, West Paris; (207) 674-3441. Year-round, daily, 9-5.

This area of Maine is noted for its wide variety of mineral and gem deposits, including tourmaline, mica, feldspar, and various types of quartz. At Perham's, you'll find out all about gem hunting and at its Mineral Museum alone have plenty of things to touch.

Bring a bag and a shovel and pick—Perham's quarry is open to the public and you're free to take home what you find. Kids love this treasure hunt.

⚞ T.A.D. Dog Sled Rides

Stratton; (207) 246-4461. Dec.-April, daily, 10-3; July-Oct., weekends, 9-1. Winter: adults, $30; 5-12, $20. Summer: adults, $15; 5-12, $10.

You'll not want to miss this experience of a lifetime. Half-hour dog sled rides through the Maine snow-covered countryside is an experience you and your family won't soon forget. The team travels about one and a half miles. In the summer, the dog sled team (four to six dogs) pulls you on carts, with a stop at a fresh, cold mountain stream.

⚞ Sandy River Railroad

Mill Hill Rd., Phillips; (207) 338-2039. May-Oct., first and third Sun. each mo., 11, 1 and 3. Adults, $3; 6-12, $1.50.

Looking for a relaxed, interesting way to spend a Sunday afternoon? Head for the Sandy River Railroad Station in Phillips. You can board the restored narrow-gauge train for a short ride up the river. There's also a picnic area, with a museum and gift shop on the grounds.

⚞ Mount Blue State Park

From Wilton or Dixfield, 15 miles off Rte. 2, in Weld; (207) 585-2261. Mid-May–mid-Oct.

This large scenic park nestled in the mountains of western Maine is popular with mountain climbers, hikers, and families looking for outdoor fun. Swim at Webb Lake and join in ranger-led activities that include gold-panning, nature walks, canoe trips, and mountain hikes. There's also a boat launch, and canoe rentals are available.

⚞ Rangeley Lake State Park

Located on the south shore of Rangeley Lake is this 691-acre recreation area with picnicking, swimming, fishing, camping, and boat launching facilities.

⚞ Sunday River Ski Resort

Rte. 2, north of Bethel, (207) 824-3000. Lift tickets: adults, $39; SKIwee (4-6), $53/day; Mogul Meisters (7-12) $53/day. Ticket prices listed are for weekends and holidays; special packages and discount rates are available.

Sunday River is fast becoming one of the premier ski resorts in the East, if not in the country. Continually upgrading and improving, the resort now encompasses six mountains spread across over 510 acres of trails. While skiing at Sunday River is geared toward the intermediate skier, beginners and experts will find plenty of action. Expert skiers will find "Agony" aptly named. Beginner's action is centered in the South

Ridge Slope area, but novices can also ski from the top of the mountain and back to the South Ridge Base via Three Mile Trail. Are there potential skiers in your group? Sunday River has a guaranteed Learn-to-Ski-in-One-Day program.

Sunday River does a great job of welcoming families, offering a variety of programs for kids of all ages and abilities. A new Children's Ski Center adjacent to the South Ridge Center serves as the base for the Mogul Meister and children's seasonal programs. Younger skiers in the SKIwee program are headquartered in the Merrill Brook II facility.

Also, snow boarders will appreciate the snow-board action park on the upper Starlight Trail on White Cap Mountain.

You won't find too many families who don't like skiing Sunday River. It's one of the best.

⛷ Sugarloaf USA

Rte. 27, Kingfield; (207) 237-2000. Lift tickets: adults, $38; Mountain Magic (4-6), $42/day; Mountain Adventure (7-16), $35/day; child-care (6 wk.-6 yr.), $35/day.

Skiing families who are tired of long waits in lift lines, crowded ski trails, and jammed parking lots should give serious thought to Sugarloaf. It's off the beaten path, and that's why it's so relaxed. The closest major cities are Portland, two and a half hours away, and Montreal, four hours away, so you miss the big crowds that head to more southerly ski mountains. Located in Kingfield in the Carrabassett Valley, Sugarloaf is a destination resort. Drive up, park your car, and spend the rest of your time on skis, on foot, or riding the Sugarloaf Shuttle to the resort's shops and restaurants.

You'll find plenty to do. The resort has a well-equipped health club (including six indoor and outdoor jacuzzis), an Olympic-size ice skating arena, and a host of eateries and shops.

Now, about that mountain: it's big, challenging, and rough and tumble if you want it, slow, easy, and relaxed if you prefer. The vertical drop is 2,837 feet, with 45 miles of trails and 81 ways down. Sugarloaf works hard at pleasing families, and succeeds. The resort offers day care and a nursery for children age 6 weeks to 6 years. Children over 3 have an introduction to skiing, combined with indoor play, arts and crafts, and storytelling. The Mountain Magic program provides all-day skiing instruction and play for kids age 4 to 6, and Mountain Adventure, for those 7 to 12, and Mountain Adventure Teen, 13 to 16, provide all-day skiing adventures.

Advance registration is suggested for all programs.

RESTAURANTS

☙ Hugs

Rte. 27, Carrabassett Valley; (207) 237-2392. Summer, Thurs.-Sat., 5-10; winter, Tues.-Sat., 5-10. Closed mid-Oct.–Nov.

This is a great place to come with friends and family. The food is nothing less than fabulous, and the staff makes you feel right at home. This friendly place dishes up big baskets of just-baked pesto bread, bowls of fresh salad and platters full of fine northern Italian cuisine. Select different entrees to pass at the table, mixing and matching to fit tastes and budgets. Dinners are served family style, and you can get all you want to eat. Save room for dessert.

☙ Cathy's Place

Main St., Stratton; (207) 246-2922. Mon.-Fri., 11-9:30; Sat.-Sun., 7 A.M.–9:30.

If you're looking for a good excuse to get off the mountain, Cathy's Place is it. It's about seven miles north from the Sugarloaf USA ski resort, and a favorite for locals and visitors both. It's not much to look at, but the food makes up for it. The menu is varied, from humble hamburg steak to fresh salmon with red pepper beurre blanc and antelope stroganoff. There are lots of familiar favorites (fried shrimp, pizza, roast pork) and a blackboard list of nightly specials. Fresh fish is always featured, and on weekends, game meat takes center stage. You may find roast venison or maybe leg of antelope. If none of this sounds like something your teenager will eat, don't worry, they offer personal-size pan pizzas, too.

☙ Red Top Truck Stop

Rte. 2, Bethel; (207) 824-2000. Mon.-Sat., 5:30 A.M.–8 P.M.; Sun., 7-6.

When you ask the locals in Bethel about a good, cheap place to eat, the answer you almost always get is the Red Top. Actually there are two Red Tops in Bethel, both on Route 2. One stands alone, the other is a combination Texaco gas station, convenience store, and restaurant. That should give you some idea of the atmosphere. But, you'll get cheap, quick service of eggs, sausage, ham, or bacon, home fries, homemade toast, and homemade muffins and donuts. Free refills on the coffee. Lunch is $1.50 burgers, hot dogs, ham and cheese sandwiches, and the like.

MOOSEHEAD AND KATAHDIN REGION

If you have a love for the great outdoors and an appreciation for the beauty of unspoiled wilderness, this northern lakes region of Maine is for you.

This is considered one of the greatest hunting, fishing, and canoeing regions in the country. You'll see few commercial tourist attractions or concessions to modern-day extravagances. Rather, it's the wealth of natural resources that draws people to the shores of mighty Moosehead Lake or into the wilderness of Baxter State Park.

You'll stand in the shadows of Mount Katahdin, one of the highest peaks in the Northeast and the legendary home of the sacred spirits of the Abenaki Indians. Mount Katahdin, meaning "greatest mountain," rises nearly one mile above Baxter State Park. You'll get a good taste of northern Maine wilderness in this 201,018-acre park, where you can swim in secluded mountain ponds, hike through forests, and picnic along babbling brooks.

You'll get your thrills not from a waterslide or a roller coaster, but from a whitewater raft trip down the West Branch of the Penobscot River, or on a floatplane ride over the undeveloped shores of Moosehead Lake. It's easy here—relatively inexpensive—to hire a seaplane for island exploring or to rent a canoe to get around the lakes and rivers. In the winter, you'll join snowmobilers, snowshoers, and ski tourers who traverse the surrounding forests on a network of trails and old logging roads. But whenever you come, be prepared to spend the time outdoors.

ॐ Moosehead Lake

Moosehead Lake is Maine's largest lake, more than 40 miles long and up to 10 miles wide. There are several large islands, bays, and inlets in the lake, surrounded by rugged mountains and miles of dense forests. Much of the 420-mile shoreline remains undeveloped and accessible only by floatplanes, boats, or canoes. But don't despair, as all are easy to rent or hire. Stop in Greenville, on the southern tip of the lake, where you'll find lots of local seaplanes for lake sightseeing tours. There's nothing formal here; just walk up to the plane of your choice and talk to the owner. In Greenville you'll also find a number of places to rent canoes and rowboats. This is a great way to see the lake and explore its many islands.

Be sure to bring a pair of binoculars for moose watching. More than 10,000 moose reportedly live in the Moosehead Lake region. The best time to see them is early morning or twilight, when they come out to feed in the lake's swampy areas. If you feel adventurous, explore some of the old logging roads around the lake; they will take you to secluded bogs.

Though moose will seldom approach people it's a good policy to watch from a distance.

⅋ Mount Kineo

While you're exploring the lake, you'll notice Mount Kineo rising dramatically out of it more than 700 feet. Located about a mile from the lakefront town of Rockwood, Mount Kineo is made entirely of green flint. Many years ago, the Abenaki Indians sought its flint to make arrowheads and tools. From here, you'll also get great views of the lake and surrounding mountains and forests.

⅋ Lily Bay State Park

East side of Moosehead Lake, 8 miles north of Greenville; (207) 695-2700. Early May–mid-Oct.

This park, located on the shores of Moosehead Lake just north of Greenville, is a fine recreation center. Its 942 acres include a small beach for swimming, canoe rentals, and boat launching facilities. The kids will enjoy taking the short path to the playground or picnicking in the pines.

⅋ S. S. *Katahdin* and Moosehead Marine Museum

Main St., Greenville; (207) 695-2716. Leave East Cove, 10 and 2. Weekends only: Memorial Day–late June. July–Labor Day, daily, 10 and 2; mid-Sept.–Columbus Day, 2 P.M. only. Adults, $12; 5-12, $6.

Known locally as *Kate*, this restored 1914 steam vessel has been converted into the floating Moosehead Marine Museum. Besides taking a ride around Moosehead Lake—the cruise takes you up the southern tip of the lake—you'll be able to see displays and photographs of the logging industry and steamboat operations. Once monthly from June to September there's an 80-mile Head of the Lake cruise, and on Thursdays and Sundays in season at 10 A.M., there's a Mount Kineo cruise.

⅋ Baxter State Park

North of Millinocket; (207) 723-5140. April-Nov.

This premier, 201,018-acre park was given to the state by Maine governor Percival Baxter in 1941, with one condition: "That it forever shall be held in its natural, wild state..." The park is an unspoiled wilderness area, dominated by Mount Katahdin, the highest mountain in the state. It includes 46 mountain peaks and ridges (18 of which exceed an elevation of 3,000 feet) and a network of about 150 miles of trails, all surrounded by natural wildlife, mountain streams, ponds, lakes, and dense forests. Visitors can wind their way through the park on a narrow road.

The auto trip through the park takes about two and a half to three hours, but this doesn't include the stops you'll want to make for picnics, swimming, and hiking along the way.

There are trails for everyone in the park, and even families with small children can enjoy a number of hikes. Daicey Pond Nature Trail is perfect for small children. The trail is level and an easy trip around Daicey Pond. Be sure to pick up the free pamphlet on the trail that points out wildlife as you go. It's available from the ranger station at Daicey Pond Campground. Little Niagara and Big Niagara Falls Trail is part of the Appalachian Trail, and it's a great one to walk on a hot summer's day. (The Appalachian Trail, the only trail in Baxter blazed in white, terminates in the park at Mount Katahdin.) You'll pick up the trail at the Daicey Pond Campground and hike along the Nesowadnehunk Stream. There are lots of places to take a refreshing dip along the way. You'll pass a logger's dam before reaching Little Niagara Falls. Go a little further down the side trail to Big Niagara Falls, a picturesque spot for a picnic. From the campground to Big Niagara Falls is 1.2 miles. Families with older children will enjoy a 3.2-mile hike up Sentinel Mountain on the Kidney Pond Sentinel Mountain Trail. It's not too steep, and the summit view, overlooking a range of mountains, is beautiful. The trail leaves from the southwest corner of Kidney Pond.

There are lots of mountain pools and streams to swim in throughout the park. Families will also enjoy South Branch Pond; this is a busy camping and picnic area also open for day use. You'll find a nice swimming area and canoes for rent. Abol Pond is a popular spot for swimming and picnicking at the southern end of the park. Take Abol Pond Road three miles in from the park's southern gatehouse entrance. Togue Pond is open for general use. It's located just outside the entrance of the park.

Baxter State Park is a great place for animal watching. There are more than 170 bird species, and you're likely to see deer and moose in the ponds feeding on aquatic vegetation. (Look for them at Daicey and Elbow ponds.) There's also a large bear population in the park. People are warned not to feed the bears or leave waste around.

Parents should be warned that there is a serious bug population from May into August, and everyone will need the protection of insect repellent, nets, or both. Finally, there are no running water, electricity, lights, food, or supplies in the park.

⇾ Lumberman's Museum
Rte. 159, Patten, at the northern entrance to Baxter State Park; (207) 528-2650. Memorial Day–Sept., Mon.-Sat., 9-4; Sun., 10-4. Oct.–Columbus Day, weekends; Sat., 9-4; Sun., 10-4.

You'll learn about the active lumbering industry at this museum. The complex of nine buildings contains a working model of a sawmill, a blacksmith shop, old tractors, and 3,000 artifacts of the lumbering industry.

Canoeing and Whitewater Rafting

In this area are some of the most spectacular whitewater rivers in the East, including the West Branch of the Penobscot River, the Kennebec, and the Allagash Wilderness Waterway. Canoe trips can last for a day, a few days, a week, or longer and are designed for beginners as well as experts. A number of licensed outfitters can arrange canoe trips. The adventurous can try a thrilling ride down rushing waters in a rubber raft. Licensed outfitters arrange and guide the trips. Minimum age is usually 12 years.

For a list of canoe trips, whitewater raft expeditions, and licensed outfitters, write the Maine Department of Inland Fisheries and Wildlife, 284 State Street, Augusta, Maine 04333; (207) 289-2043.

Blacksmith Shop Museum

Park St., off Rte. 153, Dover-Foxcroft; (207) 564-8618. May-Oct., daily, sunrise-sunset. Free.

Do your children know what a blacksmith's shop is? Here's a good place to find out. This 1863 restored Civil War period blacksmith shop retains much of the original equipment, and kids will get a quick look into the past, when four-legged animals—not engines—were the mode of transportation.

Children's Museum at the Playmill

Stagecoach Rd., Atkinson Mills, Dover-Foxcroft; (207) 564-8122. Year-round, Mon.-Fri., 9-5. Free.

You'll see crafts from around the world featured here, including an extensive array of handmade crafts from more than 20 countries. Guided tours explain the handiwork from Europe, South America, Asia and the United States. It's a great place to learn about other cultures and customs and is very popular with area school groups.

Gulf Hagas

Millinocket Rd., just north of Milo and Brownville.

Gulf Hagas, accessible only by a four-to-five-mile hike down a trail, has been called the "Grand Canyon of the East." This is where the west branch of the Pleasant River is deeply entrenched in a slate canyon, and waterfalls, sheer walls, and unusual rock formations form a spectacular site. Don't attempt this with young tots. But if you have older children and you've got the time, don't miss it.

RESTAURANTS

ॐ Auntie Em's

Main St., Greenville; (207) 695-2238. Summers, daily, 5 A.M.–9 P.M.; winters, daily, 4 A.M.–8 P.M.

Yes, you read that right...this place opens at four in the morning in the winter, five in the morning come summer. Auntie Em wants to be sure all those day hikers, hunters, and fishing enthusiasts get a good, strong start on the day. Everyone knows Auntie Em's, where you'll get homemade donuts and muffins, large-size breakfast specials, and hearty lunches and dinners. You'll find unfussy, homestyle meals offering all the basics, like fried seafood platters, steaks, chicken, sandwiches, and burgers. Breakfast anytime.

ॐ The Birches Resort and Restaurant

Birches Road, Rockwood; (207) 534-7305. Memorial Day–mid-Oct., daily. Breakfast, 7-10; dinner, 6-9.

Forget about dinner, just look at this room, a turn-of-the-century log building with giant stone fireplaces, and look at the view, a panorama of Moosehead Lake and surrounding mountain ranges. This is a great setting for a meal, and you'll likely share the dining room with fellow outdoor enthusiasts and vacationers. Actually, the food isn't bad, either. Dinners include appetizer, dessert, salad, vegetables, and potatoes. Standard menu items (steak, fish, chicken, and pasta) are offered, plus three or four daily specials.

Vermont

MANCHESTER AND THE MOUNTAINS

Long before there were ski lifts and condominiums, Manchester was an elegant summer resort—Vermont's answer to Newport, Rhode Island, and Saratoga, New York. Instead of waiting in lift lines, guests queued up for a game of croquet. Then as now, the combination of fresh mountain air and charming countryside proved too enticing to resist.

Happily, some of that gentility remains today. Visiting families can tour Manchester Village, where time seems to have stood still, in a horse-drawn carriage complete with a top-hatted driver. Guests can picnic on the manicured lawns of Hildene, the Robert Todd Lincoln estate, as past presidents once did. Or you can bundle up for a sleigh ride, stopping back at the mansion for hot mulled cider.

In Manchester Center, a more modern pastime predominates—shopping. There is a plethora of specialty stores, antique shops, craft studios, and designer outlets.

What makes this area a truly superlative place to visit is the fact that you can sample all of these pleasures and still have ample opportunity to play outside. Southern Vermont is a great place for trout fishing, canoeing, camping, swimming, hiking, skiing, horseback riding—you name it.

There's also a prominent resident your children will want to meet— Santa. Where else would the Claus family choose for a summer home?

🦌 Santa's Land

Rte. 5 (between Exits 4 and 5 off I-91), Putney; (802) 387-5550. Mid-June–Christmas, daily, 9:30-4:30; May–mid-June, weekends only. Adults, $7.50; 3-15, $5.50.

Ho! Ho! Ho! This very merry theme park has lots of child-pleasing features, including a petting zoo, a child's train ride, a carousel, and a playground. The highlight of your child's visit will likely be a chat with the Jolly Old Elf himself, who'll ask, "Do you take care of your toys?" not, "What do you want for Christmas?" To avoid the obvious North Pole questions, you might mention that Santa's Land is Mr. and Mrs. Claus's summer home. You can have lunch at the Igloo Pancake House on the grounds.

🐾 Luman Nelson Museum of New England Wildlife

Rt. 9, Marlboro; (802) 464-5494. June-Sept., daily, 8-8; Oct.-May, 8-4. Free.

This natural history museum gives a quick look at the critters that roam the forests and fly the skies of New England. In lifelike dioramas, with hand-painted scenery, you'll see stuffed bear, coyote, raccoon, fox, and an assortment of birds. It's a nice afternoon outing, and it's free.

🐾 Green Mountain Flyer

1 Depot Square, Bellows Falls; (802) 463-3069. Trains depart Bellows Falls at 11 and 2, Chester Depot at 12:10. Summer, July 1–Labor Day, Tues.-Sun.; fall, mid-Sept.–mid.-Oct., daily. Special foliage and sunset excursions scheduled, call for details. Adults, $10; 3-12, $6.

If your kids like train rides, climb aboard with them, sit back, and view the splendor of central Vermont's scenic countryside. You'll travel 26 miles, from Bellows Falls north to Chester, in a fully restored vintage train. You'll see Quechee Gorge, old covered bridges, river valleys, and rolling hillsides, and during foliage season, it's all the more spectacular.

🐾 Hildene

Rte. 7A, Manchester; (802) 362-1788. Mid-May–Oct., daily, 9:30-5:30 (last tour begins at 4). Adults, $6; 2-14, $2.

This gracious Georgian Revival mansion was built by Robert Todd Lincoln, the only one of Abraham Lincoln's four sons to live to maturity. Lincoln's descendants lived at Hildene (the name means hill and valley) until 1975. Your visit will begin with a brief slide show on Robert's life; then you can walk through the rooms of the house. Children will appreciate the toy room, decorated with fairy-tale scenes, and the 1908 player pipe organ, demonstrated for visitors. From the garden terrace, you can view the Green Mountains on one side and the Taconic Mountains on the other. Nature trails and a picnic area are also on the grounds. Open air concerts are often scheduled in summer, performed by the Vermont Symphony Orchestra. If you visit in late December, treat your family to a candlelight tour of Hildene. You'll enjoy cookies and hot mulled cider, along with a horse-drawn sleigh ride and a look at this beautiful house in its holiday finery.

🐾 Windhill Farm

North Rd., Manchester Center; (802) 362-2604. Open daily, year-round, weather permitting. Reservations are required. Sleigh rides: $35 is charged for

*the first five people; $5 per person thereafter. Trail rides: $10 per person; $2
per child for pony rides.*

This is a special place for families, no matter what the season. In
winter, a team of Belgian and Percheron horses will take you on an old-
fashioned sleigh ride. Traversing fields and woodlands, the rides are about
an hour long. The rest of the year, Windhill Farm is the perfect place to
go horseback riding. Trail rides through the countryside are offered, as
well as pony rides for the little ones.

Village Carriage Company

*Rte. 7A, Manchester. Departs daily, weather permitting, from the front of the
Equinox Hotel or from the Equinox Golf Course. Ride of 20 minutes, $20; 30
minutes, $30.*

In the grand style of days gone by, you can tour historic Manchester
Village. Step into a fancy horse-drawn carriage, complete with top-hatted
driver, for this special half-hour ride around town.

Bennington Museum and Grandma Moses Gallery

*Rte. 9 (West Main St.), Old Bennington; (802) 447-1571. Daily, 9-5;
Easter, 1-5; closed Thanksgiving and Dec. 23–Jan. 1. Adults, $5; family
rate, $12.*

You'll take a trip back to the 19th century when you view this collection of paintings, furniture, military artifacts, and toys. Even better is the
gallery devoted to Anna Mary Robertson, better known as Grandma
Moses. This legendary woman began painting seriously at age 78 and
continued to do so until her death at age 101. The story will inspire you
and her work will delight you and any aspiring artist in your group.

Sugar Houses

*Maple Tree Vermont Products, 3 miles north of Emerald Lake off Rte. 7,
Danby, (802) 293-5566; James A. Twitchell, Winhall Hollow Rd., South
Londonberry, (802) 824-3605; or Harlow's Sugar House, Rte. 5, Putney
Village, (802) 824-5852.*

Springtime is sugar time in Vermont. Warm spring days and cold
nights cause the sap to flow and set off the traditional flurry of maple
sugaring. For the most part, sap is still gathered the old-fashioned way,
and a trip to a sugar house to watch the process is a must. You'll see the
maples being tapped and the sugar makers boil the sap to make syrup.
Call ahead; the season varies, usually beginning in late February and lasting from six weeks to two months.

∞ Scenic Chairlift Rides

Stratton Ski Resort, Stratton Mountain Road, Bondville (off Rte. 30);
(802) 297-2200. July–mid.-Oct., daily, 9-4. Adults, $10; 12 and under,
$7. Bromley, Rte. 11, Peru (6 miles east of Manchester); (802) 824-5522.
Mid-May–July 4th, weekends, 9:30-6; July 4th–foliage season, daily, 9:30-
6. Adults, $4.50; 7-12, $3.50.

Grab a camera, pack a picnic, and don some sensible shoes for a trip
to the top of the mountain. On a clear day atop Bromley Mountain, you'll
be able to see five states (okay kids, name them). You'll take the Starship
Gondola to the top of Stratton Mountain for spectacular views. Work off
your picnic goodies with some hiking along the ski trails, then ride the
lift back down.

∞ Bromley Alpine Slide

Rte. 11, Peru (6 miles east of Manchester); (802) 824-5522. Mid-June–
Sept., daily, 9:30-6; mid-May–mid-June, weekends only, 9:30-6. Adults,
$4.50; 7-12, $3.50.

The action at Bromley Mountain doesn't stop when the snow melts.
Come spring, you can board the chairlift to the mountaintop, then careen
down to the bottom of the mountain on a luge-style sled. Daredevils can
take it fast, wimpier souls can take it slow.

∞ Bromley Music and Theatre Series

Bromley Mountain, Rte. 11, Peru (6 miles east of Manchester); (802) 824-
5522. July–Labor Day, Sunday concerts, 1-5. Free. Special children's theater,
July and Aug. Rates vary.

After a busy week, live music and a country barbecue are a great way
to unwind. On the deck/cafe at Bromley Mountain, you'll hear jazz, country music, and bluegrass. This informal atmosphere is just fine for families
with kids, and the festivities are free. (There's a charge if you partake of
the barbecue.) Special theater performances for children have recently been
added to the summer roster of events. Call for details.

∞ Kinhaven

Weston; (802) 824-4332.

The charming town of Weston is well known for its great summer-
stock theater, at the Weston Playhouse. But families, especially those with
young children, are better off checking out the free concerts at this summer music school, located just outside the center. Call ahead for a schedule of performances and applicable admission fees.

⅔ Stoughton Pond
Weathersfield.

For a quick dip on a hot summer's afternoon, you can't beat this big Vermont swimming hole (big by Vermont standards, anyway), in Weathersfield. You'll even find toilets and changing rooms.

⅔ Battenkill River

The infamous Battenkill, known for its great trout fishing, weaves through this southern Vermont region, inviting passersby to dip their toes or drop a line. Originating in Dorset and East Dorset, the Battenkill flows into New York State and the Hudson River. Its waters are lively, clear, and perfect for canoeing and fishing. Your best bet is to stop in at the Orvis Company in town (Rte. 7A, Manchester) and pick up a detailed map of the river. Or just chat with the sales folk here. They'll tell you the best place to access the water, whether you want to sit on a rock and dip your feet or get serious about some fishing. The store is a great place to browse, too, full of fishing gear and gadgets. You're likely to see a class or two outside by the Orvis Pond, learning the finer points of fly casting. Canoe rentals are available at Battenkill Canoe, Rte. 313, West Arlington; (802) 375-9559.

⅔ Emerald Lake State Park
Rte. 7, North Dorset; (802) 362-1655.

This 430-acre state park offers swimming, boating, and fishing at Emerald Lake, along with a playground and a marked nature trail. Picnic tables, a snack bar, and canoe and boat rentals are available.

⅔ Hapgood Pond Recreation Area
Rte. 11, Weston (2 miles north of Peru); (802) 362-2307.

Part of the Green Mountain National Forest, this popular spot offers swimming, hiking, fishing, and picnicking.

⅔ Jamaica State Park
Rte. 30, Jamaica; (802) 874-4600.

Have a picnic on the banks of the West River, or go hiking, fishing, canoeing, kayaking, or swimming. Follow the nature trail to Hamilton Falls. Boat rentals are available.

⅔ Lake Saint Catherine State Park
Rte. 30, Poultney; (802) 287-9158.

Lake Saint Catherine offers swimming, fishing, and boating. A marina on the west shore of the lake rents canoes and motorboats. You'll also find a nature trail, nature museum, playground, and picnic tables. Bring barbecue fixings for dinner; there are fireplaces and wood available.

⚜ Townsend Lake Recreation Area
Rte. 30, Townsend; (802) 874-4881.

Here you'll find swimming, boating, picnicking, hiking trails, and most notably a dam. Boat rentals are available.

⚜ Hiking
Manchester Ranger District, U.S. Forest Service, Rte. 11, Manchester; (802) 362-2307.

In southern Vermont, two legendary trails merge: the Appalachian Trail and the Long Trail. These provide opportunities for a number of day hikes. Some easy treks in the area for families include:

Grout Pond Trails; these are a series of easy loop trails, which pass Grout Pond and provide access to the north end of Somerset Reservoir. You'll find camping, picnicking, and swimming at Grout Pond. Catch the trailhead off Kelley Stand Road, just east of Route 71.

Hapgood Pond Trails; you'll begin at a picnic area, located north of Peru at the Hapgood Pond Recreation Area, Forest Highway 3. The trail loops around the north edge of the pond to a dam. (Summer admission is charged at Hapgood.)

Griffith Lake Trail; from the end of Forest Road 58, park your car and hike north on an old road to Griffith Lake. This is just over two miles and well-marked.

⚜ Sleigh Rides
The Inn at Weathersfield, Main St., Perkinsville, (802) 263-9217; Valley View Horses and Tack Shop, Northwest Hill Road, Pownal, (802) 823-4649; Stratton Mountain Resort, Stratton Mountain, (802) 297-2200; and Santa's Land, Rte. 5, Putney, (802) 387-5550.

Nestle yourself under a wooly blanket and let a beautiful draft horse pull your sleigh along snow-covered country lanes. There's nothing quite so romantically old fashioned as a winter sleigh ride. The kids will delight in the experience and in the history and tales your driver is likely to tell. Most of the places listed offer day and evening rides and charge around $10 a person. Call ahead for details and family or group rates.

❄ Snowmobiling

What an exciting, bumpy, fast, and yes, noisy thrill. It has all the elements to put a smile on any kid's face. The pristine winter scenery is great, too. Snowmobiling opportunities include: Wheeler Farm, Wilmington, (802) 464-5225, offering guided snowmobile tours on its 200-acre working dairy farm; Stan Bill's Sales & Rentals, Rte. 30, Townshend, (802) 365-7375, offering tours, moonlight rides, and trailside cookouts. Or, rent a machine and head out on your own on nearby national forest land and trails. Bob Phillips, Emerald Lake Road, East Dorset, (802) 362-3946, offers rentals for a day, week, or month for touring on more than 60 miles of trails. Guide service is also available.

❄ Memorial Park Skating Rink

Downtown Brattleboro, (802) 257-2311. Daylight hours. Free.

What's winter without ice skating? Grab those skates and mittens and head to this outdoor rink for some economical amusement and fun.

❄ Cross-Country Skiing

Southern Vermont is a Nordic skier's paradise. There are numerous ski touring centers nearby; these are great for families because you get detailed maps, advice, rental equipment, groomed trails, and lessons. Here are some possibilities:

Hildene Ski Touring Center, Rte. 7A, Manchester, (802) 362-1788; Nordic Inn Touring Center, Rte. 11, Londonderry, (802) 824-6444; Stratton Cross-Country Center, Mountain Road, Stratton Mountain, (802) 297-2200; Viking Ski Touring Center, Pond Road, Londonderry, (802) 824-3933; Hermitage, Wilmington, (802) 464-3511; Grafton Ponds, Grafton, (802) 843-2231; Sitzmark, Wilmington, (802) 464-5498; Timber Creek, Wilmington, (802) 464-0999; and White House, Wilmington, (802) 464-2135. Most charge between $7 and $12 for a weekend trail fee.

❄ Mount Snow/Haystack Ski Resort

Rte. 100, Mount Snow; (802) 464-3333. Lift tickets: adults $41; 12 and under, $20; family ticket (two adults, two juniors), $88. Pumpkin Patch day care, $45/day, including lunch; PeeWee (3-5) and SKIwee (6-12), $63/day, including lift ticket, two lessons, and lunch. Half-day rates available. Teen ski school, $21 for a two-hr. lesson. Rates listed are for weekends and holidays; special packages available.

One of Vermont's largest ski resorts, Mount Snow/Haystack offers good skiing for beginners and intermediates. Lift tickets are good for both areas, and convenient shuttle buses run continually throughout the day between the two. With a vertical lift of nearly 2,000 feet and more than 70 trails, serviced by 16 lifts, you'll have a grand time trying to cover it all. Black-diamond lovers should head for the challenging North Face area once they've warmed up. It gets crowded here on the weekends, as Mount Snow draws hordes from Massachusetts, Connecticut, and nearby New York.

Mount Snow was one of the pioneers in the nationally known SKIwee program, designed to make it fun, not fearsome, to learn how to ski. For children age 3 to 5, Mount Snow offers its PeeWee program, combining two hours of ski instruction with indoor play. Kids learn how to put on their ski gear indoors, too, where it's less slippery. Youngsters from 6 to 12 can participate in a half-day or full day of SKIwee instruction. Beginners try out their ski legs on the gentle slopes; more advanced skiers are taken to the main mountain areas to spend the day. The Pumpkin Patch provides day care for nonskiing children age 6 weeks and up. Infants, toddlers and older children (in separate rooms) take part in arts and crafts, cooking, story hours, and sing-alongs.

If possible, arrange the family vacation during one of Mount Snow's Teddy Bear Ski Weeks, when you'll get the best family deals of the season, and there are a lot of special kid-pleasing activities going on. When kids under 12 bring along their favorite teddy bear, they'll ski free. A magic show, a teddy bear parade, and a ride on a snow-grooming machine add to the fun. Most lodges in the area also allow kids to stay free in the same room with their parents.

☃ Bromley Mountain

Rte. 111, Peru (6 miles east of Manchester); (802) 824-5522. Lift tickets: adults, $32; 7-12, $20. Day care, 1 mo.-6 yr., $27/day. Beginner Discoverski, 3-5, $15 (1 hr.); Discoverski Lift, any-age child, $18 (2 hr.); Discoverski School, 6-14 (including lunch), $40-$50/day. Rates listed are for weekends and holidays; half-price weekday rates, half-day rates, and packages are available.

The best thing about skiing Bromley is its southern exposure, which makes the Alpine experience a tad warmer here than at other New England ski resorts. Amen to that. You'll find a cozy, family atmosphere here, along with 35 trails served by seven lifts.

⅋ Stratton Mountain

Rte. 11 east of Manchester to Rte. 30, Bondville (follow Stratton Mountain Road); (800) 843-6867. Lift tickets: adults, $35; 12 and under, $20. Big and Little Cub, $40/day (includes lessons and lunch; does not include lift ticket). Rates listed are for weekends and holidays; discounted weekday rates and special packages are available.

Stratton has expanded from an alpine ski resort to a full-fledged sports center, so even nonskiers will find plenty to do here. Swimming, racquetball, tennis and other activities are available. (Tennis enthusiasts take note: Stratton is the site of the Volvo International Tennis Tournament, so its facilities are first rate.)

Downhill skiers will find 86 trails, many of them rated "difficult," served by 10 lifts. Stratton offers a day-care center for children 6 months to 5 years and Cub programs for kids age 3 to 12. Little Cub participants, age 3 to 6, can enroll all day (from 8:30 to 3:45) or for a half-day, with ski lessons and supervised activities included. Big Cub skiers, age 6 to 12, take part in ski lessons geared to ability level and a variety of activities.

▶ RESTAURANTS

You'll find plenty of restaurants scattered throughout the Manchester and mountain area. Your best bet is to head for Manchester Center or Brattleboro, where a number of dining spots offer good food and fun surroundings.

⅋ Laney's

Rtes. 11 and 30, Manchester; (802) 362-4456. Sun.-Thurs., 5-10; Fri. and Sat., 5-11.

This movie-themed restaurant is decked out in film posters, many of them signed, and entrees are named accordingly. "Adam's Ribs" are deservedly popular, along with Laney's squiggly french fries. While you're mulling over the possibilities, the kids will be busily coloring the tablecloth. Not to worry—it's a big sheet of white paper set down just for that purpose. Crayons are provided. Lots of kid-pleasing choices include Dumbo (barbecued chicken) and Muppets (a child-size pizza).

⅋ Mother Myrick's

Rte. 7A, Manchester; (802) 362-1560. Daily, 10:30-5:30; Sat., 10:30-6.

This is goody heaven: an ice cream parlor, bakery, and chocolate shop all in one. Children will enjoy watching the candy makers prepare fudge and dip chocolates in the candy room. (Tell yourself this is an educational trip.) Can't decide what you want? Indulge in a scrumptious ice cream sundae now, and take some fudge home for later.

❧ Blue Benn

Rte. 7 North, Bennington; (802) 442-5140. Mon.-Tues., 6 A.M.–5 P.M.; Wed.-Fri., 6-8; Sat., 6-4; Sun., 7-4.

This is a classic diner complete with barrelled ceiling, Formica counter tops, and lots of stainless steel and chrome. But this is not your typical greasy spoon. Blackboard specials might include omelets of asparagus and cheddar or watercress and cream cheese, or whole wheat harvest pancakes, veggie enchiladas, falafel, and nut burgers. There's a lot of traditional diner fare for the kids, too, like hot dogs, meatloaf and mashed potatoes, and Jell-O. This place is often crowded, but it's worth the wait.

WOODSTOCK AREA

If your family loves the outdoors anywhere and more so where there's a healthy dose of gorgeous scenery, start packing. This is your place.

Many visitors are attracted to this region for downhill skiing; most, to mammoth Killington with its six mountains, highly regarded ski school, and extensive children's programs. And certainly you can spend days here on skis of either the alpine or Nordic variety, while your kids are merrily making snowmen, joining in sing-alongs, and perfecting their wedge turns. Not a bad way to beat the winter doldrums.

Come summer, you'll discover a whole new side of central Vermont. Actually, it's an old side. This is the time to visit the towns that existed before the ski resorts arrived, especially picturesque Woodstock, and to see a natural wonder that dates back to the Ice Age—Quechee Gorge.

Since this is Vermont, there is no need to simply play tourist. Hike, bike, swim, ride horseback, and enjoy a side of central Vermont that less savvy families usually miss.

❧ Billings Farm and Museum

Rte. 12, Woodstock; (802) 457-2355. Mid-May–Oct., daily, 10-5. Adults, $6; 6-16, $3.

Watch cows being milked, churn cream into butter, nuzzle a sheep, pet newborn calves—these are some of the pleasures awaiting your family at Billings Farm. This working dairy farm has prize Jersey cattle, sheep, draft horses, oxen, and a petting nursery. This is a great way to explore the busy life on a real working Vermont dairy farm. Be sure to visit the 1890 farm house, featuring an old-fashioned creamery. It's also the home of a farm museum, complete with an authentically restored farm home, workshop, and general store. It's a good look at the rigors and traditions of farm life in the 1890s. There are demonstrations of how to hook a rug, spin wool, and do other country chores. Visit on a weekend to have a horse-drawn wagon ride. Special events are scheduled each month. If you can, visit on Children's Day, when old-fashioned games are played. Call for details and schedule.

⁑ Vermont Institute of Natural Science

Church Hill Rd., Woodstock; (802) 457-2779. May-Oct., 10-4; closed Tues. Nov.-Apr., 11-4; closed Tues. and Sun. Adults, $5; 5-15, $1.

Most children have never seen a real live owl, seeing only the cartoon variety. Here's your chance to see a real one up close, among 26 species of owls, hawks, and eagles native to northern New England. The Vermont Raptor Center, located here, is a unique living museum offering an opportunity to learn about raptors. All the birds of prey at the center are permanently injured and unable to survive in the wild. You'll also be able to see the injured birds in the infirmary. The institute treats hundreds of injured birds of prey each year; most are released back to the wild.

Leave time for a walk on one of the many self-guided nature trails (there's 77 acres of nature preserve) and for a quick look at the visitor's center. Housed in a remodeled dairy barn, it usually has a small display of nature exhibits. Or plan your visit for the last week in September, when the institute displays New England's major Wildlife Art Exhibition. All contributions and admission fees help to support the institute's environmental education programs and natural history research.

⁑ Montshire Museum of Science

Rte. 10A, Norwich; (802) 649-2200. Year-round, daily, 10-5; Tues., 10-8. Adults, $4; 3-17, $2.

This peaceful setting has been called "one of the finest museum sites in New England" by the American Association of Museums. The entire family will enjoy learning about nature here, indoors with a wide range of exhibits and programs, or outdoors on the museum's 100-plus acres of forest along the Connecticut River.

One exhibit is a self-contained colony of more than 250,000 leafcutter ants. In the physics playground, your child will whisper over 100 feet and be clearly heard without the aid of electronic wizardry, and will create bubbles larger than a kid sister. The museum has a number of changing, interactive natural history, physical science, ecology, and technology exhibits. It's a great family outing.

Pond Hill Ranch Rodeo

Rte. 4A, Castleton; (802) 468-2449. First Sat. in July–Labor Day. Adults, $7; 6-12, $3.

Bronco busting, bull riding, calf roping—it's a real rodeo! The fact that you don't expect to find a rodeo in Vermont makes it all the more fun. Right, Buckaroo? Special events for kids include calf catching. (If you catch the tag on the calf's tail, you win a dollar.)

Wilson Castle

West Proctor Rd. (near Rutland, off Rte. 4), Proctor: (802) 773-3284. May-Aug., daily, 9-5:30. Adults, $6; 6-12, $2.

If you've ever imagined living in a fairy tale castle, you might have envisioned a place like this. Built by a local physician and his monied British wife, Wilson Castle boasts turrets, arches, parapets, and balconies, the whole thing made of imported materials, including the bricks. On the grounds are cattle barns, stables, and to the delight of children, an aviary with Indian peacocks. The Wilson Castle fairy tale, alas, has an unhappy ending. Soon after the castle was built, the lady of the house fled, taking all her money with her. The town ultimately seized the castle for back taxes and sold it.

New England Maple Museum

Rte. 7, Pittsford; (802) 483-9414. Oct.-Dec., daily, 10-4; May-Oct., 8:30-5. Adults, $1.50; 6-12, $.50.

Vermonter's call it "nature's gold," and you won't want to miss a sample of the state's sweetest product. You'll learn how the Indians first taught Vermonters how to tap the trees and turn the sap into syrup. The activity and fun are greatest during maple sugaring time from the end of February 'til early April.

Pico Alpine Slide

Rte. 4 (9 miles east of Rutland), Sherburne; (802) 775-4345. May and June, daily, 11-5; July and Aug., daily, 10-6; Sept. and Oct., daily, 12-5. Single ride: adults, $4; 6-12, $3. Unlimited riding: adults, $22; 6-12, $16.

Every kid loves a wild ride on a slide, and face it, most grown-up kids do too. In summer ride the chairlift up the side of Pico Peak, enjoying beautiful mountain views, then whoosh down the slide, where you control the pace. Try a single ride, or opt for an all-day ticket and you'll leave windburned, exhausted, and happy. (The kids will have fun, too.) You'll also find great mountain biking trails here (you're allowed to take bikes up the lift) and a minigolf course.

⚝ Killington Gondola and Chairlift

Killington Gondola Base Lodge, Rte. 4, Sherburne; (802) 422-3333. Gondola: mid-Sept.–mid-Oct., daily, 10-4. Adults, $15; 12 and under, $8. Chairlift: Memorial Day–mid-June, weekends; mid-June–mid-Sept., daily, 10-4. Adults, $10; 6-12, $5.

Summer, winter, or fall, you can ride to the summit of Killington Mountain without ever putting on a pair of skis. The gondola (an enclosed cable car) or in summer the chairlift will take you three-and-a-half miles up. At the peak you'll find a cocktail lounge, a cafeteria, and an observation deck. From the deck, you'll see the Green Mountains, the White Mountains (see if you can spot majestic Mount Washington), the Berkshires, and the Adirondacks. This is a great way for little people and non-skiers to get to the top of the mountain. The view, especially during foliage season, is spectacular.

⚝ Killington Playhouse

Killington Road, Sherburne; (802) 422-9795. July–Labor Day.

Treat your children to an afternoon of musical theater at a just-for-kids Wednesday matinee. The Green Mountain Guild performs Broadway favorites at Killington Ski Resort's Snowshed Base Lodge during the summer season. Call ahead for details.

⚝ Vermont Marble Company

Main St., Proctor; (802) 459-3311, ext. 436. Mid-May–late Oct., daily, 9-5:30; winter hours, Mon.-Sat., 9-4. Adults, $3.50; 13-18, $2; 6-12, $1.

An informative film, exhibits, and interpretive displays show the history of the marble industry in Vermont. You'll learn about marble formation, quarrying, and finishing. The kids will enjoy seeing the sculptor at work. There's also an interesting outdoor display and gallery.

⚝ Quechee Gorge

Exit 1 off I-89, then west on Rte. 4, Quechee; (802) 295-7600.

Vermont's most intriguing natural wonder, Quechee Gorge is a mile-long, 165-foot-deep channel that dates back to the last Ice Age. From the bridge spanning the gorge on Route 4, you can stare down into the seemingly bottomless chasm. Or, if your group includes older children, try the shaded mile-long trail to the bottom. It's a fairly easy hike along the fenced-in edge of the precipice. A best bet for everyone: take the short stroll to the falls at the top of the gorge and indulge in a picnic. Plan to visit in mid-June if you can, to coincide with the annual Quechee Hot-Air Balloon Festival.

⅋ Mountain Biking at Killington Peak
Top of Killington Rd., off Rte. 4, Sherburne; (802) 422-3333. Mid-June–Columbus Day, weekends.

Of course, there are lots of great places to mountain bike in the Green Mountain area of Vermont. But you can keep those bikes in high gear if you head to the Killington Peak chairlift. The lift will hoist you and your bike to the top of the second highest peak in Vermont. From there, let 'er rip, as you cruise 25 miles of marked trails. Guided tours, helmets, and rental bikes are available at the base.

⅋ Lake Bomoseen
Off Rte. 4A, north of Castleton. Call local Chamber of Commerce (802) 265-4924 for information.

So you thought in land-locked Vermont it would be tough to find places to take a dip? Not so. This nine-mile lake has a number of beaches. Our favorite is Crystal Beach, with white sand and lifeguards.

⅋ White River
Be sure to throw your bathing suit or an extra change of clothes in the trunk when you're traveling this area. The beautiful White River snakes its way through central Vermont, around bends and over rocks. There are hundreds of places along its banks to stop for a dip, to jump across its width on rocks and fallen logs, or to picnic next to a picturesque waterfall. If you're inclined, throw out a fishing line or two; with any luck you'll have trout for dinner. (Don't forget, you do need a fishing license.)

⅋ Hiking
You'll find plenty of hiking opportunities here, from easy strolls to rigorous mountain hikes. The trail around Quechee Gorge, for example, offers easy hiking with great views into the gorge itself. Quechee Village is a pleasant place to stroll; cross the covered bridge by the falls and follow the river bank upstream.

Mount Tom, in Woodstock, offers a graded footpath with benches along the way. Start at Faulkner Park and follow the switchback trail to the top of Mount Tom. Or for a guided walk, start at the Woodstock Inn

on the Green in Woodstock. The walk follows paved paths, leading gently
to the summit with a rewarding 360-degree view.

☙ Horseback Riding

From horse-drawn wagon rides to ponyrides and trail riding, there's
something for all ages and experience levels. You can ride for hours
through pastoral valleys, pine-scented forests, and along lakes and
streams. At Kedron Valley Inn & Stables, Route 106, Woodstock, (802)
457-1473, guided trail rides and hourly and daily rentals are offered.
Other places include: Brickyard Farm on South Hill, South Hill Road,
Ludlow, (802) 228-5032; and Pond Hill Stables, Route 4A, Castleton,
(802) 468-5166.

☙ Cross-Country Skiing

Nordic skiers will find abundant trails, varied terrain, and plenty of
extras at Woodstock Ski-Touring Center, Route 106, Woodstock, (802)
457-2114; Mountain Meadows, Thundering Brook Road, off Route 4,
Sherburne, (802) 775-7077; Fox Run, Ludlow, (802) 228-8871; Trail
Head, Stockbridge, (802) 746-8038; and Wilderness Trails, Quechee,
(802) 295-7620. Most downhill ski areas also have cross-country centers.

☙ Killington Ski Resort

*20 Killington Rd. (off Rte. 4), Sherburne; (802) 773-1500. Lift tickets:
adults, $41; children, $23. Children's Center rates: 6 wk.-8 yr.: all day
(lunch included), $41; half-day (no lunch), $28. First Tracks, 3-8; all day
(lunch included), $55; half-day (no lunch), $37. Rates listed are weekend
rates; weekday discounts and special packages are available.*

Killington is undeniably a popular place with skiers, and for good
reason: it's huge. With six different mountain peaks and 100 trails, there's
plenty of action for skiers of every level. Even those who are new to the
sport will find plenty of territory to cover from top to bottom. Killington
Peak, the highest mountain of the six, has a vertical rise of 3,000 feet.
Since it gets crowded here and lift lines get long, plan to hit the slopes
early. Also, you may want to head over to the less-populous Sunrise
Mountain or Bear Mountain areas, where you'll get more runs in.

The Killington's First Tracks program gently introduces the ski experience to children three to eight years old. The program includes ski lessons in the morning and afternoon, the length of the lessons depending on
the individual child. Off the slope, the children play, rest, and have lunch
at the Ski Vacation Center's licensed child-care facility. The basics of
skiing are taught in the gentle Terrain Garden practice area, complete

with hoops, cones, and obstacles designed to develop skills. Children progress from here to the surface lift and then to the chairlift. The Children's Center—for day-care and ski programs—requires reservations at all times.

⌁ Okemo Mountain Resort

815 Mountain Rd., Ludlow; (802) 228-4041. Lift tickets: adults, $42; juniors (7-12), $26. Rates listed are weekend rates; weekday discounts and special packages are available.

Nestled between the more popular and well-known Mount Snow/ Haystack and Killington resorts, Okemo has been trying hard to lure New England skiers to its own slopes. Major renovations in the past 10 years, including top-notch lift capacity and snow-making capabilities, are claiming converts and loyal, return skiers.

The mountain includes 10 lifts, accessing 71 trails. Beginners will enjoy lots of wide novice slopes, including a four-and-a-half-mile beginner's trail from the summit. Long intermediate trails and a handful for the experts complete the picture. Recent improvements have also included a new, expanded indoor kid's SKIwee facility and a special new teaching slope (complete with its own Poma lift for kids only). The half-day and full-day SKIwee sessions are for 4- to 8-year-olds of all ability levels. Group classes for children age 7 and up are organized according to ability and are offered from 9:45 to 11:30 A.M. and 2 to 3:45 P.M. Youngsters 8 to 12 of average or better ability can sign up for the Okemo's Young Mountain Explorers program. Classes provide six hours of supervised skiing and instruction and include lunch.

LAKE CHAMPLAIN VALLEY

Burlington, the largest city in Vermont, reigns over the Lake Champlain Valley region, blessed with spectacular views of mountain peaks on both sides and a large, glistening lake in the middle. The most urban of Vermont's cities sits on the eastern shore of Lake Champlain and is home to nearly a quarter of the state's population. But "urban" to most of us does not mean what it does to Vermonters. You'll find a thriving, vibrant city but one that has not lost its small-town charm and rural influences.

The rejuvenated waterfront area, once one of the country's busiest seaports, is a nice place to stroll; at dusk you'll be rewarded with breathtaking sunsets across the lake. Nineteenth-century buildings have been restored and now house cafes, specialty shops, and pedestrian marketplaces. There are five public parks from which to enjoy water views and lake activities.

Do not leave the area without visiting Champlain's Grand Islands, only a short half-hour drive away. You'll discover the rural town of South Hero, the countryside of Grand Isle, the pretty, tiny village of North Hero, and the beautiful seashore of Isle La Motte. The islands are connected by bridges, surrounded by mountains, and laced with lovely state parks and lakeside beaches.

Everywhere there are opportunities to enjoy sparkling, 110-mile-long Lake Champlain. Beaches are plentiful; there are powerboats, sailboats, and windsurfing equipment to rent; ferries and schooners to carry you across; and scenic vistas everywhere you look. Be on the lookout for Lake Champlain's legendary sea monster—Champ. In 1609, Samuel de Champlain noted in his diary the sighting of a strange creature in the lake. Since, other sightings have been made, prompting the Vermont House of Representatives to pass a resolution in 1982 protecting Champ from "injury or harassment." The Lake Champlain Chamber of Commerce annually hopes for a banner year of sightings.

Waterlogged and happy, you can travel inland to visit horse and dairy farms, a 1783 log cabin, and the popular Shelburne Museum and Farm.

ᕃᕕ Champlain Ferries

Lake Champlain Transportation Co., King Street Dock, Burlington; (802) 864-9804.

An easy way for the family to see Lake Champlain is to hop on one of the ferries that cross the lake to New York. Along the way you'll be treated to beautiful vistas of the New York Adirondacks on one side and the Green Mountains of Vermont on the other.

There are three crossings on Lake Champlain. Catch the ferry in Charlotte just south of Burlington, for the 20-minute ride to Essex, New York. You'll enjoy the stopover in Essex—it's a charming lakeside village. The drive from Burlington to Charlotte is worthwhile, too, and you might want to visit a few other sites (Wildflower Farm, Mount Philo State Park) in Charlotte, before or after the ferry ride. The ferry leaving Charlotte is open April through December.

A 12-minute ferry between Grand Isle and Plattsburgh, New York, is open all year. This is a good side trek to remember on your visit to Grand Isle.

A longer, one-hour ferry between Burlington and Port Kent operates mid-May through Columbus Day and provides great views of Lake Champlain.

❧ *Spirit of Ethan Allen*

Departs from Perkins Pier, Burlington; (802) 862-9685. Late-May–mid-Oct.
This is a lively, narrated lake excursion aboard a replica of a vintage stern-wheeler. With children, you might want to opt for the shorter day cruise or perhaps the sunset ride. On either one, you'll see fine scenery. Keep your eyes and ears open for the elusive Lake Champlain sea monster "Champ," whom only a favored few have seen. The sea serpent is said to be about 20 feet long with a horselike head.

❧ Burlington Perkins Pier

This small waterfront park in town is a good place for lake viewing and sunset watching. The children will also enjoy watching the many boats that come in and go out.

❧ Burlington Farmer's Market

College St. (next to City Hall Park), Burlington. Wed. and Sat., 9-2.
You can see some local color and pick up some local fruit and vegetables at this lively market held every Wednesday and Saturday. Give the kids a few bags and a dollar or two and have them do their own bartering at the stands. This is also a good time to wander the side streets and browse the gourmet shops, bakeries, and specialty stores.

❧ Burlington Bike Path

This 10-mile recreation path follows the lake from the mouth of the Winooski River. You'll share the route with strollers, joggers, and bikers. Pick up the path at Perkins Pier, Leddy Park, Oakledge Park, or North Beach.

❧ Burlington Public Beaches

There are five public beaches in Burlington where you can enjoy the clear, cool waters of Lake Champlain. North Beach is the largest and most popular of the town's beaches. It has a sandy area for sunbathers and swimmers. You'll also get a view of the Adirondacks in the distance. Oakledge Park is a more rugged, scenic beach. It has a picnic area and rocky ledges to toss your towel on. Red Rocks, a small, sandy beach in South Burlington, is good for kids. Lifeguards are always on duty. Leddy Park has a playground and a small beach area. There's also an ice skating rink, if you've brought your skates, open mid-July through March. Ethan Allen Park is close to Leddy Park. At this one you can climb up a turret for a view of the city and lake.

≋ Ethan Allen Homestead

Off Rte. 127, Burlington; (802) 865-4556. Mid-May–June 15, Tues.-
Sun., 1-5; June 16–Labor Day, Mon.-Sat., 10-5; Sun., 1-5; after Labor
Day–late Oct., daily, 1-5. Adults, $3.50; 5-17, $2; per family, $10.

You'll learn all about Ethan Allen, Vermont founder and hero of the
American Revolution, as you tour his restored 1787 farmhouse. The
struggles of 18th-century Vermont farm families come alive as you recon-
struct their day-to-day chores and travails at this famous Vermont homestead. (Maybe the kids will stop complaining about making their beds
and picking up their toys after seeing this. Sure.) Through exhibits and
shows, visitors also learn about the Indians, French colonists, and English
settlers in the Champlain region. Some in your family will enjoy the authentic working gardens on the grounds; others will delight in the archae-
ology projects now in progress at the homestead. Bring a picnic basket of
goodies to complete the outing; besides plenty of hiking trails with river
access, there's a picnic area.

≋ Champlain Chocolate Company

431 Pine St., Burlington; (802) 864-1807. Mon.-Sat., 9:30-5:30. Free.

Okay, we all know the real reason for entering this factory and store.
It's to sample some of the yummy, fresh chocolate treats and to bring
some of those factory seconds home. But, you'll also get to see these
chocolates being hand-made and to talk to the folks who are doing it.
That's educational, isn't it?

≋ Champlain's Grand Islands

You'll not want to miss a drive through these peaceful lakeside gems.
Traveling north from Burlington, you'll cross the lake to the islands of
South Hero, Grand Isle, North Hero, and Isle La Motte. These island
villages, connected by bridges, form one county, 30 miles long and eight
miles wide. Surrounded by water, with views of the Adirondacks to the
west and Mount Mansfield to the east, they offer some of the best in water
activities, solitude, and scenery. Parks and beaches on the islands include:

Grand Isle State Park, with great views, a small beach cove, and
rowboats to rent; U.S. 2, Grand Isle; (802) 372-4300;

Knight Point State Park, a good family beach with a large, sandy
swimming cove, picnic area, nature trails, concession stand, and boat
rentals; U.S. 2, North Hero; (802) 372-8389;

North Hero State Park, where the beach is open to campers only and
others can fish, hike, and rent boats; U.S. 2, North Hero; (802) 372-8389.

Even if shrines are not high on your list of attractions you'll want to stop at the Saint Anne Shrine on Isle La Motte, for its peaceful setting. The shrine, which draws crowds of worshipers on Sundays, is the site of Fort Saint Anne, the earliest settlement in Vermont. You'll enjoy a walk around the grounds and the surrounding lake views. There's even a picnic area, small beach and snack bar.

ૐ The Hyde Log Cabin on Grand Isle

Rte. 89, Grand Isle. July–Labor Day, daily, except Tues. and Wed., 9:30-5:30. Free.

Built in 1783, this is probably the oldest log cabin in the country. It was certainly one of the first homes on the island. It's now maintained by the local historical society and filled with 18th-century antiques. This is a good place to stop and stretch your feet on your drive through the islands.

ૐ Royal Lipizzan Stallions

North Hero, (802) 372-5683.

If you haven't seen these beautiful leaping steeds from Austria, here's your chance. The stallions and their riders make North Hero their summer home and visitors are treated to a running commentary on the history and the delights of the Royal Lipizzans. For a summer schedule, contact the Lake Champlain Islands Chamber of Commerce, (802) 372-5683.

ૐ Birds of Vermont Museum

Sherman Hollow Rd., Huntington; (802) 434-2167. May-Oct., daily (closed Tues.), 1-5. Adults, $3.50; 3-12, $1.50.

Bring your binoculars and hiking shoes and try your luck at spotting some of Vermont's most common birds on the museum trails. Inside you'll find a lovely display of wood-carved Vermont birds and lots of information on these native friends.

ૐ Shelburne Museum and Heritage Park

Rte. 7, Shelburne; (802) 985-3344. Mid-May–Columbus Day, daily, 10-5. Adults, $15; 6-14, $6.

This is a museum for people of all ages. The children will enjoy its parklike setting, covering 45 acres and filled with an interesting collection of buildings and memorabilia. You'll be able to board the 220-foot steamboat *Ticonderoga,* cross a covered bridge, peek in a a typical New England one-room schoolhouse, shop in an 1840s general store, circle the round barn, and climb the lighthouse. There are 37 exhibit buildings in all; most have been moved here from other sites. The buildings are filled with wonderful collections of treasures. You'll see old dolls and toys, a first-rate quilt collection, antique wagons and tools, and some of the best of American primitive antiques.

The museum, set on 45 scenic acreas, leaves lots of room for strolling and includes one of the finest lilac gardens in New England, as well as several perennial and herb gardens. It's a fun peek at our past, and a great family outing.

⁓ Shelburne Farms
Bay and Harbor roads (off Rte. 7), Shelburne; (802) 985-8442. July and Aug., daily; mid-May–June, Sept. and Oct., weekends. Farmyard: adults, $3.50; 3-12, $2.50. Tours: adults, $5.50; 3-12, $3.50.

This is a true gentleman's farm, with 1,000 acres of rolling hills, gracious gardens, and lake views. Always on the kids'-favorite list, the open-air wagon tour stops at the dairy barns where you can try your hand (literally) at milking, at the Coach Barn Education Center, and at the beautiful Shelburne House gardens. You'll see cheese-making and dairy operations and majestic 19th-century buildings and landscapes along the way. Save time for the walking tour; it begins at the Visitor's Center and winds through fields and woodlands about a mile, past the Farm Barn to the top of Lone Tree Hill for a magnificent view of Lake Champlain and the Adirondacks. The kids will delight in making friends with the animals at the newly opened family farm animal area at the Farm Barn.

Stop by the gatekeeper's cottage on your way out to pick up some cheese made from the herd of Brown Swiss on the farm. If you have the time, the slide presentation on the history and evolution of the farm is worth seeing.

⁓ The Vermont Teddy Bear Company
2031 Shelburne Rd., Shelburne; (802) 985-3001. Year-round, Mon.-Sat., 10-4; Sun., 1-4. Free.

Few can resist a peek at the cuddly inhabitants of this company. The factory that makes these soft, Vermont handcrafted teddy bears has opened its doors, allowing a look inside the magical business of teddy bear making. On the guided tour, you'll discover how each bear is hand-made, from the selection of the material and its first cut to sewing and stuffing. A fun look at a fun business.

⁓ Bixby Memorial Free Library
Vergennes; (802) 877-2211. Mon.-Fri., 12:30-8; Wed., 10-5; Tues. and Thurs., 12:30-5. Free.

Among all the kinds of high-adventure stories the very best may be frontier Indian tales, and the tales you'll hear at this library are all true. The library displays a large collection of Indian artifacts, paintings, and old maps, all proudly telling the action-packed history of this region.

⚞ The Discovery Museum

51 Park St., Essex Junction; (802) 878-8687. Sept.-June, Tues.-Fri. and Sun., 1-4:30; Sat., 10-4:30. July and Aug., Tues.-Sat., 10-4:30; Sun., 1-4:30. Adults, $3; 2-14, $2.

This wonderful hands-on museum includes a natural science area with live animals; a physical science area, where kids can make giant bubbles or work at WFUN-TV station; and an art hall, with changing art exhibits and programs. The museum is best enjoyed by children age two to 12. In July and August, the outdoor animal wildlife center is open, where you can meet native Vermont critters like the great horned owl, fox, and raccoon.

⚞ UVM Morgan Horse Farm

R.D. 1 (Weybridge Rd.), Middlebury; (802) 388-2011. May-Oct., daily, 9-4. Adults, $3.50; 13-19, $2; under 12, free.

This farm, once owned by Joseph Battell, an eccentric local landowner, was one of the first centers for the development of the purebred Morgan Horse. Now operated by the University of Vermont, the stables are open for guided tours to see the Morgan descendants. From the short audiovisual presentation shown on the tour you'll learn that the Morgan was the first breed of horse developed in America.

⚞ Robert Frost Trail

Rte. 125, west of Middlebury Gap.

"[A]nd I—I took the one less traveled by..." Whatever road you travel, don't miss the short (three-quarters of a mile) walk on this commemorative trail. You'll wind through the woods and across a beaver pond, coming upon seven mounted Robert Frost poems along the way. Why here? Poet Frost spent 39 summers in a log cabin just down the road and surely must have walked the same path years ago. While you're here, visit nearby Texas Falls.

⚞ Texas Falls

Rte. 125, east of Middlebury Gap.

These falls must have been an inspiration to long-ago resident poet Robert Frost. You'll see a sign marking the falls on Route 125 and a designated parking area; walk across bridges to view the series of falls. There are picnic tables along the way.

✺ M/V Carrillon

Departs from Teachout's Lakehouse Store & Wharf, Larabee's Point (end of Rte. 74); (802) 897-5331. Mid-May–late-Oct.

While other Champlain boat charters opt for the wide-open waters and expansive lake views, this special excursion boat takes a different route. The *Carrillon,* a 1920s lakeboat, moves up and down the narrowest stretch of Lake Champlain. In a vivid history lesson along the way, the boat makes stops at Fort Ticonderoga on the New York side and at several Vermont Revolutionary War battlefields. Call for schedule and rates.

✺ Vermont Wildlife Farm

Rte. 7, Charlotte; (802) 425-3500. Early April–late-Oct., daily, 10-5. No admission fee until May. Adults, $3; under 12, free.

This farm is well known to many New England gardening aficionados. The farm's seed catalog is the bible for wildflower growers. In July and August, the farm is ablaze with color and the air filled with accompanying music. You'll walk the self-guided pathways through acres of wildflowers and trees. Not the place to spend hours with rambunctious toddlers or bored teens, but worth a stop. (Promise them ice cream when you depart.) Before leaving the area, stop by Mount Philo State Park.

✺ Dakin Farm

Rte. 7, Ferrisburg and the Champlain Mill, Winooski; (802) 425-3971. Year-round, daily, 9-5:30. Free.

Vermont is known worldwide for some of its farm products. At this family-owned farm, you'll gain a greater understanding of the processing of food between the farm field and the grocery shelves. Farm products include corncob–smoked ham, bacon, poultry, syrup, and cheeses. And there are free samples. Lots of local folk and visitors alike stop by just to shop the store and stock up on the farm's specialty items.

✺ Taproot Morgan Horse Farm

Off of Falls Rd., Hinesburg; (802) 482-2168. Year-round, daily, 9-5 (call ahead to be sure someone's there to show you around). Free.

This is Morgan horse country—and for a look at a real breeding farm it's hard to beat Taproot. You'll get an up-close and personal look at these beautiful horses, and a glimpse at the business of breeding.

✣ Catamount Family Center

Governor Caittenden Rd., Williston; (802) 879-6001. Year-round: Tues.-Fri., noon-8; Sat.-Sun., 10-4. Adults, $5; under 17, $2.50.

At this 500-acre recreation center, you can run, mountain bike, hike, cross-country ski, golf, and more. There are cross-country ski and mountain bike rentals on the premises. Refreshments and services are available in the summer kitchen of the Catamount family's 1796 historic farmhouse.

✣ Lake Champlain Maritime Museum

Basin Harbor, (802) 475-2317. Mid-May–Oct. 15, daily, 10-5. Adults, $3; under 12, free.

This small museum is dedicated to the preservation of the Lake Champlain region and includes exhibits, artifacts, and special programs on Lake Champlain's maritime past. Of special interest are the active boatbuilding activities at the lakeside.

✣ Mount Philo State Park

Off Rte 7, Charlotte; (802) 425-2390.

Mount Philo is the only mountain available to climb in this region, and it's small at that. But don't let that stop you from driving to its 980-foot summit. There's an access road in the state park (you pay a nominal toll) that will take you to some of the best views in the area.

✣ Kill Kare State Park

Rte. 36, Saint Albans; (802) 524-6021.

A good place, if you're in the Saint Albans area, to stop for a picnic and swim. You can also catch a ferry to Burton Island from here.

✣ Burton Island State Park

For those who like a solitary look at natural beauty this island is paradise. There are no cars allowed on the island; you reach it by boat or a launch service from Kill Kare State Park: Town Road, off Rte. 36; (802) 524-6021. Pitch a tent or come for the day to enjoy its scenery and solitude. There are hiking trails, great fishing, and a small nature center on the island.

✣ Ice Skating

There are lots of places to ice skate along the shores and inlets of Lake Champlain. Also, you'll find skating at Leddy Arena in Leddy Park, Burlington, (802) 864-0123; Essex Junction Education Center, Essex

Junction, (802) 878-1394; Fenton Chester Ice Arena, Lyndon, (802) 626-9361; and at the Collins-Perley Sports Center, Saint Albans, (802) 527-1202.

RESTAURANTS

Stroll through Burlington's downtown pedestrian marketplace and you'll find all kinds of things to eat at lots of delis, take-out stalls, candy shops, sidewalk cafes, and indoor and outdoor restaurants. Two family favorites are featured below, as is a restaurant recommendation for your tour of Champlain's Grand Isles.

Carbur's

115 Saint Paul St., Burlington; (802) 862-4106. Mon.-Sat., 11-10; Sun., noon-10.

Like no other, this zany restaurant is perfect for families. From the moment you glance at the menu (a 16-page newspaper entitled the *National Injester*) 'til the moment you wipe your face and hands with the fluffy hand towels, you'll enjoy your meal here. There are close to 200 items on the menu. (The staff recommends you glance at the table of contents, decide what you're in the mood for, and turn to the pages for descriptions.) The favorite items on the kid's menu are the peanut butter, jelly, honey, and sliced banana sandwich or the peanut butter and fluff sandwich (fluff of marshmallow). If these offend your good taste, there's the kid's bowl of tricolored pasta and sauce, minipizza, fish and chips, and more.

Henry's Diner

Bank St., Burlington; (802) 862-9010. Daily, 11-10.

A real diner, with real diner food and with pocket-pleasing prices. Try the pig-in-a-poke—a hot dog wrapped in bacon and cheese on a grilled roll. The kids will just love swinging around on those stools at the counter.

Sandbar Motor Inn and Restaurant

Rte. 2, South Hero; (802) 372-6911. Wed.-Sun., dinner, 5-9; Sat., breakfast, 8-11; Sun., brunch, 8-1.

On Lake Champlain, in a pretty harbor in South Hero, this popular restaurant offers fresh seafood and meat dishes. The food is fine; the location is great. You can walk off your meal on the sandy beach across the street.

MONTPELIER AREA

Take a deep breath, let it out, and relax. As you gaze up at Montpelier's elegant, gold-domed capitol building, you'll get a sense that time has passed you by. The nation's smallest state capital is nestled in the valley of the Winooski River and surrounded by the green hills. There's a simple elegance and beauty about Montpelier. But it's not at all pretentious; it's a friendly place to be. Your family will feel comfortable running about the town streets or tumbling on the front lawn of the capitol. Best of all, from here you have all of central Vermont to explore. You won't need to look hard, or far, for recreation. The area mountains, forests, lakes, and streams offer great skiing, hiking, biking, swimming, fishing, and sightseeing.

Meander the back roads for a view of rural Vermont's rolling farmlands and tiny villages. Follow the winding mountain road through dramatic Smuggler's Notch or the twisting side road that follows the Lamoille River over scenic covered bridges. If you're looking for something more lively, visit the cosmopolitan, four-season resort town of Stowe. (Stowe is also one of many places in the area for families to ski.)

This is also a great place to learn about how things are made. Visit the Cabot Farmers' Cooperative Creamery to see cheese being made. At the Maple Grove Museum, you'll see a maple-sugaring operation. In nearby Barre, you can visit the world's largest granite quarries. Take the tour of the capitol and learn how laws are enacted. And everyone's favorite is a tour of Ben & Jerry's Ice Cream Factory, which includes samples.

⁂ Vermont State House Tour
State St., Montpelier; (802) 828-2228. July-Oct., Mon.-Fri., 8-4. Free.

On this friendly, 20-minute tour of the State Capitol, you'll get an introduction to how state government works. You'll see old Civil War flags in the governor's ceremonial office and take a look at Representatives' Hall. If you are here when the Legislature is in session (January to April), you can watch the proceedings, although tours are not given at this time.

⁂ Morse Farm Sugar House
Country Rd. (3 miles from the State Capitol), Montpelier; (802) 223-2740. Year-round, daily, 9-5; summers, 9-6. Free.

The Morse family members have been maple sugar makers for seven generations and they love to tell the story of maple syrup. The best time to visit this rustic sugar house is in March or April, when the sap is gathered and transformed into syrup. But you can tour the farm and learn about the equipment and process of maple sugaring at all times. There's a short slide show and a chance to taste samples of the syrup.

☃ Vermont Historical Society Museum
State St., Montpelier; (802) 828-2291. Free.

You'll get a peek at Vermont history in this small, hands-on museum, located at the Pavilion Office Building. The city band plays here on summer evenings, too. Call for details.

☃ Hubbard Park

This 121-acre network of trails, directly behind the State Capitol, is a favorite place to go for short hikes. Pack a picnic to enjoy en route; there are scenic places along the way to stop.

☃ Rock of Ages
Exit 6 off I-89, Barre; (802) 476-3121. May-Oct., daily, 8:30-5; tours, June–mid-Oct., Mon.-Fri. Free.

You can stand atop an observation platform and look over the world's largest granite quarry. From a 350-foot pinnacle of the 20-acre quarry, you'll watch skilled granite miners carve out huge blocks with machines, then lift up to 150 tons with giant granite derricks towering 150 feet above the quarry's edge.

Rock of Ages has been operating since the Civil War, producing granite for buildings and monuments around the world. On the guided walking tour, you'll see and hear (this is a noisy place) the work being done here. You can also take an open-air rail car to the work areas farther uphill. Visit the Craftsman Center on your way out to see how granite is used in final products. Just the sheer size of things here will amaze the children.

☃ Stowe Gondola and Alpine Slide
Mountain Rd., Stowe; (802) 253-7311. Memorial Day–June, weekends and July-Oct., daily, 10-5. Adults, $8.50; 13-19, $7; 6-12, $5.

Take a scenic ride to the summit of 4,393-foot Mount Mansfield aboard the enclosed, four-person gondola. For a faster ride, take the alpine slide down Spruce Peak. You control your own speed through the woods and fields and around turns and curves.

☃ Mount Mansfield Auto Road

This four-and-a-half-mile gravel road twists and turns its way to the top of Mount Mansfield. At the top—put on your coats, it's cold up here—take a look at the 33,881-acre Mount Mansfield State Forest that stretches before you. Because of the cold climate, you'll see alpine plants found only in arctic temperatures.

Bingham Falls

This is a nice hiking trail down to a beautiful gorge. Pick up the trail on Route 108, just past the Mountain Toll Road entrance.

Stowe Aviation

Rte. 100 (7 mi. north of Stowe); (802) 888-7845. May–mid-Nov., daily, 8-sunset. Rates vary.

For a bird's-eye view of Mount Mansfield, stop by Stowe Aviation and inquire about their airplane, sailplane, and hot-air balloon rides. If you've always wanted to soar above mountaintops or float silently across treetops, this is your chance.

Top Notch Riding Stable

Mountain Rd., Stowe; (802) 253-8585. Memorial Day–Oct., daily, 9-5.

Top Notch offers one- and two-hour guided horseback tours through the pretty Vermont countryside. You'll trot up hills, ford streams, and cross bridges on your way. Call for rates.

Stowe Recreation Path

Get a good tour of this mountain city as you walk or bike its recreation path. The 5.3-mile handicapped-accessible path meanders back and forth over Stowe's West Branch River on 11 gracefully arched bridges. It connects and links a considerable number of attractions in the scenic town of Stowe. In winter, it's a popular cross-country tour. The path begins behind the white-steepled Community Church on Main Street.

Ben & Jerry's Ice Cream Factory

Rte. 100 (Exit 10 off I-89), Waterbury; (802) 244-5641. Year-round, daily, 9-5. Over 12, $1. Note: There's no ice cream production on Sun.

It's not quite Willie Wonka's Chocolate Factory—but close enough. For ice cream lovers, it's next to heaven. The fun-filled tour takes you through the factory where all that famous Ben & Jerry's ice cream is made. You'll learn the steps it takes to produce the ice cream, and just when you think you can wait no longer, you've reached the Scoop Shop. (The tour does include free samples of ice cream, but just enough to make you want more.) Enjoy your Chunky Monkey cone (or your other favorite flavors) at a picnic table overlooking a pasture of cows with a backdrop of mountains. In the summer, Ben & Jerry's offers free outdoor family movies, once a week at dusk. Call ahead for a schedule. If you're here in June, inquire about the timing of the Ben & Jerry's annual ice cream festival— lots of fun.

ꙮ Cold Hollow Cider Mill

Rte. 100, Waterbury; (802) 244-8771. Year-round, daily, 8-6. Free.

Cold Hollow is Vermont's largest producer of fresh apple cider. Come here to watch the cider being made and to partake of a barnful of homemade Vermont goodies, including fresh pies, donuts, jams and jellies, cheeses, ham, syrup, and more.

ꙮ Lamoille Valley Railroad

Rte. 100, Railroad Depot, Morrisville; (802) 888-4255. Mid-July–mid-Oct., daily, 10 and 1. Two-hour trips: adults, $15; 2-12, $7. One-hour trips: adults, $10; 2-12, $5.

Take a scenic mountain trip aboard these 1920 rail cars. The 60-mile excursion takes about two hours and is very popular during foliage season. Call ahead for reservations.

ꙮ Cabot Farmers' Cooperative Creamery

Rte. 2, Cabot; (802) 563-2231. Mid-June–mid-Oct., Mon.-Sat., 8-4:30; Sun., 11-4:30. Winter, Mon.-Sat., 9-5. Closed Sun. Donations accepted.

If your family has not tired of factory visits, go to the Cabot Creamery, where you'll see all kinds of dairy products being made. The cooperative comprises more than 400 farmers and nearly 30,000 cows. And from this small, quiet Vermont village comes award-winning, world-renowned cheddar cheeses. The countryside setting is pleasant, the staff friendly, and the video presentation interesting. Of course, you'll not want to leave without sampling the creamery's excellent products.

ꙮ Groton State Park

Rte. 232, Groton; (802) 584-3822.

This is one of the best places for outdoor family recreation in the region. The 28,000-acre area is the state's largest recreational center, covering six towns. There are several lakes in the forest for swimming and boating (you can rent boats and canoes in the park) and more than 40 miles of hiking trails. The summer nature programs are fun for the entire family.

⌇ Lake Elmore State Park

Rte. 12, Lake Elmore; (802) 888-2982.

A pleasant park about 25 minutes from Stowe. You can swim in Lake Elmore, rent boats, hike, and walk up a lookout tower for a view of the Green Mountains.

⌇ Smugglers Notch

If you can endure the hairpin turns and narrow curves on a steep, winding scenic drive, you'll be rewarded with a dramatic view of Smuggler's Notch. Travel Route 108 just beyond Spruce Peak, where you'll begin your climb to the top of the notch. It's said to have been used as a hideout and, during the War of 1812, as a passageway between Canada and the United States. At the top, there's a small rest area from which to view the gnarled chasm created by glacial waters. You'll be at an elevation of 2,162 feet, where the air begins to cool. On the way down the back side, you'll pass a waterfall before reaching the Smuggler's Notch Ski Resort. The road is closed from late fall until May.

⌇ Smuggler's Notch Ski Resort

Rte. 108, Smuggler's Notch; (802) 644-8851. Smuggler's specializes in multiday family resort packages, offering a variety of options. Please write or call for free brochures, listing packages and rates.

Smuggler's has accumulated just about every "best family resort" award given out. It's always rated at the top of the list for quality and fun. Basically, if you're looking for a winter outing and your get-away includes kids, this is the place to go. It has everything children want—lots of activities, lots of freedom, and lots of other kids. Drive your car up to the resort (the drive itself is beautiful), and park. You'll need to go no farther to find dining, swimming pools, games, sledding, ice skating, movies, arcades, saunas, hot tubs, tennis, and top-notch resort lodging. The really nice part? While the kids are off having fun (everything is within walking distance), the parents are free to do the same. Smuggler's basically takes care of your kids, and all the details, so you can relax and have fun, too.

There's plenty of skiing here, too, three interconnected mountains with 56 trails in all. Serious skiers will find nothing too spectacular, but ski the morning and head to the Scandinavian Spa and Massage. The staff does a great job with the youngsters. Kids and parents alike will enjoy Alice's Wonderland, the large nursery and day-care center. The bright nursery, for children age 3 months to 6 years, is open daily from 8:30 to 4. Activities center on toys and crafts, books, a closet of costumes, and a water/sand table. For indoor exercise, padded mats, a ski ramp, and jungle gym are used. The smallest children do their first skiing indoors on the carpeted ski ramp. They get the feel of sliding on skis before they head outdoors for their first 20- to 30-minute lesson. Three- to 6-year-olds can join Discovery Ski Camp; 7 to 12-year-olds, Adventure Ski School. Activities for both programs include ski lessons, lunch, games, sleigh rides, story-telling, guided skiing, and on-mountain games. Smuggler's also offers Parents Night Out, available on selected evenings and limited to kids 3 and older.

🎿 Sugarbush Resort

Warren; (802) 583-2381. Lift tickets: adults, $39; minibear (4-5), $50; Sugarbear (6-11), $60; Catamount (12-16), $24; day care (6 wk. to 10 yr.), $40/day.

If it's been a good season for snow, you'll enjoy a trip up to Sugarbush. It averages more than 200 inches of snow each season, and when it's been coming down, Sugarbush is a great place to ski. The area encompasses two mountains, 105 trails, and a variety of terrain. Black-diamond skiers will be challenged here on more than 30 runs. In fact, Sugarbush boasts more expert terrain than other top resorts in the East, and runs like Ripcord, Paradise, Rumble, and Middle Earth will challenge the best. But there's also a good selection of intermediate trails. Beginners are limited to the lower areas of the mountain, but the kid's learn-to-ski programs get them on the mountain fast, executing just-taught wedge turns. Programs are offered for all ages and abilities.

This is a full-fledged resort with lots of amenities and activities to coax you to stay overnight, including deluxe lodging and dining, a full sports center and puppet shows, parades, sledding, and a night club for teens.

🎿 Stowe Mountain Resort

Stowe; (802) 253-7311. Lift tickets, adults, $32. Mountain Adventure (6-12), $62/day. Infant care (2 mo.–3 yr.), $40/day; child care (3-12), $40/day with 1 lesson, $52/day with 2 lessons.

You'll get real spoiled skiing at Stowe. It makes skiing as easy, convenient, and comfortable as possible. You'll find the finest in on-mountain services (like homemade pizzas, and fresh-baked pastries and cookies at the boutique-style Midway Cafe), the fastest gondola in the world (no need to brave the brutal New England weather), and the deluxe mountaintop Cliff House Restaurant (where the views and fare are equally suberb). And you'll find some great skiing—big-time skiing. You'll tackle a 2,360-foot vertical drop, offered in a variety of terrain. The intermediate runs at Stowe ski long and hard all the way down. The black-diamond trails will challenge you, and beginners have an entire mountain area to explore. Stowe has been called one of the best ski resorts in the country, and its reputation as a world-class area draws plenty of trendy, lively crowds. But in recent years, Stowe has actively targeted the family business, offering special family vacation packages and top-notch day-care and children's ski programs. (Check into the multiday lift and lodging package; kids ski and stay free.) Also, children age 6 to 12 can join Mountain Adventure, where kids take off for the day, exploring the mountain with their instructors and learning along the way. The Children's Learning Center offers infant care (for tots from 2 months to 3 years) and child care (for children 3 to 12 years) that includes activities, supervised play, and ski lessons.

⅋ Bolton Valley Ski Resort

Bolton Valley Access Rd., off Rte. 2; (802) 434-2131. Lift tickets, adults, $30. Bolton Cubs (5-7), $50/day; Bolton Bears (6-12), $50/day; Mountain Explorers (10-15); $50/day; pre-ski program (4-5), $40/day. Day care, $32/day.

The familiar, friendly atmosphere of Bolton Valley is especially appealing to skiing families. Tucked away high in the mountains of Vermont, Bolton offers two mountains to ski with 46 trails. This is a relaxing, effortless skiing experience, with gentle cruising runs and an emphasis on the slow and easy. Bolton loves families and goes the extra mile in welcoming them. It was one of the first ski resorts in America to offer a full-service day-care and instruction program for kids. The slopeside HoneyBear Child Care Center offers programs and care for infants and preschoolers. Children age 4 and 5 will enjoy the combined HoneyBear Child Care Center and Pre-Ski program featuring all-day care and two hours of outdoor play and pre-ski fun. From age 5, kids are on the slopes, either in the Bolton Bears or Cubs. Older kids, age 10 to 15, join the Mountain Explorers Ski Team.

Bolton is an all-inclusive self-contained resort, offering dining, recreational facilities, and nightlife. An added plus: there's night skiing at Bolton; you can ski from nine in the morning until 10 at night.

▶ RESTAURANTS

The Stowe area is well known for its vast array of restaurants. You'll find a variety of cuisines, from elegant, highly rated eateries to casual, take-out delis. You'll also find these fine, family-friendly restaurants in the area:

≈3 The Shed
Mountain Access Rd.; (802) 253-4364. Daily, 8-10.

More families eat here than probably any other restaurant in Stowe. It serves breakfast, lunch, and dinner, offering a wide variety of dishes, and in particular goes through lots of barbecued baby-back ribs and mighty Shed burgers (voted "Best in Stowe"). The seafood strudel is also worth trying.

≈3 About Thyme Cafe
40 State St., Montpelier, (802) 223-0427. Mon.-Fri., 7:30-7:30; Sat., 9-7:30. Closed Sun.

This gourmet take-out/eat-in cafe is probably the most exciting thing that's happened on the culinary scene in recent years here. Since opening, and it started out great, it has only gotten better. This is high-quality international cuisine. The sandwiches come on thick-sliced homebaked bread; the salads—an impressive array is always offered—are fresh, creative, and great tasting. Breakfast is homemade muffins, waffles, fresh fruit, and more. With dinner comes a selection of at least 10 daily entrees, reflecting About Thyme's international flavor.

≈3 Tubs, La Brioche, Elm Street Cafe
The Jailhouse Common, Elm Street, Montpelier. Tubbs: Mon.-Sat., 11:30-2 and 6-9:30. La Brioche: Mon.-Fri., 7:30 A.M.–3; Sat., 7:30 A.M.–1. Elm Street Cafe: Mon.-Sat., 7-10, 11:30-1:30, and 5:30-9.

These are the three restaurants operated by the students of the New England Culinary Institute, all located near each other in downtown Montpelier. If you're in the mood for something creative, stop by. The food is prepared fresh with a flair and is reasonably priced. The atmosphere is casual in all three, and there's always something the kids enjoy: how about the turkey-apple-topped-with-cheese sandwich?

NORTHERN VERMONT

Some call it the Northeast Kingdom. Some call it the quiet corner. Some call it the only vestige left of "real" Vermont. Whatever you call it, you can't mistake its scenic, unspoiled beauty. The territory closest to the Canadian frontier offers the most variety of terrain and range of topography, from rolling hills to high mountaintops to wide, flat rural regions. There are places where you'll be able to see for miles without a trace of civilization and others where you'll find surprising pockets of lively culture, interesting museums, and frolicking activity. Your options for travel are just as diverse, from aloft in a hot-air balloon or gondola seat to car or train, mountain bike, or foot. And poking about through the vast rural vistas you'll discover some unexpected pleasures, like an extraordinary natural history museum, a top-notch arts and film festival, a challenging and comfortable ski resort, and a hidden mountain lake to enjoy.

✌ Fairbanks Museum and Planetarium

Main St., St. Johnsbury; (802) 748-2372. Museum: year-round, Mon.-Sat., 10-4; Sun., 1-5. Adults, $4; under 12, $2.50; families, $9. Planetarium: Sept.-May, Sat. and Sun., 1:30 show; July and Aug., daily, 1:30. Admission, $1.50.

This museum was founded by Colonel Franklin Fairbanks, a naturalist and born collector of wildlife. This is a must-see for any families traveling in the area. The building itself, a red sandstone Victorian with 30-foot barrel-vaulted oak ceiling, is something to see, but you'll be dazzled by the exhibits inside.

Here you'll be nose to nose with stuffed polar bears, wild boars, alligators, penguins, bison, foxes, moose, opossums, an armadillo, and more. You'll be surrounded by an unbelievable collection of mounted birds and mammals peeking out through holes, from under limbs, and from behind glass in environmental displays. The eclectic collection also includes mosaic pictures made of insect parts, Indian artifacts, dolls, photomicrographs of tiny snowflakes, dinosaur bones, Fairbanks scales, and lots of folklore.

Be sure to visit the lower level, where you'll see one of the country's oldest continuously operated weather stations and get a glimpse of regional weather broadcasts being prepared. If you have time, travel to the stars at one of the ongoing planetarium shows, offered daily in July and August and on weekends the rest of the year.

✌ Maple Grove Maple Factory

Rte. 2, E. Saint Johnsbury; (802) 748-5141. Museum: Memorial Day–Oct., daily, 9-5. Factory tours: year-round, Mon.-Fri., 9-5. Museum, free. Tours, $.75.

Vermont is maple syrup country, and you can't leave the area without at least one visit to where it is being made. Maple Grove is one of the world's largest. You'll learn how the sap is gathered—a tap is driven into the tree and a tin bucket hung from it. When the bucket is full, it's emptied into a vat, transported to the shack, and boiled down. The Maple

Grove Maple Museum recreates this process. Housed in an original sugar shack, the museum includes displays of both antique and modern sugar-making equipment. You'll also see how maple syrup is converted into candy (and get a free sample) on the tour.

⅋ Catamount Arts
60 Eastern Ave., Saint Johnsbury; (802) 748-2600.

In this tiny, sleepy town, you can find some of the best film and per-formance art in the region. Catamount Arts, a nonprofit organization, has been able to bring internationally known performers to its stage for more than two decades. Catamount also hosts an impressive series of children's plays. Call ahead for its performance schedule and appropriate rates.

⅋ Bread & Puppet Museum
Glover; (802) 525-3031. May-Oct., daily, 10-5. Donations accepted.

Show us a kid that doesn't like a puppet or can resist the lure of full-size masks, and we'll show you a kid that hasn't seen them. As you travel the Northeast Kingdom and find yourself near the tiny town of Glover (just off I-91), stop by this small museum. You'll enjoy looking at the nice collection of puppets and masks in all sizes.

⅋ Lake Willoughby
Near Westmore.

Okay, you've been traveling through the northern region of Vermont, gazing at gorgeous scenery, rolling hills, and rural pastures. Nice, but now it's time to get out of the car for fresh air, a little exercise, maybe even a swim. This is the place. Although a bit off the major highways, Lake Willoughby is worth the extra time it takes to get there. This is a 600-foot deep lake carved by ancient glaciers, tucked between two moun-tain ranges. Secluded and undiscovered, it has great views.

⅋ Jay Peak Ski Resort
Rte. 242, Jay; (802) 988-2611. Various package rates available.

Ready to get away from it all? Want to escape the southern crowds? Longing for some skiing on real, natural snow? Consider a trip up to Jay Peak. This area is famous for receiving the greatest natural snowfall of any Eastern ski resort. This is a relatively small resort, unpretentious, relaxed. You'll find 2,153 vertical feet of skiing, 40 diverse trails and glades (yes, there's glade skiing here), and numerous slopeside accommodations and amenities.

Jay Peak welcomes families and offers SKIwee programs for all ages and abilities. Family specials are offered, including "children stay free" programs and complimentary day and evening child care.

RESTAURANTS

⚞ Miss Newport Diner

E. Main St., Newport; (802) 334-7742. Mon.-Fri., 5:30 A.M.–1 P.M.; Sat., 6-noon; Sun., 7-noon.

This authentic 1947 dining car has been a favorite watering hole for many a year. Here you can have homemade, old-fashioned food at old-fashioned prices. It's a great place for families. In fact, the food is pretty close to home-cooked. You'll feast on hot turkey sandwiches, real mashed potatoes and gravy, fresh baked breads, burgers, fries—even Jell-O.

⚞ Miss Vermont Diner

Memorial Dr., Saint Johnsbury; (802) 748-9751. Mon.-Thurs., 6 A.M.– 8 P.M.; Fri.-Sat., 6 A.M.–9 P.M.; Sun., 7 A.M.–8 P.M.

This is the quintessential cheap-eats restaurant—and the kids will love the swivel seats. Clean, bright, and cheery, Miss Vermont serves up huge portions of homemade food at yesteryear prices. You'll get jumbo eggs, thick slices of toast, and chunks of ham, or for lunch a fresh, flaky haddock sandwich or thick, marinated chicken breast with roasted potatoes and cole slaw. At dinner you're likely to find roast turkey, homemade soups and chowders, and fresh pies for dessert.

MYSTIC AND THE SHORELINE

The Mystic area is tremendously popular with families, and for good reason: it boasts two world-class attractions, Mystic Seaport and Mystic Marinelife Aquarium. Downtown Mystic—sliced down the middle by the Mystic River—has a seafaring charm all its own. Here you can participate in the town's most popular spectator sport, watching boats go by. You may not have a choice regarding this activity: the bridge goes up in the middle of downtown approximately every hour and a quarter in summer.

Neighboring towns, including Stonington, Norwich, Groton and New London, offer appealing attractions, too, such as the Thames Science Center, the Nautilus Submarine Museum, and Ocean Beach Park.

Where there's lots of fun and activity, you can bet there'll be crowds. This is especially true of Mystic Seaport. So arrive early, and be prepared to spend some time waiting in lines if you visit in summertime. Or plan your trip to Mystic in the less-hectic spring or fall. Another possibility: consider Christmastime. Mystic makes the most of it. Mystic Seaport holds Children's Victorian Christmas Tours, and downtown Mystic recreates the spirit of a 19th-century Christmas, complete with carolers and yuletide refreshments.

⚓ Mystic Seaport

Exit 90 off I-95, Mystic; (203) 572-0711. Year-round, daily, except Christmas Day. Open April–mid-June, 9-5; mid-June–Sept., 9-8; Sept. and Oct., 9-5; Nov.-March, 9-4. Adults, $14; 6-15, $8.75. Horse-and-carriage ride: adults, $2 (15-min. ride) or $1 (10-min. ride.); children, free. Steamboat Sabino river cruise: adults, $3; 6-15, $2; under 6, free.

Many visitors have the mistaken notion that the name Mystic Seaport refers to a Connecticut town. It's actually the name of America's largest maritime museum, a 17-acre site boasting tall ships and a recreated 19th-century seaport village. If you're visiting Mystic Seaport in summer, stop at the gate for your copy of *Kids Today*, a chronological guide to all the fun stuff scheduled for kids. This might include a session on tying sailors' knots or helping set sails, and special planetarium shows. Small fry will adore the quaint Children's Museum (despite the long wait to enter it in high season). A treasure trove of 19th-century toys and games awaits inside; outside, on the green, children can try rolling a hoop or walking on stilts.

Your family could spend a whole day at Mystic Seaport and not be bored. For starters, you'll want to explore the seaport's historic homes and village, where "role-players" demonstrate such 19th-century skills as boatbuilding and wood carving. Climb aboard the 1841 whaleship *Charles W. Morgan,* and you'll see the magnificent result of one of the lengthiest restoration projects in the seaport's history. The *Morgan* is the last of the wooden whaleships. You won't want to miss a river cruise on the *Sabino,* the last coal-fired steamboat in America. The *Sabino* departs hourly for 30-minute cruises, from mid-May to mid-October.

A great way to end your day at Mystic Seaport: give your legs a rest and take a ride on a horse-drawn carriage at Chubb's wharf. Children will enjoy clip-clopping around the seaport village, and you'll get one last look at this special place before heading back to the 20th century.

ᘓ Mystic Marinelife Aquarium

Exit 90 off I-95, Mystic; (203) 536-9631. July 1–Labor Day, 9-5:30; rest of year, daily, 9-4:30. Closed Thanksgiving, Christmas, New Year's Day, and last full week in Jan. Adults, $8; 5-17, $5.

More than 6,000 marine animals live here, and the best part about this aquarium is that you can get really close to most of them. The aquarium houses 49 exhibits, with every kind of fish and sea creature you can imagine, including a blue lobster and an octopus.

Most kids are fascinated by sharks, and they'll love exchanging menacing stares with three kinds of them in the Open Sea exhibit. There's even a special step up, alongside the tanks, so that toddlers won't miss anything. Of course, you'll want to see as many of the marine mammal shows as possible. Dolphins, sea lions, and whales perform here; children are especially delighted when the dolphins walk on their tails and the Beluga whale kisses its trainer. Outside, Seal Island features five species of seals and sea lions in natural settings, and the Penguin Pavilion houses a colony of African black-footed penguins. Plan to spend a couple of hours here to see it all.

ᘓ Denison Pequotsepos Nature Center

Pequotsepos Rd., Mystic: (203) 536-1216. Nature Center: May-Oct., Mon.-Sat., 9-5; Sun., 12-5; Nov.-April, Tues.-Sat., 9-4; Sun., 12-4; closed Mon. Adults, $1; children, $.50; under 6 free. Homestead open mid-May–mid-Oct., Wed.-Sat. and Mon., 12-4; Sun., 1-4. Adults, $2.50; children, $1.

If you're worn out from fighting the crowds at Mystic Seaport and Mystic Marinelife Aquarium, the peaceful Nature Center could provide the perfect respite. You'll find more than 125 acres of wildlife sanctuary and four miles of hiking trails, with ponds, fields, and lowland and upland woods to explore. The Nature Center maintains a year-round trailside museum, where you'll learn about birds, insects, reptiles, and pond and marine life. The nonprofit center is dedicated to environmental awareness. Special programs are offered on weekends throughout the year; call ahead. Nearby, the Denison Homestead (1717) showcases heirlooms from several generations of the Denisons, one of Connecticut's first families.

⚘ Old Lighthouse Museum

Water St., Stonington Village; (203) 535-1440. May-Oct., Tues.-Sun., 11-4:30. Adults, $2; 6-12, $1.

Drive out to the Lighthouse Museum on Stonington Point (a short trip from downtown Mystic on Route 1) and you can see three states at the same time: Fisher's Island, New York, to the south; Watch Hill, Rhode Island, to the east; and Connecticut, under your feet. Stonington Lighthouse was operated as a lighthouse until 1889; now it's a museum, housing 19th-century portraits, a collection of whaling and fishing artifacts, swords and firearms, and, in the children's room, toys and a dollhouse. To most kids, the best part is just being inside a lighthouse.

⚘ Rocky Neck State Park

Rte. 156, exit 72 off I-95, Niantic; (203) 739-5471. Parking fee, Memorial Day–Sept.; off season, free.

The best feature of this park is a mile-long crescent beach. Enjoy hiking, fishing, picnicking, a boardwalk, and concessions.

⚘ Millstone Information and Science Center

278 Main St., exit 74 off I-95, Niantic; (203) 444-4234. Year-round, Mon.-Fri., 9-4; special evening and weekend hours in summer (call for times). Free.

The Millstone Nuclear Power Station offers exhibits on nuclear energy and other energy sources, computer games, multimedia shows, and more.

⚘ Maple Breeze Park

Rte. 2, exit 92 off I-95, Pawcatuck (near Stonington); (203) 599-1232. May and June, weekends; July–Labor Day, daily, 10-10.

Here's just the place for the kids to expend some pent-up energy after a too-long road trip or museum session. This amusement park offers a waterslide, go-cart tracks, bumper boats, and minigolf. All this, and an ice cream shop, too.

⅍ Seal Watching and Whalewatching

Wildlife watchers will want to check out these intriguing adventures, offered by Captain John's Sport Fishing Center. In March and April, take a three-hour cruise to visit harbor seals, departing from Waterford. From May through Labor Day, excursion boats head to the waters of Montauk Point for all-day whalewatching, departing from Captain John's dock near the Niantic River bridge, Route 156. Call (203) 443-7259 for information.

⅍ U.S.S. *Nautilus* Memorial Museum

Exit 86 off I-95, Groton; (800) 343-0079 (recorded information), (203) 449-3174. Mid-April–mid-Oct., Wed.-Mon., 9-5; mid-Oct.–mid-April, 9-3:30. Closed Tues.; also closed the third full wk. of March and Sept., first full wk. of June, and second full wk. of Dec. Closed Thanksgiving, Christmas, and New Year's Day. Free.

Many a child has fashioned a periscope out of a cardboard tube and played submarine. At the *Nautilus* Memorial Museum—part of the U.S. Naval Submarine Base—kids can peer through real periscopes and tour a real submarine, the U.S.S. *Nautilus.* The world's first nuclear-powered vessel, the *Nautilus* was commissioned into the U.S. Navy in 1954. Once on board (you might have to wait in line, as only 60 people are allowed aboard at one time), you'll carry an electronic wand that activates narration about each area of the submarine. You'll see the navigation center, the radar room, the attack center, and more. Elsewhere in the museum, there are working periscopes, an authentic submarine control room, and several midget submarines.

⅍ Project Oceanology

Cruises depart from Avery Point off Eastern Point Rd., Groton; (203) 445-9007. Late June–Labor Day, daily, 10 and 1. Adults, $13.50; under 12, $10. Reservations recommended.

Climb aboard a 50-foot Enviro-Lab research vessel for a cruise you won't forget. Marine scientists and instructors will teach you how to use oceanographic instruments, test seawater, identify fish, and measure lobsters. You'll also help take core samples from the bottom of the ocean and examine them. Best for kids age five and up, the trips last two and a half hours.

⅍ Fort Griswold State Park

Monument St., exit 85 off I-95, Groton; (203) 566-2304. Park open year-round. Museum and monument: Memorial Day–Labor Day, daily, 9-5; Labor Day–Columbus Day, weekends only, 9-5. Free.

This 17-acre park was the scene of a massacre in 1781. Benedict
Arnold led an attack by the British forces, taking the fort and burning
Groton and New London. On the hilltop near Fort Griswold, a 135-foot
monument dedicated to the victims of the massacre bears their names.
Today you'll find the spot a considerably more pleasant place, with beautiful views of the Thames River and Fisher's Island from the memorial
tower. Bring a picnic.

⅔ Bluff Point State Park
Depot Rd., off Rte. 1, Groton; (203) 566-2304.

Located between Mystic and Groton on Long Island Sound, this unspoiled stretch of shoreline is a great place to take a hike or nature walk,
have a picnic, or fish from the shore. Take to the trails on cross-country
skis in winter.

⅔ Lyman Allyn Museum
*625 Williams St., New London; (203) 443-2545. Year-round, Tues.-
Sat., 11-5; Sun., 1-5. Free. (A donation of $3 per adult, $1 per child is
suggested.)*

This small museum, a memorial to whaling captain Lyman Allyn,
houses period furniture, a glass collection, and displays of Oriental, Greek,
Egyptian, and Roman art. We recommend it for families because of the
terrific collection of dollhouses and toys including an exhibit of rare 19th-
and 20th-century dolls. At Christmas, a special exhibit, "The Victorian
Toy Shop," is featured.

⅔ Connecticut Arboretum/Thames Science Center
*Gallows Lane off Williams St., exit 83 off I-95, New London; (203) 442-
0391. Arboretum: daily, dawn-dusk. Science Center: Mon.-Sat., 9-5; Sun.,
1-5. Adults, $2; 5-12, $1.*

Two sites on the Connecticut College campus are worth a visit. The
415-acre arboretum offers several hiking trails, including one that leads to
Balles Wood, a hemlock forest. The Thames Science Center features a
marine touch tank, where kids can make friends with local sea creatures.
Also thrilling: a working beehive under Plexiglas, squirming with life.
Kids will enjoy hearing bird calls on tape, and you're sure to hear kiddie
versions of same, long after you've left the Science Center.

⅔ U.S. Coast Guard Academy
*Mohegan Ave. and Rte. 32, exit 83 off I-95, New London; (203) 444-
8270. Visitor's Pavilion: May-Oct., daily, 9-5. Free.*

There are two advantages to visiting the academy in spring and fall: you might see the cadet corps on dress parade (usually on Friday afternoons), and you can board the 295-foot training barque, *Eagle,* Fridays through Sundays from 1 to 4 P.M. when it's in port. (Call first to avoid disappointment.) The Visitor's Pavilion features a multimedia show depicting cadet life, while the museum at Waersbe Hall displays historical nautical items.

⅔ Ocean Beach Park

Ocean Ave., exits 75N and 83S off I-95, New London; (203) 447-3031; (800) 962-0284 (CT only). Memorial Day–Labor Day, 9 A.M.–10 P.M. Adults, $2; 18 and under, $1.

You can have family fun galore at one of the most popular recreation areas on Long Island Sound. In addition to a wide white-sand beach, you'll find a boardwalk, eateries, a pool, a triple waterslide, minigolf, a playground, and lots more. The kids won't leave willingly.

⅔ Harkness Memorial State Park

Rte. 213, 4 mi. south of New London, Waterford; (203) 443-5725. Year-round. Parking fee, Memorial Day–Sept.; off season, free.

Once a private summer estate, this grand Italian-style villa is set on 116 acres on Long Island Sound. Grown-ups will enjoy poking around the 42-room mansion and formal gardens; kids will like beachcombing, picnicking, and fishing.

⅔ Garde Arts Center and Vangarde Gallery

329 State St., New London; box office; (203) 444-7373.

The historic Garde Theatre, the region's last remaining vaudeville/cinema house, offers a family theater series among its program of performances. Call for a schedule and showtimes.

⅔ Mohegan Park

Rtes. 2 and 32, Norwich; (203) 886-2381. Year-round. Free.

The best feature of this 385-acre park, overlooking the city, is a children's petting zoo. In season, don your suits for swimming in Mohegan Park Lake. A beautiful rose garden, honoring World War II dead, is in full bloom from late June to early July. Other features include hiking trails, picnic areas, and a playground.

⅔ Slater Memorial Museum

108 Crescent St., Norwich; (203) 887-2506. Sept.-June, weekdays, 9-4; Sat. and Sun., 1-4. July and Aug;, Tues.-Sun., 1-4. Closed holidays. Free.

Visit the Norwich Free Academy with your kids for a look at the Slater Museum complex's Joseph P. Gualtieri Children's Gallery. Appointed with work that appeals to children, the gallery features authentic African masks, a parade of circus figures carved in wood, sculpture and painting, and porcelain dolls. The Romanesque Slater Memorial Museum houses sculpture; Egyptian, Greek, Roman, and Native American artifacts; American primitives; and African and Oriental art. Kids will be inspired to get out the Play-doh and modeling clay once they get home.

⁀ Tantaquidgeon Indian Museum

Rte. 32, Montville; (203) 848-9145. May-Oct., Tues.-Sun., 10-4. Donation requested.

This unique museum offers a personal look at the Mohegan Indians. Begun in 1931 by direct descendants of Uncas, chief of the Mohegan Nation, the museum houses numerous artifacts. Among the unusual and beautiful objects here are headdresses made of deer hair and tiny, intricate straw baskets. Objects made by Plains and West Coast Indians are also displayed, including a wolf kachina doll. Behind the museum are replicas of Indian dwellings.

⁀ Boat Cruises

From Mystic, sail aboard a windjammer schooner on Long Island and Block Island sounds. Or, from Groton, cruise past the U.S.S. *Nautilus* up to the Coast Guard Academy and back on a replica of *The African Queen*— among other possibilities. Cruise companies include: Mystic Whaler Cruises, (203) 536-4218 or (800) 243-0416, departing from Whaler's Wharf, Mystic; Voyager Cruises, (203) 536-0416 or (800) 243-0882, departing from Steamboat Wharf, Mystic; and *Mystic River Queen,* departing from Thames Harbor Inn, 193 Thames Street, Groton, (203) 445-9516. And don't forget the steamboat *Sabino* at Mystic Seaport, (203) 572-0711.

◢ RESTAURANTS

⁀ Abbott's Lobster in the Rough

117 Pearl St., Noank (10 minutes from Mystic off Rte. 215); (203) 536-7719. May–Labor Day, daily, 12-9; Labor Day–Columbus Day, Fri. and Sat. only, 12-7.

This waterfront, eat-in-the-rough restaurant has won fans far and wide, including the folks at *Gourmet* magazine. Eat at a picnic table outdoors, where you might see lobster boats bringing in their catch, or grab a table indoors if the weather is foul. The bill of fare includes boiled lobster, hot lobster rolls (excellent), shrimp, clams, mussels—and hot dogs. Ice cream, too.

Avanti's
Rte. 1, Mystic; (203) 536-2639. Daily, lunch and dinner.

Most children love Italian food, and this small family restaurant is a local favorite. There's nothing fancy, but all your favorite pasta dishes are on the menu, as well as Avanti's popular pizza.

Peter's Family Restaurant
Rte. 33, Montville; (203) 848-1411. Daily, lunch and dinner.

Picky eaters in your brood? They'll have no excuse here, where the menu boasts more than 100 items. Seafood, pasta, chicken, wiener-schnitzel, you name it, and it's all cheap, cheap, cheap.

Goldy's
556 Colman St., New London; (203) 442-7146. Daily, breakfast, lunch, and dinner.

Friendly and homey, Goldy's serves up food to match—all-American diner fare like honey-dipped fried chicken, baked haddock, and meatloaf with mashed potatoes. There's a killer salad bar, too.

HARTFORD AND CENTRAL CONNECTICUT

When most people think of Hartford, they think "insurance," not "vacation wonderland." However, the city of Hartford—Connecticut's second largest—offers several attractions that will delight visiting families. Museums are the main event, with a wonderful hands-on science museum, the Mark Twain house, a fire museum, and an art museum with a super program for kids. Hartford also serves as a good base for exploring other sites in central Connecticut. They're varied and loaded with kid appeal, ranging from a state park with real dinosaur tracks to an aviation museum.

What you probably won't see are stag roaming the streets. Although an insurance company has perpetrated this image in their advertising, locals assure us it's just not true.

State Capitol and Legislative Office Building
210 Capitol Ave., exit 48 off I-84 or exit 29A off I-91, Hartford; (203) 240-0222. Tours Sept.-June, Mon.-Fri., every hour, 9:15-2:15; July and

Aug., Mon.-Fri., 9:15-2:15. Open Sat., April-Oct., 10:15-2:15. Closed state holidays and Thanksgiving–New Year's Day. Free.

Visiting a state capitol building makes history lessons come alive. Connecticut's state executive offices and legislative chambers are housed in an impressive gold-domed structure built in 1897. See bullet-riddled battle flags and more on a guided hour-long tour.

⅋ Mark Twain and Harriet Beecher Stowe Houses (Nook Farm)

351 Farmington Ave., exit 46 off I-84, Hartford; (203) 525-9317. Year-round, Tues.-Sat., 9:30-4; Sun., 12-4; also open Mon., June–Columbus Day and month of Dec. Closed New Year's Day, Easter, Labor Day, Thanksgiving, and Dec. 24 and 25. Call for rates.

Twain's bright red Victorian-Gothic house reflects the eccentricity of its owner. For example, Twain slept with his head at the foot of his bed so he could admire the ornate Venetian headboard, and he kept his telephone in the closet because it drove him crazy. You'll see the study where Twain wrote about Tom Sawyer and Huckleberry Finn—and took billiards breaks at the full-sized pool table. Visitors soon realize that the author enjoyed drinking, smoking, and billiards at least as much as he liked writing. The Twain House is part of Nook Farm, an intellectual community formed in the mid-19th century by Twain and cultural luminaries Isabella Beecher Hooker, who was a women's rights activist; William Gillette, a playwright; author Harriet Beecher Stowe; and others.

Adjacent to the Mark Twain House at 73 Forest Street, is the restored cabin of *Uncle Tom's Cabin* author Harriet Beecher Stowe. Most of Stowe's original furniture is here, including the small desk where she wrote 33 books.

⅋ Science Museum of Connecticut

950 Trout Brook Dr., exit 43 off I-84, West Hartford; (203) 236-2961. Tues.-Sat., 10-5; Sun., 12-5. Open Mon. holidays; closed major holidays. Adults, $5; 3-15, $4; under 3, free. Gengras Planetarium: star shows, $1 per seat; laser shows, $2 per seat.

From kinkajoos to computers, this science center offers lots to see and do. Explore the mysteries of the solar system and the planetarium, shake hands with a starfish in the touch tank (part of a 25-tank aquarium), and learn by doing in the Discovery Room, where there's an echo tunnel and a walk-in kaleidoscope. The center also has a computer laboratory, and a small indoor/outdoor zoo with 50 species of animals. Many kids take a shine to Teddy, the kinkajoo; other zoo inhabitants include a mountain lion, a raccoon, an eagle, ferrets, owls, and snakes.

Special Note: In 1995 or 1996, the museum is scheduled to move to Commerce Center in East Hartford, where plans include an IMAX Theater, a planetarium, and expanded exhibit space.

☙ Travelers Tower

700 Main St., 1 Tower Sq., Hartford; (203) 277-2431. Tours conducted May–mid-Oct., Mon.-Fri., on the hour and half-hour between 10:30 and 3. Closed holidays. Reservations requested for groups of 4 or more. Free.

At 527 feet, this building—home of Travelers Insurance Company— is one of the tallest in New England. Climb up 72 steps to the observation deck for a panoramic view of the city.

☙ Bushnell Park

Jewel St., Capitol Area exit off I-84, Hartford; (203) 246-7739 or (203) 249-2201. Mid-April–mid-May and Sept., weekends only, 11-5. Mid-May–Aug., Tues.-Sun., 11-5. Carousel rides, $.50.

What child doesn't adore a carousel? And the one at Bushnell Park, built in 1914, is something special, with 48 hand-carved horses and ornate lovers' chariots. It operates daily in summer and weekends in spring and fall. Also on the grounds are two Farragut cannons. Located in the center of the city, within steps of the capitol, the park is a great place to people watch or just relax under a tree. Grab a hot dog and a soda from a pushcart vendor.

☙ Elizabeth Park

915 Prospect Ave., exit 44 off I-84, Hartford; (203) 722-6514.

Another urban oasis, this park features gorgeous rose gardens (more than 10,000 plants of 50 varieties), in full bloom late June through early July. Lots of space to play; lawn bowling, perhaps? Ice skating in winter.

☙ Wadsworth Atheneum

600 Main St., Hartford; (203) 247-9111. Tues.-Sun., 11-5. Adults, $3; under 13, free. Free to all Thurs. and Sat., 11-1.

America's first public art museum (more than 150 years old), the Atheneum's collections include paintings, sculpture, furniture, costumes, bronzes, firearms, and even mummies. Items date from prehistory to the present. For kids, the staff has prepared specials tours on cassette tapes, designed to make art more accessible. The tapes combine fun (treasure-hunt-type questions and clues about the works) and facts (design concepts, how art is made). Wearing the headphones makes kids feel involved, not merely dragged along. Adults can plug in, too. On your way out, don't miss Alexander Calder's huge stegosaurus exhibit.

New England Air Museum

Bradley International Airport, 10 miles north of Hartford on Rte. 75, off I-91, Windsor Locks; (203) 623-3305. Year-round, daily, 10-5. Adults, $5.50; 6-11, $2.

Older kids who think airplanes are neat will enjoy taking a look at the aircraft exhibited here. More than 75 examples are on display, including bombers, fighters, helicopters, and a modern commercial jet. All have been meticulously restored. Children (and adults) will get a kick out of playing with the flight simulator; a museum staffer will supervise you. Aviation-related films are shown several times a day.

Connecticut Trolley Museum

58 North Rd., Rte. 140, exit 45 off I-91, East Windsor; (203) 627-6540, (800) 252-2372. Memorial Day–Labor Day, Mon.-Fri., 10-4; Sat., 10-6; Sun., 12-6. Labor Day–Memorial Day, Sat. and Sun., 12-5. Adults, $5.50; 5-12, $3; under 5, free.

Take a three-mile ride on an antique trolley car a la "Mister Rogers' Neighborhood," or say "Allllllll aboard!" and ride the steam passenger train. (Steam trains operate on selected weekends; call for a schedule.) The Halloween special, "Rails to the Dark Side," is a howlin' hoot.

Connecticut Fire Museum

58 North Rd., Rte. 140, exit 45 off I-91, East Windsor; (203) 623-4732. June-Aug., Mon.-Fri., 10-4; Sat. and Sun., 12-5; April and May, and Sept. and Oct., Sat. and Sun., 12-5. Adults, $2; 5-12, $1.

It's 100 years of fire-fighting history, with old-time fire trucks and models dating from 1850 to 1950.

Allen's Cider Mill

Mountain and N. Granby rds., Rte. 189, Granby; (203) 653-6438. Mid-Sept.–Dec., Sat. and Sun., 9-5. Call to confirm they're pressing cider before you visit.

Watch cider being pressed and, even better, sample the results at this 1919 mill.

Massacoh Plantation

800 Hopmeadow St., Rte. 10, Simsbury; (203) 658-2500. May-Oct., Sun.-Fri., guided tours 1-3:30. Phelps House open Mon.-Fri., 1-4 P.M., all year. Adults, $5; 5-18, $2.

This complex represents three centuries of local history. Older children will enjoy the Phelps House (1771, formerly a hotel and tavern), the one-room schoolhouse (1741), and the stocks and pillory. Also on the grounds are an herb garden, a 1683 meeting house, and a Victorian carriage house. Guided tours, from 1 to 3:30, are lively and geared toward children.

⅋ Talcott Mountain State Park and Heublein Tower
Rte. 185, Simsbury. Memorial Day–Labor Day, daily, 10-5; (203) 677-0662. Call for fall schedule.

For the best view in the state, take a one and a half mile hike to Heublein Tower in Talcott Mountain State Park. Once the summer home of the Heublein family, the tower offers panoramic views of four states and the Farmington River.

⅋ Stratton Brook State Park
Rte. 305, Simsbury. 8 A.M.–sunset.

Have bikes, will travel? This small park is best known for its extensive bike trail, winding through white pines and over brooks. Hiking, swimming, fishing, and, come winter, cross-country skiing and ice skating are other possibilities here. There are boathouses and a concession stand, too.

⅋ Old Newgate Prison and Copper Mine
115 Newgate Rd., exit 40 off I-91, East Granby; (203) 653-3563. Mid-May–Oct., Wed.-Sun., 10-4:30. Adults, $3; 6-17, $1.50.

This colonial copper mine served as a Revolutionary War prison—the nation's first state prison—housing British sympathizers. Prowl the dungeonlike chambers to see where the prisoners ate and slept, and hear of their attempted escapes. You can take a tunnel stairway down to the celebrated Simsbury copper mine and walk the narrow mine paths. The mine was worked from 1707 to 1773. Later the Newgate prisoners were kept in the mine at night. It's an unusual glimpse of American history. Today the crumbling jail walls set against a backdrop of foothills and valley forests appear picturesque. The picnic area on the grounds is a pleasant setting. If you have time, take the Newgate Wildlife Trail from the parking lot. The six-mile self-guided nature trail winds around Newgate Pond.

⅋ Lutz Children's Museum
247 South Main St., Rte. 83, exit 59 off I-89, Manchester; (203) 643-0949. Tues. and Wed., 2-5; Thurs., 2-8; Fri., 9:30-5; Sat., 12-5. Adults, $2; 1-7, $1. Free admission Thurs. nights.

Don't look, just touch…what is it? Yes, deer antlers. The "feel boxes" are just one of many exhibits children can get their hands on here. This little charmer is chock-full of fun possibilities: children can put on life jackets and steer a boat through a storm, climb aboard the Alphabet Express, or put on their own puppet show. The museum also has a live animal exhibit. Many of the animals are part of a rehabilitation and release program, making this an ever-changing exhibit. Nearby, the museum's Oak Grove Nature Center offers self-guided trails through woods, swamps, and a hemlock grove, and over a covered bridge. Little ones will want to run—not walk—to the outdoor playscape.

⚞ Wickham Park

1329 W. Middle Tpke., exit 92 off I-384, Manchester; (203) 528-0856. April-Oct., daily, 9:30-dusk. Parking fee.

An aviary, a small zoo, and a 1927 log cabin are the featured attractions at this unusual park. The 215-acre site has beautifully manicured grounds with Oriental and lotus gardens, toddler play areas, and picnicking facilities. Cross-country skiing in winter.

⚞ Old Tolland Jail Museum

Town Green, exit 68 off I-84, Tolland; (203) 875-7559. Jail museum: May–mid-Oct., Sun., 1-4. Hicks-Sterns House: mid-May–mid-Oct., Wed. and Sun., 1-4. Donations accepted at both.

This site on Tolland Green housed prisoners until the 1960s; now visitors can go into the jail's cells (c. 1856) and tour the country house connected to it where the jailer and his family lived. Across the street, the Hicks-Sterns Family Museum is worth a visit. This colonial-tavern-turned-Victorian-summer-cottage houses family heirlooms (including toys) and souvenirs of European travel. Summer lawn concerts here are a local tradition.

⚞ Benton Homestead

Metcalf Rd., exit 68 off I-84, Tolland; (203) 875-7559. May–mid-Oct., Sun., 1-4. Donations accepted.

The best feature of this historic house is its romantic-yet-spooky ghost story. The guide tells it well, and locals swear it's true. Visit and decide for yourself whether or not the Benton house is haunted.

⚞ Dinosaur State Park

West St., exit 23 off I-91, Rocky Hill; (203) 529-8423. Park: year-round, daily, 9-4:30. Free. Museum: year-round, Tues.-Sun., 9-4:30. Adults, $2; 6-17, $.50.

Imagine finding real, 185-million-year-old (Jurassic Period) dinosaur tracks! That's what happened here in 1966 during excavation for a new state building. The fossil tracks, three-toed impressions ranging from 10 to 16 inches in length, are now protected in a large geodesic dome. What type of dinosaur made these tracks? Nobody knows for sure, but you'll see a full-size replica of the scientists' best guess, a dilophosaurus, on display here. Bring 10 pounds of plaster of paris and one-quarter cup of vegetable oil, and make your own cast of a dinosaur footprint. The park also has nature trails and a gift shop.

⁂ Holland Brook Nature Center

1361 Main St., exit 7 off Rte. 2, Glastonbury; (203) 633-8402. Tues.-Fri., 1-5; Sat., 10-5; Sun., 1-4. Free. Discovery Room: $1 per person for nonmembers.

"Green" tots (and aren't they all, these days?) will love connecting with nature at this center, run by the Connecticut Audubon Society. Best for kids up to the third grade or so, the hands-on Discovery Room offers do-it-yourself craft projects (make footprints with inkpads, for example), a skull collection, a puppet theater, and live animals. Other exhibits feature native flora and fauna and the Connecticut River ecosystem. Wear walking shoes and plan to hike the nature trails in adjacent Earle Park; maps are available at the center.

⁂ Mill Pond Falls

Garfield St., Newington; (203) 666-4661. Year-round.

Once surrounded by Indian wigwams, this area is now a lovely town park with its own natural waterfall. Enjoy a picnic here, as ducks paddle across the pond.

⁂ New Britain Youth Museum

30 High St., New Britain; (203) 225-3020. Year-round, Tues.-Fri., 1-5; Sat., 10-4. Donations requested.

A doll collection, a miniature circus display, multicultural exhibits, and a small petting zoo are featured here, along with changing exhibits. The museum is affiliated with the Hungerford Outdoor Center in Kensington.

⁂ Hungerford Outdoor Center

191 Farmington Ave., exit 35 off I-84, Kensington; (203) 827-9064. Year-round, Tues.-Fri., 1-5; Sat., 10-5. April-Oct., also open Sun., 1-5. Summer, open Tues.-Sat., 10-5. Closed Mondays and holidays. Adults, $2; 2-17, $1; under 2, free.

Take a walk on the wild side, with exotic animals and Connecticut wildlife, friendly farm animals, hiking trails, and (best) a pond with an observation station.

❧ Fruit Picking

There's plenty of picking outside the city of Hartford, especially to the south of town. Here are some possibilities: Bell Town Orchards, 475 Matson Hill Rd., S. Glastonbury, (203) 633-2789 (apples and blueberries); Riverview Farm, 593 Tryon St., S. Glastonbury, (203) 633-0200 (apples and strawberries); and Rose's Berry Farm, Matson Hill Rd., S. Glastonbury, (203) 633-7467, (strawberries, blueberries, and raspberries). For a complete directory, contact the Connecticut Department of Agriculture, Marketing Division, at (203) 566-3671.

❧ Roaring Brook Nature Center

70 Gracey Rd. off Rte. 44, Canton; (203) 693-0263. Tues.-Sat., 10-5; Sun., 1-5. Closed Mondays during the school year. Adults, $2; children (up to age 12), $1.

This interpretive center features an Indian longhouse and live animals, along with seasonal exhibits and self-guided nature walks.

▶ RESTAURANTS

❧ The Pavilion

State House Square, Hartford. Daily, 7-midnight.

For variety and ease, you can't beat Cafe Court on the second floor of the Pavilion. The building is smack in the middle of all the action at State House Square and is an architecturally interesting bit of art deco, featuring lots of plants, glass, and lights. Ride the glass elevator to the second floor and take your pick of fare: deli sandwiches, tacos and enchiladas, salads, pizza, and more. Save room for dessert; on the first floor, you'll find Ben & Jerry's ice cream and Jessica's Cookies.

❧ Brown, Thomson & Co.

942 Main St., Hartford; (203) 525-1600. Daily, lunch and dinner; Sunday brunch.

It looks like a T.G.I. Friday's but more so, with lots of stuff—stuffed (real) animals, department store mannequins, old musical instruments, and such. In fact, this used to be a department store. It's fun, it's noisy, and the menu is fun, too, especially the "Food from the Fifties" column. Don't arrive too late on Friday or Saturday night or you'll run into the singles crowd, which will only depress you.

❧ Sharpy's Lobster Spa

159 Rainbow Rd., Rte. 20 West, East Granby. Mon.-Fri., 9-6; Sat., 9-5.

This take-out place is north of Hartford, convenient to visitors going to Newgate Prison or the New England Air Museum. At front is a fish market (kids can take a peek at the lobster pool), while out back is a take-out sandwich counter. Best bets: the lobster croissant or, for hearty appetites, the lobster grinder. From the picnic tables outside you'll get a run-way view of planes taking off from Bradley International Airport.

⌁ Manchester Seafood Market and Restaurant
43 Oak St., Manchester; (203) 649-9937. Daily, 11-5.

Nothing fancy here, just good, fresh seafood at this local fish market and restaurant. It's a quick, inexpensive place to stop before or after you visit the Lutz Children's Museum. Try the clam fritters or chowder.

⌁ The Heavenly Hog
520 Center St., Manchester; (203) 649-1212. Lunch and dinner, Mon.-Sat.; closed Sun.

A great place to pig out if you love frisky barbecue. Wonderful Texas-style chili (with sirloin tips) and that guaranteed kid pleaser, grilled foot-long hot dogs with fries.

ESSEX AND THE CONNECTICUT RIVER VALLEY

A visit to charming, postcard-pretty Essex is like a trip to the past. Stroll down tree-lined Main Street, and you'll see gracious old colonial homes where sea captains and shipbuilders once lived with their families. Once an important shipbuilding town, Essex is where America's first warship, the *Oliver Cromwell,* was built.

Stand at the lower reaches of the Connecticut River and you can almost picture an old side-wheeler riverboat churning up the river on its voyage from New York to Hartford. Although schooners have been replaced by pleasure craft and riverboats have given way to automobiles, it's possible for visitors to get a taste of the river's glory days. You can even take a ride on an authentic riverboat. Combine your cruise with a steam-train ride, and you'll get a delightful tour of the Connecticut River Valley, albeit the 20th-century version. For more river lore, visit the River Museum. Or for something completely different, tour the fantasy castle-turned-state-park or the museum that's positively nutty.

⌁ Steam Train and Riverboat
Valley Railroad Co., exit 3 off Rte. 9, Essex; (203) 767-0103. Schedules change depending on season; check locally for exact departure times. Every train connects with the riverboat except the last train of the day. No boat service with Christmas train rides. Adults, $14 (train only, $8.50); 2-11, $7 (train only, $4.25).

There's an old-fashioned magic about a steam train ride. Kids find it exciting—the smoke billowing and whistles blasting—while adults find it relaxing. This attraction combines a steam-train ride from Essex to Chester with a riverboat cruise; the whole trip lasts about two and a half hours. The scenery is beautiful and includes rolling hills, flowering meadows, and local attractions such as Gillette Castle and the Goodspeed Opera House. Bring a picnic to enjoy on the riverboat, if you wish. Off season, visit in fall for an unforgettable view of autumn foliage. Or come at Christmastime, when you'll share the train with Santa, Mrs. Claus, and their elves.

‍ Connecticut River Museum

Main St., Essex; (203) 767-8269. Year-round, Tues.-Sun., 10-5. Adults, $3; under 12 free.

At the foot of Main Street in Essex, where the old steamboat dock has been restored, you'll find a full-size replica of America's first submarine. Constructed in 1775, *American Turtle* was clumsy and ineffective against the British; still, it's interesting to look at. The River Museum also houses ship models, navigational instruments, shipbuilding displays, and special exhibits.

‍ Gillette Castle State Park

Off Rte. 82, Hadlyme; (203) 526-2336. Castle: Memorial Day–Columbus Day, daily, 10-5; weekends, 10-4. Columbus Day–last weekend before Christmas, weekends, 10-4. Park: weekends, 10-4. Castle: adults, $2; 6-11, $1. Park only: free.

Your kids may not know who actor William Gillette was—for that matter, you might not remember him, either. But visiting his 24-room fantasy castle is a fun way to get acquainted. Best known for his role as Sherlock Holmes, Gillette was a rather eccentric character himself, and the house is full of creative mechanical touches. It's also full of feline-themed artifacts; Gillette shared the castle with 15 cats during his residence from 1919 to 1937. After his death, the estate was designated a state park. Now, you can picnic here, take a hike, go fishing, or, for a real adventure, rent a canoe here and camp at Selden State Park, a 528-acre island near Gillette Castle that's accessible only by water.

‍ Goodspeed Opera House

Rte. 82, East Haddam; (203) 873-8668. Tours offered on Mon., 1-3 P.M., and Sat., 11-1:30, June-Aug. Adults, $1; under 12, $.50.

This wonderful Victorian "gingerbread" structure was a popular riverside theater from the late 1800s to the 1920s. Nearly demolished in the

1950s, this unique landmark was rescued, restored, and now features musical theater productions. Take a behind-the-scenes tour of the opera house or take in a show. Older children who enjoy the performing arts will find a visit to the Goodspeed a real treat.

Devil's Hopyard State Park
Three miles north of junction of Rtes. 82 and 156, East Haddam; (203) 873-8566.

This scenic area offers 15 miles of hiking trails—one steep side, one gentler side. Hike along the stream to Chapman Falls, a 60-foot cascade. Fish in the trout-stocked stream, enjoy a picnic, or bring camping gear and spend the night. Beware: legend has it that the devil lived here. That should inspire some interesting ghost stories around the campfire....

Connecticut Yankee Information & Science Center
Injun Hollow Rd., off Rte. 151, Haddam Neck; (203) 267-9279. July and Aug., Mon.-Fri., 9-4; Sat., 9-5; Sun., 12-5; Sept.-June, Mon.-Fri., 9-4. Closed holidays. Free.

Part of the Connecticut Yankee nuclear power plant, the center offers several hands-on exhibits for kids, and films, science demonstrations, and computer games. Making the most of its location on the east bank of the Connecticut River, the center maintains a self-guided nature trail, picnic area, and boat dock.

Haddam Meadows State Park
Rte. 154, Haddam; (203) 566-2304. Daily, 8 A.M.–sunset.

Fly a kite, toss a Frisbee, or just stretch your legs; this 175-acre meadowland (the river floodplain) offers lots of room to roam, along with fishing, picnicking, boating, and, in winter, cross-country skiing.

Mary's Doll House
56 Neptune Ave., Moodus; (203) 873-8301. Sat. and Sun. For hours, and weekday schedule, please call. Free.

If someone in your group is a doll fanatic, stop by this family-run doll and miniature museum.

Special Note: While in Moodus, listen for the "Moodus Noises." These strange, subterranean rumblings have been variously explained as the threats of evil spirits (according to Indian legend), witches in the mountain (according to early white settlers), and emanations from pearls (according to a British scientist, who disappeared while researching the subject). Modern scientists believe the sounds are caused by movement along intersecting fractures in the earth's crust.

🥢 Fruit Picking

One of the busiest spots in the area is Lyman Orchards, Routes 147 and 157 in Middlefield, (203) 349-1566; it offers pick-your-own sweet corn, raspberries, tomatoes, squash, pumpkins, apples, peaches, and strawberries in season. The farm store sells produce and baked goods and hosts special events in summer and fall. For a complete directory of pick-your-own farms, roadside stands, and cider mills, call the Connecticut Department of Agriculture, Marketing Division, at (203) 566-3671.

🥢 Chatfield Hollow State Park

Exit 63 off I-95, .5 mi. west of Killingworth Center on Rte. 80, Killingworth; (203) 566-2304. Daily, 8 A.M.–sunset.

An old waterwheel, a covered bridge, a pond, a brook, and red pine groves make this a truly exceptional park. Swim in Schreeder Pond, walk the nature trail along the brook, or hike the well-marked trails (a four-and-a-half-mile loop passes points of interest). The pond is stocked with trout. The park is part of Cockaponset State Forest, where you'll find additional hiking trails, cross-country skiing, and snowmobiling in winter.

🥢 Wadsworth Falls State Park

Rte. 157, Middlefield; (203) 566-2304. Daily, 8 A.M.–sunset.

A beautiful waterfall with a scenic overlook is the most outstanding feature here. Also enjoy fishing, hiking, swimming, picnicking, and, in springtime, colorful laurel. There are ice-skating and cross-country skiing in winter.

🥢 Hurd State Park

Rte. 151, East Hampton; (203) 566-2304. Daily, 8 A.M.–sunset.

Located on the east bank of the Connecticut River, this park features several hiking trails—some through the woods, some along the river, and some to high points with scenic views. Pack your gear and fish in the Connecticut River. There's cross-country skiing in winter.

🥢 Boat Cruises

In addition to the riverboat ride previously described, several other cruise options are available. Choose a one-and-a-half-hour trip to Essex Harbor or a two-hour trip around Long Island Sound, departing from Dock 'N Dine Restaurant at Saybrook Point. Contact Deep River Navigation Company, River St., Deep River, (203) 526-4954. Cruises are offered late June to Labor Day and weekends in September.

Cruise from Haddam to the ports of Sag Harbor and Greenport, New York, across Long Island Sound. Explore for three hours, then return to

Haddam. The trip lasts all day. Contact Camelot Cruises, One Marine Park, Haddam; (203) 345-4507. This cruise is offered June through Labor Day.

RESTAURANTS

Many of the restaurants in this area of Connecticut are found in fine country inns—not the best of choices if you're dining with small fry. Your best bet is to head to Old Saybrook, where you'll find fast-food franchises and some casual family restaurants.

Dock 'N Dine
Old Saybrook Point; (203) 388-4665. Lunch and dinner; Sunday brunch, 11-2.

The ocean view from the dining room can't be beat. For a special treat, try the locally famous Sunday brunch and feast on on Belgian waffles topped with fresh strawberries or omelets made to order. The brunch spread includes several breakfast items, plenty of homemade bread, salads, crepes, and meat dishes. Reservations are suggested.

Pat's Kountry Kitchen
Mill Rd. and Rte. 154, Old Saybrook; (203) 388-4784. Mon.-Sat., 6 A.M.–9 P.M. Sun., 'til 12:30 P.M.

There's a little bit of everything on the menu here: steaks, Italian specialties, seafood, soups, sandwiches. It's a quick breakfast stop, and great for early birds since it opens at six. Children's lunch and dinner menus offer the usual burgers, dogs, and grilled cheese. The setting is casual; the daily specials are good and cheap.

Oliver's Taverne
Oliver's Corner Shopping Center, Plains Rd., Essex; (203) 767-2633. Mon.-Thurs., 11:30-10:30; Fri. and Sat., 11:30-11; Sunday brunch, 11:30-4.

A bit fancier than the other two recommendations, this "eating and drinking emporium" (the tavern's words) is a big, multilevel barn-wood affair with lots of wood, brass, and cozy fireplaces. Blackboard specials include everything from fried clams to pot roast to baked stuffed lobster; prices are moderate.

GREATER NEW HAVEN

The next time you lick a lollipop, fish with a steel fishhook, or pop open a
bottle with a corkscrew, thank the folks of New Haven. Those items were
invented here, along with the first steamboat and rubber footwear. The
city also takes credit for creating the sports of football (dreamed up by a
Yale rugby coach) and Frisbee throwing (inspired by Yalies tossing their
pie plates into the air). Of course, New Haven residents have a couple of
other reasons to boast. The most obvious is Yale University, one of the
country's oldest and most respected colleges. Yale's outstanding museums
are not to be missed, especially the Peabody Museum of Natural History.

New Haven is also a center for regional theater, the most famous
being the Yale Repertory Theater, where many top-flight actors have
honed their skills, and the Long Wharf Theater, birthplace of several
Broadway plays over the years. Whether you're in town for museum hopping, theater going, or attending the Harvard-Yale game, you'll realize
that New Haven is a college town—and more.

Don't forget your lollipop.

☃ Peabody Museum of Natural History
*Yale University, 170 Whitney Ave., exit 3 off I-91, New Haven; (203)
432-5050. Mon.-Sat., 10-5; Sun. and holidays, 12-5. Adults, $2.50; 3-
15, $1. Free hours Mon.-Fri., 3-5 P.M.*

You don't have to know a pterodactyl from a triceratops to be im-
pressed by this museum. A massive mural provides a dramatic backdrop
for life-size prehistoric creatures in the Hall of Dinosaurs. Youngsters will
be amazed, and delighted, by the sight of the 65-foot brontosaurus skeleton. Elsewhere the natural history of our planet is traced through miner-
alogy, meteorites, and zoology. The Peabody is one of the best museums
of its kind in the country. Don't miss it.

☃ Yale Collection of Musical Instruments
*15 Hullhouse Ave., New Haven; (203) 432-0822. Sept.-July, Tues.-Thurs,
1-4. Closed Aug. and during University recesses. Free.*

Budding musicians will be inspired by this collection of 850 exquisite instruments, some dating back to the 16th century. Included are historical violins, harpsichords, and woodwinds, with Western and non-
Western pieces on display. Concerts are presented periodically; call for a
schedule. The building is located on Hullhouse Avenue, the street described by Charles Dickens as the most beautiful in America.

⅋ The Only Game in Town

275 Valley Service Rd., exit 11N/12S off I-91, North Haven; (203)
239-GOLF. March-Nov., Mon.-Fri., 11-10; Sat. and Sun., 10:30 A.M.-
11 P.M., weather permitting. Free admission; activities charges.

This is one of those mega sports complexes that attract older kids and
sports-happy moms and dads. Miniature golf, a driving range, indoor
batting cages—it's all here, waiting for you to test your prowess.

⅋ New Haven Colony Historical Society

114 Whitney Ave., New Haven; (203) 562-4183. Tues.-Fri., 10-5; Sat.
and Sun., 2-5. Adults, $2; 6-16, $1.

Local antiques are the focus here, including beloved playthings of
New Haven children who lived 300 years ago. In addition to the antique
dolls and toys, older children will enjoy seeing the photographs of old
New Haven and comparing them to the city of today. Other noteworthy
items are Eli Whitney's cotton gin and the sign from Benedict Arnold's
drugstore on Chapel Street.

⅋ Shore Line Trolley Museum

17 River Rd., exit 51E off I-91, East Haven; (203) 467-6927. Memorial
Day–Labor Day, daily, 11-5. May and Dec., Sat. and Sun.; April and
Nov., Sun. only; Sept. and Oct., Sat., Sun., and holidays; all 11-5. Adults,
$5; 2-11, $2.

Kid-appeal is guaranteed here, where the highlight is a three-mile
ride on a vintage 1911 trolley car. Adults will get a chuckle out of the old
advertising slicks posted in the cars. More than 100 trolley cars are on
view, many antique, from the United States and Canada. If you dare, sign
up for a special "Terrifying Trolley Trip" at Halloween. Wear a suitably
bewitching costume.

⅋ Connecticut Children's Museum

22 Wall St. (corner of Wall and Orange), exit 3 off I-91, New Haven;
(203) 562-KIDS. Summer, Tues.-Thurs., and Sat. and Sun., 10-4. Fall,
winter, and spring, Sat. and Sun., 10-4. Per person, $3.

This delightful museum is set up like a little village where kids can
indulge in imaginative role playing. There's a hospital, a grocery store, a
school, a restaurant, and more, each equipped with plenty of props and
dress-up clothing. Parents won't feel silly joining in—in fact, the museum
staff encourages it. Young visitors will learn by doing, and have lots of fun
in the process. The recommended age range is toddler to seven years.

✺ Grove Street Cemetery

227 Grove St., between Prospect and Ashmun streets, New Haven. Gates close at 4.

Visit the gravesites of Eli Whitney, Charles Goodyear, Noah Webster, and other famous figures here. Established in 1796, this cemetery is a good place to try your hand at grave rubbing.

✺ Hammonasset Beach State Park

Exit 62 South off I-95, Madison; (203) 245-2785. Daily, 8 A.M.–sunset. Parking fee, Memorial Day–Sept.; off season, free.

A two-mile stretch of white, sandy beach is the main attraction at this popular recreation area, which is Connecticut's largest shoreline park. Swim in Long Island Sound, try your luck at fishing, or hike along marked trails through salt marsh areas. There's even a nature center with interpretive center: boating, camping, scuba diving, and concessions, too.

✺ East Rock Park

East Rock Rd., Willow St. exit off I-91, New Haven; (203) 787-6086. Daily, sunrise-sunset. Summit closed to vehicles Nov. 1–April 1, weekdays; open weekends, weather permitting.

The best feature of this city park is its height. Drive up and you'll get an aerial view of the city, the harbor, and Long Island Sound. Also on the grounds are an arboretum, a bird sanctuary, playgrounds, nature trails, and picnic facilities.

✺ West Rock Park and West Rock Nature Center

Wintergreen Ave., New Haven; (203) 787-8016. West Rock Park: daily, 9 A.M.–sunset. Free. Nature Center: Mon.-Sat., 10-4; Sun., 12-4. Free.

You can have loads of family fun here, including at Judges Cave, on hiking trails, and at a small zoo with native animals. West Rock Park surrounds West Rock, which is 428 feet high. The summit is reachable by hiking, biking, or by car. Along the ridge you'll enjoy excellent views of New Haven harbor and Long Island Sound. West Rock Nature Center has displays of birds, insects, butterflies, and native animals. The center is surrounded by 40 acres of woodland with nature trails, ponds, and meadows.

✺ Lighthouse Point Park

Two Lighthouse Rd., exit 50 off I-95, New Haven; (203) 787-8016. Memorial Day–Labor Day, 6 A.M.–9 P.M. Parking fee.

This 82-acre waterfront park and beach has a delightful attraction: an antique carousel, set in a turn-of-the-century beach pavilion. You'll also find nature trails, playgrounds, and lots of happy kids splashing in the ocean.

✌ Fort Nathan Hale and Black Rock Fort

Woodward Ave., exit 50 off I-95 North, New Haven; (203) 787-8790. Daily, Memorial Day–Labor Day. Free.

These reconstructed Revolutionary War and Civil War forts give kids a chance to play soldier with reasonable authenticity. Located on the eastern shore of New Haven harbor, the forts have bunkers, gun emplacements, breastworks, and there's even a Civil War–era drawbridge that really works.

✌ Sleeping Giant State Park

Rte. 10, Hamden; (203) 789-7489. Daily, 8 A.M.–sunset. Parking fee charged on weekends and holidays.

Two miles of mountaintop form the outline of a "sleeping giant" along the skyline. The park is a popular hiking area, with a 25-mile network of nature trails. A one-and-a-half-mile trail leads to a stone lookout tower on the peak of Mount Carmel, offering great views of Long Island Sound. You can go rock climbing and stream fishing, too.

✌ Wharton Brook State Park

Rte. 5, Wallingford; (203) 566-2304. Parking free.

Quiet and peaceful, this park is a pleasant out-of-the-city escape. Fish, swim, or enjoy a picnic here in relative solitude. Ice skating in winter.

✌ Ansonia Nature & Recreation Center

10 Deerfield Ln., Rte. 243 or Rte. 115, Ansonia; (203) 736-9360. Park: daily, sunrise-sunset. Center: daily, 9-5; closed major holidays. Free.

This lovely, 104-acre park boasts an interpretive center, two miles of nature trails, a fishing pond, picnic pavilions, and beautiful fern and wildflower gardens. Cross-country skiing in winter.

✌ Milford Amusement Center

Boston Post Rd., exit 39B off I-95, Milford; (203) 877-3229. Daily: Sun.-Thurs., 10 A.M.–1 A.M.; Fri. and Sat., 10 A.M.–2 A.M. Kiddie Land open Sun.-Thurs., 10-9 or -10 P.M.; Fri. and Sat., 10 A.M.–midnight.

When they've had enough wholesome outdoor activity and need a little high-tech fun, this is the place. You'll find amusements ranging from video and pinball games (300 or so) to a giant laser-tag arena. Kiddie Land has coin-operated games and rides and miniskeeball; other options include miniature golf, bumper boats, and batting cages. (Some of these are outdoors, so kids will get a little fresh air in spite of themselves.) For refreshments, there's a Nathan's Famous Restaurant.

⌘ Boat Cruises

If you want to see the area by sea, you have several options. Tours of New Haven harbor and Long Island Sound are offered on the *Liberty Belle,* departing from Long Wharf Dock in New Haven. Visit Liberty Belle Cruises on Long Wharf (exit 46 off I-95) or call (203) 562-4163. Several cruise companies offer 40-minute, narrated tours of the 27 tiny Thimble Islands in Long Island Sound. Boats depart from Stony Creek Dock in Branford; most run May through October. Sign up with the captain or vessel that strikes your fancy at Stony Creek Dock, or call *Sea Mist II,* (203) 481-4841; *Sea Venture,* (203) 397-3921; or *Volsunga III,* (203) 488-9978, 481-3345.

⌘ Hayrides and Sleigh Rides

Who can resist the lure of a bumpity hayride in autumn or a cozy sleigh ride through the season's first snowfall? Here are some options: Field View Farm, 707 Derby Avenue (Route 34) in Derby, hosts hayrides every Friday night from August through October, weather permitting. Rides run from 6:30 to 9:30 P.M. "Haunted Hayrides" happen at Halloween. Call (203) 795-5415 for a schedule and rates. The oldest operating farm in Connecticut, Field View, has hayrides plus a petting zoo and homemade ice cream. Neubig Farms, 111 North Hill Road, North Haven, features farm animals, a picnic area, pick-your-own pumpkins, hayrides, and sleigh rides. Call (203) 234-0018 or (800) 4-HAYRIDE. Maple View Farm, 603 Orange Center Road, Orange, offers hayrides, sleigh rides, and pony rides by appointment. Call (203) 799-6495.

◀ RESTAURANTS

⌘ Louis' Lunch

263 Crown St., New Haven; (203) 562-5507. Sept.-July, 12-4; closed Aug.

Do your kids consider burgers one of the four major food groups? Take them to the place where America's first hamburger patty was slapped on a bun in 1898 (the original broilers are still in use). There's a children's menu, too. The restaurant is located downtown, in the theater district.

⌘ Chuck's

341 Whalley Ave., New Haven; (203) 776-6851. Daily, 6 A.M.–7 P.M.

This Jewish deli is a favorite local spot for breakfast, lunch, or a low-key dinner. Chuck's specialty is a three-egg omelet stuffed with lox, onions, and cream cheese, with crispy home fries on the side. While that may not appeal to the kids (their loss), the potato pancakes or cheese blintzes probably will.

⛉ Jimmies of Savin Rock

5 Rock St., West Haven; (203) 934-3212. Lunch and dinner.

How can you get this close to the water and not do the "seafood-with-a-view" dinner thing? Since 1925, local families and tourists have flocked to this huge fish house, for its views of Long Island Sound and great seafood. Get it fried, broiled, baked, stuffed—there are plenty of choices, including a luscious lobster roll. Landlubbers can have chicken and steak, and of course there's a children's menu. Moderate prices.

SOUTHWEST CONNECTICUT

The southwest corner of Connecticut offers attractions aplenty for visiting families. State-of-the-art interactive museums and old-fashioned amusement parks wait to be explored; enticing natural attractions include beaches, woodland trails, and wildlife sanctuaries. You could bypass this area on the way to the Big Apple, but look what you'd miss: touring an 1868 lighthouse; taking a sleigh ride on a working farm; playing astronaut at the Challenger Learning Center; admiring the Siberian tigers at the Beardsley Zoo; and seeing a tube worm face to face at Norwalk's Maritime Center. Intrigued? Here are the details, and lots more to tempt you to meander a bit.

⛉ Beardsley Zoological Gardens

Noble Ave., exit 27A off I-95, Bridgeport; (203) 576-8082. Daily, 9-4. Closed Thanksgiving, Christmas, and New Year's Day. Adults, $3.75; 5-15, $2; 3-4, $1; 2 and under, free. Parking fee.

There are 300 reasons to like the Beardsley Zoo, Connecticut's largest —the 300 species that call this zoo home. From the Siberian tigers to the pony offering rides at the quaint, New England farm-themed children's zoo, your kids are sure to make a new friend or two. If you're in the area, don't miss it.

⛉ The Discovery Museum

4450 Park Ave., exit 27 off I-95, Bridgeport; (203) 372-3521. Tues.-Sat., 10-5; Sun., 12-5. Closed Mon. and major holidays. Adults, $5.50; 4-18, $3.50.

Wow. This interactive art-and-science museum features 100 permanent exhibits, not to mention a planetarium, art galleries, changing exhibits, and more. A major attraction is the Challenger Learning Center, where kids can play astronaut with computer-simulated space missions.

☸ The Barnum Museum

820 Main St., exit 27 off I-95, Bridgeport; (203) 331-1104. Tues.-Sat., 10-4:30; Sun., 12-4:30. Adults, $5; 4-18, $3.

Your kids may never have heard of tiny Tom Thumb, but they'll probably get a kick out of this circus history "lesson," dedicated to P.T. Barnum and "the Greatest Show on Earth." The most child-pleasing space here is the third floor, with Tom Thumb's tiny carriage and furniture and a 20-by-40-foot, hand-carved miniature circus. The Clown Corner has clown props and costumes; put your nose to the clown's make-up mirror and see yourself in clown-face.

☸ Audubon Center of Greenwich

613 Riversville Rd., Greenwich; (203) 869-5272. Tues.-Sun., 9-5. Adults, $3; children, $1.50.

Families flock to the bird observation window here (sorry), and you're sure to find some new additions for your bird book—the whole place is a bird sanctuary. There are guided walks for families on weekends, with 15 miles of hiking trails, along with an exceptional visitor's center and a bookstore and gift shop.

☸ Wilton Heritage Museum

249 Danbury Rd., Rte. 7, Wilton; (203) 762-7257. Tues.-Thurs., 10-4; call for Sun. openings. Adults, $2; children free when accompanied by an adult.

A tour of this 1756 classic center-chimney house can be endurable for kids thanks to permanent exhibits of dolls, toys, and dollhouses from 1750 to 1850. (You know your offspring better than we do…you decide.)

☸ Quassy Amusement Park

Rte. 64, exit 16E/17W off I-84, Middlebury; (203) 758-2913, (800) FOR-PARK. April-June, Sat. and Sun., 10-10; July and Aug., daily, 10-10. All-day ride ticket: $9.75. Beach passes: adults, $2.50; children, $1.50. Parking fee.

Hot dogs, sno-cones, cotton candy, stomach-churning rides—what more could any kid (or young-at-heart mommy or daddy) ask for. Well, how about swimming and boating in Lake Quassapaug, a video arcade, a petting zoo, and miniature golf? It's an old-fashioned, all-American good time, complete with wandering minstrels, magic acts, and, on Friday nights, live music (heavy on the oldies acts and country western).

➔ Stamford Museum & Nature Center

39 Scofieldtown Rd., Rte. 15, exit 35, Stamford; (203) 322-1646. Mon.-
Sat. and holidays, 9-5; Sun., 1-5. Planetarium shows: Sun., 3:30. Closed
Thanksgiving, Christmas, and New Year's Day. Adults, $4; 5-13, $3.

The showpiece of this 118-acre complex is a 19th-century working
farm. You'll enjoy poking around the country store and seven galleries
(including one highlighting Native American customs) and meandering
the woodland trails. Be sure to visit the zoo, and catch a show at the planetarium. Seasonal activities, like maple-syrup-making demonstrations, are
a special delight here. If you're in town, don't miss it.

➔ Cabaret Children's Theatre

263 Golden Hill St., exit 27A off I-95, Bridgeport; (203) 576-1636.
Shows Sat., 12 and 2:30; Sun., 12. Per ticket, $7.50.

Catch your favorite fairy tales and fables here, updated for the 1990s
and presented with original music. Recent productions have included *The
Little Mermaid, The Phantom of the Opera, Snow White,* and *The Jungle Book.*
Performances are geared toward kids age two to 12. It's a lovely way to
spend an afternoon and a splendid rainy-day activity.

➔ Seaside Park

Exit 27 off I-95, Bridgeport; (203) 576-7233. Parking fee.

Open year-round, this pretty 370-acre park was donated to the city of
Bridgeport by P.T. Barnum. Notable features include a beautiful beach
and picnic areas.

➔ The Maritime Center at Norwalk

10 North Water St., exit 14N/15S off I-95, S. Norwalk; (203) 852-0700.
Memorial Day–Labor Day, daily, 10-6. Fall and winter hours, 10-5. Closed
Thanksgiving, Christmas, and New Year's Day. Adults, $7.50; children,
$6.50. Theater admission: adults, $5.50; children, $4.50; under 2, free.

Explore the marine life of Long Island Sound at this family-friendly
waterfront museum. Attractions include an IMAX theater, an aquarium,
and a hall dedicated to maritime history with several interactive exhibits.
Your kids will love the close-up glimpses of underwater inhabitants; you
may be inspired to build your own wooden boat after watching the
craftspeople here demonstrate their techniques.

➔ Sheffield Island Lighthouse

Ferry service from Hope Dock, corner of Washington and North Water streets,
Norwalk; (203) 838-9444. Mid-May–Oct.; call for daily ferry schedule.
Adults, $9; 2 and under, free.

Could you handle living in a lighthouse? (Hint: you wouldn't need a Stairmaster.) Take a scenic ferry boat ride to this three-acre park with an 1868 lighthouse. Explore the lighthouse's four levels and 10 rooms; bring along a picnic.

❦ My Three Sons' Family Fun Center
250 Westport Ave., Norwalk; (203) 846-9810. Memorial Day–Labor Day, daily, 11 A.M.–midnight. Labor Day–Memorial Day, Sun.-Thurs., 11-11; Fri. and Sat., 11 A.M.–midnight. Pay as you go, with tokens.

This place has gotten many a local parent through a rainy summer week or school vacation, with 8,000 square feet of games and amusements. There are 70 interactive games, sports-themed games, bumper cars, kiddie rides, a pop-a-shot basketball cage, and (by the time you read this), more. Best for kids age four and up.

❦ Sherwood Island State Park
Exit 18 off I-95, Westport; (203) 226-6983. Daily, 8 A.M.–sunset. Parking fee, Memorial Day–Sept.; off-season, free.

When you need a beach break, this one can't miss. It's a mile and a half of beachfront on Long Island Sound, suitable for swimming and saltwater fishing. Large, open fields are a great natural playscape—bring a ball and glove and a picnic. Services include a bathhouse and concessions.

❦ Sportland America
40 Mill Plain Rd., Danbury; (203) 730-0730. Memorial Day–Labor Day, Mon.-Thurs., 10-10; Fri. and Sat., 10-midnight; Sun., 12-10. Skating day pass: adults, $4; under 6, $2.50. Evening pass: adults, $5; under 6, $2.50.

Remember how much fun it was to go to a roller rink? Turn your kids on to same here, or take advantage of the bumper cars and miniature golf course.

❦ Hayrides and Sleigh Rides
Thrill to an old-fashioned, horse-drawn hayride or sleigh ride at Gems Morgans, 75 North Poverty Rd., Southbury; (203) 264-6190. Call for rates and reservations.

▶ **RESTAURANTS**

❦ The Restaurant at Captain's Cove
1 Bostwick Ave., exit 26 off I-95, Bridgeport; (203) 335-7104. Memorial Day–Oct., Mon.-Thurs., 11 A.M.–midnight; Sat., 11 A.M.–1 A.M.; Sun., 11-11.

Captain's Cove is a great place to knock around, with its boardwalk, charter boats to gawk at, and little Victorian shops. The restaurant fare ranges from a boxed lunch to a lobster bake; kids love the old-fashioned arcade games and rides.

ॐ Sycamore Drive-In

282 Greenwood Ave., Bethel; (203) 748-2716. Year-round. Summer hours: Mon.-Fri., 6 A.M.–9:30 P.M.; Sat., 7 A.M.–9:30 P.M.; Sun., 7 A.M.– 7:30 P.M. Winter hours: Mon.-Wed., 6 A.M.–8:30 P.M.; Thurs.-Sat., 6 A.M.–9:30 P.M.; Sun., 7 A.M.–5 P.M.

Picky about your upholstery? Forget this place and skip ahead to the next listing. The Sycamore is one of the last places on the planet where they offer car hop service; you flash your lights, they take your order, and eventually the car hop will attach a big (yeah, greasy) tray of food to your window. This isn't just a restaurant, it's a cultural experience. And the food's not bad; try the chicken-in-a-basket with a mug of the Sycamore's secret-recipe homemade root beer. Anybody seen the Fonz?

ॐ Bacco's

1230 Thomaston Ave., Waterbury; (203) 755-0635. Tues.-Thurs., 11:30- 10; Fri., 11:30-11; Sat., 4-11; Sun., 12-8:30. Closed Mon.

This is a homey, family-style Italian place, with an absolutely killer pizza. The sublime pie is covered with fresh clams and garlic, and baked to perfection in a brick oven. Not bad for a place that's been around for more than 60 years. Kids won't touch clams or garlic? Order a pizza for the grown-ups, and get the kids a nice order of lasagna. Mangia!

LITCHFIELD HILLS AREA

The village of Litchfield could be a movie set entitled "Quaint New England Town." It has the requisite white clapboard homes, a town green, even pristine 18th-century mansions that could be museums but in fact are private homes. The area is, without question, one of New England's most richly blessed when it comes to natural beauty.

If your children consider the appeal of a picturesque colonial village on par with a trip to a plumbing supply store, not to worry. Litchfield County, and the surrounding area, offers more than just a pretty face. Northwestern Connecticut is studded with state parks where you can camp, fish, hike, swim, ride, and picnic. Round out your visit with a museum, take in the action at Lime Rock race track, and stop at a local pick-your-own farm to load up on fresh produce.

New England Carousel Museum

95 Riverside Ave., exit 31 off I-84, Bristol; (203) 585-5411. April-Sept., daily, 10-5; Sun., 12-5. Oct.-March, closed Mon.-Tues., except for Bristol school holidays. Adults, $4; 4-13, $2.50.

Remember the thrill of your first carousel ride? Probably not, but you'll have a real appreciation for those painted ponies after a visit here. Housed in a restored, turn-of-the-century factory are wonderful examples of antique carousel art, where painters and carvers work painstakingly to restore old pieces to their past glory. Tours run every half-hour; "Kidstuff" programs offer classes in papier-mâché. Call for a schedule.

Lake Compounce Festival Park

Lake Ave., exit 31 off I-84, Bristol; (203) 583-6000. (This attraction was closed at press time but may reopen; please call ahead to confirm.)

Ready for some action? You'll find thrills aplenty at Lake Compounce, claiming to be America's oldest continually open amusement park. The park is still an appealing blend of Victorian charm (old-time shops, a carousel) and wild rides like the flume waterslide and the Wildcat roller coaster. There are live stage shows and eateries galore; the lake itself adds a touch of serenity.

White Memorial Foundation and Conservation Center

Rte. 202, Litchfield; (203) 567-0857. Conservation Center: Spring-fall, Tues.-Sat., 8:30-4:30; Sun., 11-5. Winter hours, Tues.-Sat., 9-5; Sun., 11-5. Adults, $1; under 12, $.50. Sanctuary open year-round, daily. Free.

This 4,000-acre wildlife sanctuary—including half the shoreline of Bantam Lake and the Bantam River—offers 35 miles of hiking trails. Take a guided tour or set your own pace, with time out for a picnic along the way. Bantam Lake is great for swimming, or rent a rowboat or canoe at Point Folly Marine. Be sure to stop by the Conservation Center near the entrance. It has lots of kid appeal, with a working beehive, an aquarium with turtles, and snakes, fish, and stuffed hawks and owls on display.

American Indian Archaeological Institute

Curtis Rd. off Rte. 199, Washington; (203) 868-0518. Mon.-Sat., 10-5; Sun. 12-5. Adults, $3; 6-16, $2.

If your children harbor any Western-movie notions about Native Americans, this museum will open their eyes. Exhibits highlight the Native American experience in New England, with artifacts spanning 10,000 years. Most kids are intrigued by the recreated Onondaga Indian longhouse filled with household objects and appearing as though the family will return home any minute. Dino-philes will delight in the mastodon skeleton, unearthed in nearby Farmington. Walk along an Indian trail, visit a 17th-century Indian village, and view a simulated archaeological dig.

✂ Gunn Historical Museum

On the Green, Washington; (203) 868-7756. March-Dec., Thurs.-Sat., 12-4. Free.

Of course you'll want to get a peek inside one of the lovely homes here; this 1781 house is furnished with memorabilia from several Washington homes, including exquisite dolls and dollhouses.

✂ Lime Rock Park

Rte. 112, Lakeville; (203) 435-2571. Racing on most weekends, early May–Oct. Call for schedule. Rates vary with event: $10 and up for adults; 12 and under, free.

If your kids love fast cars, lots of noise, and action, head to the track. Pro national and regional racing is held here. If you're bringing a small child, consider a regional race (not to mention earplugs); they're shorter (30 minutes as opposed to 2.5 hours) and less crowded than other spectator events. Spectators are also welcome at Tuesday practice sessions. Your ticket entitles you to a walk around the paddock area, where drivers and crews are at work on their cars.

✂ Northeast Audubon Center

Rte. 4, Sharon; (203) 364-0520. Mon.-Sat., 9-5; Sun., 1-5. Closed major holidays. Trails open daily, dawn to dusk. Adults, $4; children, $2. (Free to Audubon Society members.)

This is a hiker's paradise, with miles of nature trails. A stand-out: the Bog Meadow Trail, a short (1.25 miles), moderately challenging hike through some beautiful territory. Clearly marked, the trail is at its best in autumn, when the maples and aspens are in their fall colors. Walk along the boardwalk and beside a pond that's home to ducks, turtles, minks, and beavers. The center maintains a small zoo of animals either injured or too old to live in the wild, and some stuffed specimens. You may also see the four timber wolves in residence, Rasta, Wolfie, Timber, and Raven. They're not on display, but they're taken for daily walks by their keeper.

Lake McDonough
Beech Rock Rd., Rte. 219, Barkhamsted; (203) 379-3036. Boating, mid-April–Labor Day; fishing, mid-April–Nov.; swimming, Memorial Day–Labor Day. Parking fee.

Rent a rowboat or paddleboat and putter around this pretty, popular lake. Or go swimming, fishing, hiking, picnicking—this place has it all.

Macedonia Brook State Park
Rte. 341, Kent; (203) 566-2304. Daily, 8 A.M.–sunset.

Beautiful and wild, this park is blessed with forests, mountainous terrain, a deep gorge, upper and lower falls, wildlife, and, of course, a brook. It offers great views of the Catskill and Taconic mountain ranges, too. Hiking trails here are plentiful and color coded, and some extend along the Appalachian Trail. There's fishing, and there's cross-country skiing in winter.

Peoples State Forest
East River Rd., Barkhamsted; (203) 566-2304. Daily, 8 A.M.–sunset.

More great hiking, with trails leading past caves and springs. Drop a line into the trout-stocked Farmington River, or look for beavers building dams in the marsh. Stop for a picnic among the 200-year-old white pines in Mathies Grove. Cross-country skiing in winter.

Topsmead State Forest
Rte. 118, 2 miles west of Rte. 8, Litchfield; (203) 567-5694.

The principal attraction here is an English Tudor–style cottage, the summer home of Edith Morton Chase. Miss Chase donated the 514-acre forest to the state upon her death in 1972. The cottage is open to visitors during the summer; call first to confirm the schedule. The grounds include a 40-acre wildflower preserve and nature trail. Have a picnic at one of the tables, or spread a blanket wherever you choose. Cross-country skiing and snowshoeing in winter.

Burr Pond State Park
Rte. 8, 5 miles north of Torrington; (203) 566-2304. Daily, 8 A.M.–sunset.

Features here include trout-stocked Burr Pond, a sandy beach, streams, rivers, and interesting rock formations. Swimming, boating, and fishing are permitted. A scenic path encircles the 88-acre pond. The cross-country skiing is easy, and there's also ice skating in winter.

✨ Haystack Mountain

Rte. 272, 1 mile north of Norfolk; (203) 566-2304. Daily, 8 A.M.–sunset.

Drive halfway up the mountain and enjoy the view, especially lovely during fall foliage season. From there, active types can hike the half-mile trail to the top of the mountain. At the summit, you'll see a 34-foot-high stone tower; climb it for dramatic vistas of Long Island Sound and the Berkshires.

✨ Housatonic Meadows State Park

Rte. 7, 1 mile north of Cornwall Bridge, Sharon; (203) 566-2304. Daily, 8 A.M.–sunset.

If your group enjoys fly fishing, the clear, cold Housatonic River is a great place to test your skills on trout and bass. A two-mile stretch of river is limited to fly fishing. Enjoy a picnic under the pines on the riverbank. There are hiking and canoeing, too.

✨ Kent Falls

Rte. 7, 3 miles north of Kent; (203) 566-2304. Daily, 8 A.M.–sunset.

This cascading waterfall draws thousands of visitors each year. Climb the stairs adjacent to the falls for great views at all levels. This is a favorite scene for professional and amateur photographers.

✨ Lake Waramaug State Park

Rte. 478, 5 miles north of New Preston, Kent; (203) 566-2304. Daily, 8 A.M.–sunset.

Picturesque, placid Lake Waramaug is a super setting for a day—or weekend—of swimming, fishing, hiking, and picnicking. Ice skating in winter.

✨ Mohawk Mountain State Park and Forest

Rte. 4, Cornwall; (203) 566-2304. Daily, 8 A.M.–sunset.

In summer or, even better, during peak fall color, drive to the mountaintop for enchanting views. An abandoned fire tower serves as a lookout. There are plenty of hiking opportunities throughout the forest, with several loop trails and a section of the Appalachian Trail. Don't miss Black Spruce Bog, near forest headquarters, home of a unique community of insect-eating plants. Cross-country ski on forest roads and trails or join the downhill skiers at Mohawk Mountain Ski Area.

᠍᠍᠍᠍ Mohawk Mountain Ski Area

46 Great Hollow Rd., off Rte. 4, Cornwall; (203) 672-6100. Daily, except Christmas, generally Thanksgiving weekend–Easter. Lifts run Mon.-Sat., 8:30 A.M.–10 P.M.; Sun., 8:30-4. Lift tickets (anytime): adults, $29; 6-15, $25; under 6, $8. Partial-day passes (morning, 8:30-1; afternoon, 1-6:30; twilight, 4-10): adults, $19; 6-15, $15; under 6, $8.

Family skiing is the name of the game at Mohawk Mountain. Run by a mother-daughter team, the resort does not serve alcohol, and it offers a friendly, low-key atmosphere. Noteworthy features include night skiing (except on Sundays), snowmaking over 95 percent of the mountain's ski-able terrain, and ski programs for kids as young as age three.

Tiny tots can get into the act with Mohawk's "Try-and-see" program; kids from age five to 12 can participate in the SKIwee program, run on weekends and holidays from 10 to 3. Youngsters who can handle the chairlift with ease and make controlled wedge turns can graduate to SKIwee Tigers, a multiday instruction program, while junior speed demons can sign up for Christmas Racing Camp, a five-day course designed to hone racing skills. Group and private lessons are offered daily, and lest you doubt that Mohawk emphasizes learning, group lessons are offered four times a day.

This managable, family-friendly resort is a great place to build your confidence on skis, or to introduce your kids to this exhilarating activity. In summer, the resort offers mountain biking (including a race series) and hiking.

᠍᠍᠍᠍ Cross-Country Skiing

Connecticut's numerous state parks and state forests are open to Nordic skiers, as are several nature centers and preserves. There are also a number of cross-country ski centers, offering groomed trails, equipment rentals, and snack bars. Recommended destinations include Mohawk Mountain ski resort with more than 40 miles of trails, in Cornwall, (203) 672-6100; the Blackberry River Inn in Norfolk, (203) 542-5100, with more than 10 miles of trails, and rentals and lessons; and White Memorial Foundation in Litchfield, with 35 miles of trails through varied and beautiful conservation land. Call (203) 567-0857 for information.

◣ RESTAURANTS

᠍᠍᠍᠍ Litchfield Food Company

West St., across from Village Green, Litchfield; (203) 567-0448. Mon.-Sat., 9:30-5.

By now, you've got the idea that this area is loaded with great picnic spots; why not pack your basket here? You can select from a wide variety of gourmet take-out food. Spread your blanket, open the basket, and feast on smoked salmon with capers, artichoke salad, duck a l'orange, and chocolate mousse balls. Choose from salads, pasta dishes, sandwiches, soups, and more.

ᘔ Deer Island Gate Restaurant

Rte. 209, on Bantam Lake, Morris; (203) 567-4622. Wed.-Sat., 5-10 P.M.; Sun. buffet, 1-7; open for lunch, Memorial Day–Labor Day, Wed.-Sun., 12-2.

This is a large, casual restaurant with great views of Bantam Lake. The menu is ambitious, offering daily fish specials, steaks, pork, duck, chicken, lamb, and German dishes. Prices start at around $10 and up for entrees; there's no children's menu, but they're happy to offer half-portions of most entrees for half price. Local folks love the Sunday German buffet.

ᘔ La Tienda Cafe

Rte. 202, Federal Square shopping center, Litchfield; (203) 567-8778. Tues.-Thurs., 11:30-2:30 and 4:30-9:30; Fri. and Sat., 11:30-10; Sun., 12-9:30; Mon., 3-9.

Modern kids seem to love Mexican food, as do most grown-ups, and this little place is a happy find. You can tell a lot about a Mexican restaurant by the quality of its tortilla chips; La Tienda's are homemade and just great. Try a Mexican pizza, Arizona-style nachos (topped with ground beef), or a soup-and-appetizer combination. All the Mexican favorites are offered, along with some unique house specialties, all very reasonably priced. There's also a children's menu, but what child doesn't like tacos?

NORTHEAST CONNECTICUT

"Off the beaten track." "Where the crowds aren't." These phrases describe Connecticut's quiet corner. If modern life-with-children has left you worn out, strung out, and in need of escape, this might be the perfect place to reconnect. Besides, how could you miss showing your kids the statue honoring General Israel Putnam, who said, "Don't fire until you see the whites of their eyes?" And life is far to short to miss indulging in a home-made ice cream at U-Conn's dairy bar—the perfect reward for hiking local hills and biking country roads.

Rolling countryside, working farms, and historic inns give a pastoral feel to this undiscovered corner of Connecticut; we'll provide suggestions for some pleasant diversions as you roam.

✣ Connecticut State Museum of Natural History

University of Connecticut, Rte. 195, exit 68 off I-84, Storrs; (203) 486-4460. Videoplace: Mon., Thurs.-Sat., 12-4; Sun., 1-4. (Call ahead to confirm hours.) Shark exhibit: Mon.-Fri., 8-4. Closed July 4th, Thanksgiving, Christmas, and New Year's Eve. Free.

Great white sharks, a life-size wigwam, mounted birds of prey—these totally cool exhibits will surely capture your child's attention, along with the minerals and fossils on display at the University of Connecticut's natural history museum. And did we mention the 20 life-size interactive video games? Awesome. Special children's workshops and family festivals are held periodically; call for a schedule of events.

✣ University of Connecticut Dairy Bar and Animal Farm

(See previous listing.) Dairy bar: Mon.-Sat., 10-5; Sun., 1-5. Animal barns: daily, 10-4. Closed July 4th, Easter, Thanksgiving, and Christmas.

The University of Connecticut began as a land-grant school of agriculture; part of that heritage remains today. Visit the friendly farm animals housed at U-Conn's barns, then head to the dairy bar for the local delicacy—wonderfully sinful homemade ice cream.

✣ James F. King Indian Museum

332 Turnpike Rd., exit 47E off I-91, Somers; (203) 749-4129. April-Dec., Wed.-Fri., 11-5; Sat., 10-5; Sun., 1-5. Adults, $2; children, $1; under 5, free.

Most children will find something to grab their interest in this collection; perhaps the intricate beadwork pieces, lovingly crafted dolls, or weaponry from the French-Indian War. You'll also find nature trails and a picnic area.

✣ Nathan Hale Homestead

South St., off Rte. 44, Coventry; (203) 742-6917. Mid-May–mid-Oct., daily, 1-5. Adults, $2; under 18, $1.

Explore the life and times of Connecticut hero Nathan Hale at his 1776 family farm. The best feature for kids is a walled-in, grassy field where they can try hoop-rolling and walking on stilts. (Many parents can't resist these stilts, either.) You can picnic on the grounds. Plan your visit to coincide with one of the special events held here: "Hale to Spring," featuring baby animals; "Muster and Colonial Encampment," with tents and musket shooting, in July; and the "Lantern Tour," a house tour by candlelight, in October. Call for dates.

❧ Quinebaug Valley Trout Hatchery

Trout Hatchery Rd., exit 89 off I-395, Central Village; (203) 564-7542. Daily, 10-4. Free.

Fish-o-rama! Nearly 300,000 pounds of trout are produced here each year. Watch them in action through glass viewing walls.

❧ Roseland Cottage

Rte. 169, exit 72 off I-84, Woodstock; (203) 928-4074. Mid-May–Labor Day, Wed.-Sun., 12-5. Adults, $4; 6-12, $2.50; 5 and under, free. Half-price to state residents. Children's Teas: $10 per person.

This is one of those local landmarks that just can't be missed. Roseland is pink, pink, pink—what else?—and is Gothic revival in style. It was built by publisher Henry Bowen as a summer home. Kids will get a kick out of the indoor bowling alley, in the barn. Presidents Grant, Hayes, Harrison, and McKinley visited Roseland (wonder if Bowen made them wear those goofy bowling shoes?). A nice feature for families: Children's Teas are held throughout the summer, on various Wednesdays and Sundays, lasting two hours. Kids learn how to brew a proper pot of tea and get a friendly lesson in table etiquette. Children age three to 14 take part; parents can join the tea party if they desire.

RESTAURANTS

❧ Stoggy Hollow General Store

Rte. 198, Woodstock Valley; (203) 974-3814. Daily, 7-7.

Hard to find but worth it, this general store and eatery is cute as can be. But wait, there's more. The oversized sandwiches are messy and delicious, and the home-baked sweets are sheer heaven. Sit in the parlor of this 1836 colonial and enjoy the food and atmosphere. Need sunscreen or a fishing license? The general store, next door, has both.

Rhode Island

You might be tempted to pass by the Providence area, in a hurry to get to the more famous Rhode Island resorts of Newport, Narragansett, or Block Island. Yet this quiet, urban pocket, often named as one of America's most livable cities, has much to offer young visitors. The biggest city in the smallest state boasts a revitalized downtown area with landscaped parks and waterfront brick walkways that are perfect for strolling. Window shop along South Main Street, where historic colonial buildings have been authentically restored and now house unique boutiques, art galleries, and restaurants; visit the animals at the Roger Williams Park and Zoo; or let the little tykes run loose at the nearby Children's Museum.

🐾 Roger Williams Park, Museum & Zoo

950 Elmwood Ave. (off I-95), Providence; (401) 785-9450. Park: daily, 7 A.M.–9 P.M. Zoo: Nov.-March, 10-4; April-Oct., 10-5. Closed Thanksgiving, Christmas, New Year's Day, and during inclement weather. Adults, $3.50; 3-12, $1.50.

It's easy to spend a pleasant, busy day exploring this wonderland of parks, ponds, lakes, and gardens that cover more than 430 acres. But Roger Williams Park is more than a nature tour; a growing collection of exotic animals lives here. Elephants, giraffes, and zebras roam a replica of the African savannah. Polar bears, seals, and penguins frolic in their pools, while llamas, lemurs, wolves, bison, and flamingoes can be seen roaming within the zoo. Small fry love the International Farm. Indoor exhibits include Tropical America, a rainforest pavilion, and the Nature Center. One of the oldest zoos in the country, this one keeps getting better.

Don't go home yet—there's more to see and do. Walk the wetlands trail and try to spot native animals and plants. Visit the Museum of Natural History and the Cormack Planetarium. Don't forget the carousel, or the antique railroad train. Or—a must on muggy days—rent a boat at the Dalrymple Boathouse and explore the park's connecting waterways.

⅋ Rhode Island State Capitol

82 Smith St., Providence; (401) 277-2357. Mon.-Fri., 8:30-4:30, except holidays. Tours, 9:30-3:30.

Many believe that this impressive, white-domed Georgian marble structure is the most beautiful capitol building in America. Inside, see the full-length portrait of George Washington painted by Rhode Islander Gilbert Stuart.

⅋ Children's Museum of Rhode Island

Pitcher-Goff Mansion, 58 Walcott St., Pawtucket; (401) 726-2590. Year-round, Tues.-Sat., 10-5; Sun., 1-5. Closed the first two weeks following Labor Day. Per person, $3.50; under 1, free.

This warm, lively museum, housed in a 19th-century Victorian mansion, is a place where children can touch, draw, paint, explore, bounce, read, imagine, and learn. Have a make-believe tea party in Great Grandmother's Kitchen, explore Rhode Island on your hands and knees in the room-size map, play hide-and-seek in a climbing maze of tunnels and platforms, and more. The museum hosts good traveling exhibits, too.

⅋ Crescent Park Carousel

At the end of Bullock's Point Ave., East Providence; (401) 434-3311, (401) 433-2828. Easter Sunday–Memorial Day, Sat. and Sun., 12-9. After Memorial Day, Fri.-Sun., 12-9. July–Labor Day, Wed.-Sun., 12-9; closed Mon.-Tues., except for summer holidays. Labor Day–Columbus Day, Sat. and Sun., 12-9. $.35 per ride or 3 rides, $1.

This is a treasure. Nearly a century old, it's one of the few complete carousels of its type still operating, with the original, hand-carved and -painted horses. The neo-baroque-style band organ is carved with one-of-a-kind moving figures.

⅋ Slater Memorial Park

U.S. Rte. 1-A, Pawtucket; (401) 728-0500, ext. 257. Memorial Day–Labor Day, 8 A.M.–9 P.M.; Labor Day–Memorial Day, 8 A.M.–dusk. Carousel hours vary.

Alas, the Slater Park zoo has closed, but this is still a nice spot for a picnic, a paddle boat ride, a pony ride, and a whirl on the restored 1894 Loof carousel.

⅋ Pawtucket Red Sox Baseball

McCoy Stadium, 1 Columbus Ave., Pawtucket; (401) 724-7300. Box seats: adults, $5; 12 and under, $4. General admission: adults, $4; 12 and under, $3.

This is the AAA International Baseball League farm team of the Boston Red Sox, so you never know if one of the young hotshots on the field will make it to the majors. Cheer on your favorites from April to September.

Slater Mill Historic Site

Roosevelt Ave., Pawtucket; (401) 725-8638. Hours for general public: June–Labor Day, Sat., 10-5; Sun., 1-5. March-May and Labor Day–third Sun. in Dec., Sat. and Sun., 1-5. Adults, $4; 6-14, $2; under 6, free.

This excursion is for older children who like the sounds of and are intrigued by the mechanisms of machinery. (You know who we're talking about: the kids who can't resist a construction site and adore dismantling small home appliances.) Billed as the birthplace of American industry, the site includes the Sylvanus Brown House (1758) an early skilled-worker's home; the Wilkinson Mill (1810), which houses an authentic 19th-century machine shop; and a working, 16,000-pound waterwheel. The 90-minute tour includes demonstrations of early textile machinery, hand-spinning, and weaving.

Fruit Picking

A number of Rhode Island farms offer fruit-picking possibilities—mostly raspberries, strawberries, blueberries, blackberries, and apples in season. Pick-your-own produce farms are located throughout the state, including several in Providence County. For listings, contact the Rhode Island Division of Agriculture, 22 Hayes Street, Providence, 02908; (401) 277-2781.

RESTAURANTS

The Arcade

65 Weybosset St., Providence. Mon.-Sat., 10-6; Thurs. 'til 8.

Located in the heart of downtown Providence, the Arcade (1828) was the first enclosed shopping center in the United States. Today, you'll find a collection of eateries, offering soup (Jen's Great Soups) to nuts (J. Phib's Candy and Gourmet Ice Cream). Whether your bunch likes Greek or Chinese food, pizza, or burgers, you'll find it here. Find a table at Center Court and enjoy. Warning: when the business crowd rolls in for lunch on weekdays, the place gets mobbed.

Angelo's Civita Farnese

141 Atwells Ave., Providence; (401) 621-8171. Mon.-Sat., lunch and dinner.

This comfortable family restaurant is located in the heart of "Little Italy," and it's a true classic, known for megaportions and miniprices. All your favorite pasta dishes are on the menu, available in half-size portions for kids. (That may not be necessary if you have a small child—regular portions are huge enough to share.) Mangia, bambini!

NEWPORT

America's First Resort. Millionaire's Playground. Queen of American Resorts. Yachting Capital of the World. Visit Newport, and you'll soon understand why this island seaport has earned such superlative titles. The city echoes its past, first as a 17th-century colonial town of merchants and traders, later as the summer resort of America's richest society members. You'll find the narrow streets surrounding its harbors lined with clapboard houses that were once home to sea captains and traders. You'll also see magnificent Gilded Age mansions hugging the shoreline, extravagant summer homes for the wealthy American aristocracy during the Industrial period.

Newport remains a prestigious East Coast resort community; opulent sailboats and powerboats dot its harbors. The 17th-century mercantile harbor has turned into a contemporary center of fine restaurants, boutiques, and outdoor cafes. The beauty of the island, with its dramatic views of Narragansett Bay and the Atlantic Ocean, remains.

The summer season is crowded and congested, which is fine for people watching, but you'll want to find time to venture beyond the town center. Tour one of the mansions, by all means, but take a drive to Fort Adams Park for a picnic, take a harbor cruise, or walk the dunes at Second Beach for a pretty (and unhurried) view of this elegant coastal community.

⅋ Newport Mansions

Plan on seeing only one or two mansions (otherwise known as summer "cottages"). Children will quickly tire of the hour-long tours and the inevitable summer crowds that flock to see how the Vanderbilts, Belmonts, and Berwinds lived. You'll enjoy the tours most with older children (eight years and up), but if you're taking an infant or toddler, be prepared to carry them—most mansions are not stroller accessible. Ten mansions are open to the public. Here are three that families will enjoy the most:

⚏ The Breakers

Ochre Point Ave.; (401) 847-1000. May-Oct., daily, 10-5. Adults, $7.50; 6-11, $3.50.

The Breakers, built for Cornelius Vanderbilt, is the most palatial of Newport's mansions. You'll marvel at this 70-room castle of marble, mosaic, alabaster, and mahogany. Included is a music room, a library, bathrooms that deliver both salt and fresh water, a magnificent double loggia with commanding ocean views, and a glittery, opulent dining room.

⚏ The Beechwood

Bellevue Ave.; (401) 846-3772. Late May–Oct., daily, 10-5. Call to confirm closing time. Adults, $7.75; 6-12, $6.

Kids enjoy The Beechwood; it's a living history tour. Instead of roped-off displays and dry narration, you'll encounter the Astors' staff of servants, who will show you around the house. You are the Astors' guests for their 10th anniversary ball. The Beechwood Theater Company reenacts how life would have been at the Beechwood in the summer of 1891. If your children love make-believe, and what child doesn't, you'll have a good time here. The annual Children's Day features games, story-telling, and special activities.

⚏ Hammersmith Farm

Ocean Dr. (adjacent to Fort Adams State Park); (401) 846-7346. April–mid-Nov., daily, 10-5. Memorial Day–Labor Day, daily, 10-7. Call to confirm closing time. Adults, $6.50; 6-12, $3.

Hammersmith Farm, the Auchincloss family's summer cottage, is the only working farm left in Newport. The informal tour provides personal glimpses into the lives of the Kennedy family. When John Kennedy was in office, Hammersmith was often referred to as the "Summer White House." Its seaside location and gardens are beautiful, and children love visiting the miniature horses that graze in the fields. Or, arrive in style: combine your tour of Hammersmith Farm with a *Viking Queen* cruise. The hour-long narrated cruise passes through the harbor and bay to a private dock at Hammersmith. There, you'll disembark and tour the farm for an hour. The cost is $13 for adults and $6 for kids age four to 11.

⚏ Cliff Walk

Put the baby in a backpack and grab the little ones' hands for this dramatic walk overlooking the Atlantic Ocean. On this steep, picturesque hike, you'll see the rocky coastline at its best and pass by some of

Newport's mansions. The three-mile trail runs from Memorial Boulevard
and Eustis Avenue to Bailey's Beach. Walk it all or just part of it.

⚛ Fort Adams State Park

Ocean Dr.; (401) 847-2400. Year-round, sunrise-sunset.

Built in 1824, the fort was designed to accommodate 2,400 soldiers
with 468 mounted cannons. It is not open for public viewing, but its park
remains a great place for a picnic. There are a small beach, fishing pier,
barbecue grills, picnic tables, and lots of room here for the kids to run and
play while you savor the oceanside setting.

⚛ Rhode Island Fisherman and Whale Center

*144 Spring St.; (401) 849-1340. Daily, except Wed., 10-5. Adults, $2;
5-13, $1; under 5, free.*

Ahoy, mate! Young salts will enjoy this interactive exploration of the
sea. See—and touch—Rhode Island marine life (horseshoe crabs, starfish,
sea urchins), and take a turn at the wheel of a fishing boat. Listen to recorded "fish stories," go on a (videotaped) whale watch, and try your hand
at tying a bowline and other nautical knots. Or eavesdrop on real fishermen chatting over the marine radio.

⚛ International Tennis Hall of Fame

*194 Bellevue Ave.; (401) 846-4567. Year-round, daily, 10-5. Adults, $5;
under 16, $2.50; family rate, $10.*

Tennis buffs will not want to miss this. Housed in the Newport Casino
Building, it's billed as the birthplace of United States tennis tournaments.
There are exhibits and displays of trophies, tennis fashions, and equipment.
Old Davis Cup films are shown in a 450-seat theater. The site also boasts
the only grass courts in the United States that are open to the public.

⚛ Shamrock V

*Moored in front of the Museum of Yachting, Fort Adams State Park; (401)
847-1018.*

Whether she's moored in front of the museum or sailing on
Narragansett Bay, this sailing yacht is an impressive sight. The 120-foot
J-class sloop challenged *Enterprise* in the 1930 America's Cup races.

⚛ Green Animals Topiary Gardens

*Cory's Lane (off Rte. 114), Portsmouth; (401) 847-1000. Late April to
Nov., daily, 10-5. Holiday schedule, Thanksgiving weekend to Dec. 22, Sat.-
Sun., 10-4. Adults, $6; 6-11, $4.*

This maze of charming sculptured geometric figures and animal shapes is sure to delight young children and amaze adults. The gardens contain nearly 80 plant sculptures that have been lovingly pruned and shaped. The gardens are located in the nearby town of Portsmouth. Drive it yourself or take the Old Colony and Newport Railway, a 1930s train, from downtown Newport.

⌇ Old Colony and Newport Railway

America's Cup Ave. (across from the Gateway); (401) 624-6951. May-Dec., Sun. and holidays, 1 P.M. Adults, $6; 14 and under, $4; family rate (2 adults, kids age 14 and under), $15.

Board a vintage 1930s railway car for this eight-mile scenic trip to Portsmouth. The two-hour round trip includes a stopover at Green Animals Topiary Gardens.

⌇ Sailing

Fort Adams State Park, Ocean Dr.; (401) 849-8385.

Visit the Yachting Capital of the World and not get out on the water? Unthinkable! Plus, you'd miss seeing Newport from the water side. Rent a sailboat from Newport Sailing Association; they offer six- to 24-foot vessels by the hour or half-day. Call ahead to reserve one during busy summer weekends. Rate information is available by phone.

⌇ Viking Queen

Goat Island Dock; (401) 847-6921. May-Oct., daily. Adults, $7; 4-11, $3. Call ahead for cruise times.

If a ferry boat cruise is more your style than a sail, relax aboard the *Viking Queen*'s bay and harbor cruises. Or tie in your cruise with a visit to Hammersmith Farm. (See Hammersmith Farm, above.)

⌇ Beavertail State Park and Lighthouse

Rte. 138, Beavertail Point, Jamestown; (401) 423-99441. June-Aug.; tours daily, Wed.-Sun.

The centerpiece of this park is the lighthouse at Beavertail Point. Park naturalists give tours three times daily; you'll also enjoy panoramic views of the Atlantic coastline.

⌇ Norman Bird Sanctuary and Museum

583 Third Beach Rd., Middletown; (401) 846-2577. Memorial Day–Labor Day, daily, 9-5; Labor Day–Memorial Day, Tues.-Sun., 9-5. Trail use: adults, $2; under 12, free. Museum is free.

This 450-acre refuge is a wonderful outdoors spot for families, with seven miles of walking trails. Don't miss Hanging Rock Trail—this gently sloping hike (one mile each way) will take you to a dramatic rock formation overlooking the ocean. Before leaving the sanctuary, stop in at the museum, housed on the second floor of the large barn. You'll see specimens of local birds and animals mounted on the walls, with explanations of their habitats and habits. Kids can crawl into the authentically reconstructed bark wigwam.

ꙮ Beaches

Kids might find that the best thing to do in Newport is to head for one of its sandy beaches. Besides swimming at Fort Adams State Park, you can ride the waves (or just dunk your toes) at First Beach (Memorial Boulevard, running from Cliff Walk to Middletown); the three-mile long, sandy Second Beach (Sachuest Point Area in Middletown); and Third Beach (Sachuest Point Area on the Sakonnet River).

RESTAURANTS

ꙮ Inn at Castle Hill

Ocean Dr.; (401) 849-3800. Barbecue, Memorial Day–Labor Day, Sun., 2:30-6, weather permitting.

If it's a sunny Sunday afternoon, don't miss the barbecue at this ocean bluff restaurant. It has the best view in town—a panorama of Narragansett Bay, Newport Harbor, and the Atlantic Ocean. Sit on the grassy hill overlooking the water while listening to live jazz and awaiting barbecued chicken, hamburgers, and other favorites. Or, if your kids are older, mom and dad can dine on fresh fish in one of the inn's dining rooms or outside on the terrace while the youngsters feast on picnic food on the lawn.

ꙮ Newport Creamery

208 West Main St., 49 Long Wharf Mall, and 181 Bellevue Ave.; (401) 846-6332. Daily, 7 A.M.–11 P.M.

Everybody's tired, hungry, and sandy. Where do you go to eat? This local chain is fine for a quick, inexpensive bite. Best known for ice cream, these casual restaurants also offer sandwiches, hot dogs, kid's meals, and salads.

ꙮ Bannister's Wharf

In the heart of downtown Newport you'll find lively Bannister's Wharf. Sit outside under a colorful umbrella and order oysters on the half-shell, lobster rolls, fresh shrimp cocktail, or a bowl of chowder. You can get sandwiches, salads, hors d'oeuvres, and sweets from the outdoor cafes while you watch the harbor activity.

SOUTH COUNTY BEACHES AND ATTRACTIONS

From Narragansett Pier to Watch Hill, the southwestern coastline of Rhode Island is nearly one continuous stretch of beautiful white sand, offering beaches for every taste.

Two good family beaches are right in Narragansett—Sand Hill Cove and Narragansett Town Beach. Both are calm—no heavy surf—and offer all the facilities you'll need, from lifeguards and bathhouses to snack bars. Arrive early to snare a parking space.

In South Kingston, off Route 1, you'll find controversial Moonstone Beach, where bathing suits are optional. It's a small strip of sand for those who like to sunbathe and swim au naturel. The Charlestown Beach, at the edge of the Minigret National Wildlife Refuge, is popular with residents and visitors alike. You'll find it clean and spacious, with changing rooms, showers, and a small store for refreshments. If you'd like to get away from the ocean beach crowd, pack a picnic basket and head for the Minigret National Wildlife Refuge. You'll find peaceful walking trails to the small pond beach.

You won't be alone at East Beach, but the crowd is a mellow one. Located at the eastern edge of the Minigret Refuge, East Beach is considered one of the best beaches in the country. You'll find nearly three miles of white sand and lots of dunes to climb on. Kids enjoy the walk to Minigret Pond, where they can watch windsurfers sail the protected waters. There are no facilities at this beach, and the small parking lot fills up fast (before nine) on weekends, so arrive early. Right next to East Beach is Blue Shutters Beach, where many East Beach–goers trek to for refreshments and rest rooms. Blue Shutters has nearly four miles of clean sand, plus lifeguards, bathhouses, concessions, and kids, kids, kids.

Like to be where the action is? Proceed to busy Misquamicut Beach, where the air is laden with the smell of suntan lotion and the sound of boom boxes. This is a blanket-to-blanket, towel-to-towel sea of sunbathers. Of course, the kids will love all this, especially the snack bars and activities along the beach—including minigolf, kiddie rides, and a Ferris wheel. The total opposite experience is at Watch Hill, a quiet Victorian town on the western border of the state. Watch Hill Beach is small and rarely crowded, with showers, changing rooms, and a cluster of restaurants and shops nearby. Generations of kids have enjoyed the beach's Flying Horse Carousel.

Beyond the beaches, here's a look at some other favorite South County attractions.

⚡ The Enchanted Forest

Rte. 3, exit 2 off I-95, Hope Valley; (401) 539-7711. May–mid-June, call for schedule. Mid-June–Labor Day, daily, 10-5; month of Sept., Sat. and Sun., 10-5. Also open for Christmas, early–mid-Dec. Per person, $7.50; under 2, free. Extra charge for go-carts.

Too, too cute, this fairyland-themed amusement park will delight the small fry (age two to 12) in your bunch. Fun features include storybook exhibits, horse-drawn sleigh rides, a jump castle, a carousel, tame roller coasters, a Ferris wheel, a petting zoo, miniature golf, go-carts, and batting cages. There's a snack bar and a picnic area, too.

⚡ Adventureland

Point Judith Rd., Narragansett; (401) 789-0030. Weekends, mid-April–mid-June and Labor Day–mid-Oct., 11-6. Daily, mid-June–Labor Day, 10-10. Prices, $1.50-$20; discount tickets available.

Junior sports fiends will be in heaven at this attraction. If yours are into minigolf, they'll find the course here a hoot, with waterfalls, caves, streams, and an island. Bumper boats, batting cages, and a state-of-the-art go-cart track round out the offerings. This attraction is recommended for ages seven and up; go-carts require a height of 56 inches.

⚡ Canonchet Farm and South County Museum

Off Boston Neck Rd., Scenic 1-A, Narragansett; (401) 789-1044, (401) 783-5400. Farm: open daily. Museum: May-Oct., Wed.-Sun., 11-4. Adults, $2.50; 6-16, $1.50; family maximum, $8.

Spread over this 174-acre park is a 19th-century working farm, a cemetery with graves dating to 1700 (which are great for making grave rubbings), nature trails, picnic areas, and the South County Museum. The museum features articles of early Rhode Island life, including antique toys and dolls and a collection of antique carriages. Special events and demonstrations are frequently held; call for a schedule.

⚡ Water Wizz

319 Atlantic Ave., across from Misquamicut Beach, Westerly; (401) 322-0520. Memorial Day weekend–mid-June, Sat. and Sun., 11-4. Mid-June–Labor Day, daily, 10-6:30. Per person, $6.75 for 40 min. of riding, or $15 for an all-day pass (allowing you to go back and forth from the beach).

If they're feeling hot, sticky, and crabby after a couple of hours at the beach, this will cool them down—and give mom and dad a chance to sip an iced tea in peace. Watch them squeal and splash down six giant waterslides, twisty serpentine slides (including a kiddie version), and two 50-foot-high speed slides. It's best for bigger kids, but little ones can ride with a grown-up.

⚞ Flying Horse Carousel

Bay St., Watch Hill. Mid-June–Labor Day, weekdays, 1-9; Sat., Sun., and holidays, 11-9. Per ride, $.75.

This 1867 merry-go-round is one of the oldest in America and is designated as a National Historic Landmark. Each hand-carved horse has a real tail and mane; horses are suspended from a center frame, swinging out or "flying" when in motion. Grab the brass ring and win a free ride.

◤ RESTAURANTS

⚞ Olympia Tea Room

Bay St., Watch Hill; (401) 348-8211. April-Oct., daily, 8 A.M.–10 P.M.

Sick of picnics and beach food? Ready for something civilized? You'll find it at this charming classic, part bistro and part soda fountain. Sit at a wooden booth and enjoy the timeless quality of the place, with its black-and-white floor and waitresses garbed in tea room attire (black uniforms, white lace collars). Despite the gentility of the place, it's casual; you can even sit outside at a cafe table and enjoy the added bonus of a view of the bay. A children's menu is offered, along with enticing soda fountain creations and the Olympia Tea Room's trademark dessert, the Avondale Swan (a hot fudge sundae in a swan-shaped puff pastry).

⚞ George's of Galilee

250 Sand Hill Cove Rd., Port of Galilee; (401) 783-2306. Mid.-Feb.–Memorial Day, 11:30-9; Memorial Day–mid.-Oct., 11:30-10; mid-Oct.–mid-Feb., Fri. and Sat., 11:30-9.

This is one of those big, bustling, shore-dinner-with-a-view outposts. Ferries headed for Block Island depart here, so it gets busy; rather than wait in the lines, we advise you to head upstairs to the deck for an inexpensive menu and great views of Long Island Sound. Menu offerings include fish and chips, marinated seafood salad, fried clams, and more. Smell the aroma of fish-frying mingling with salt air—ahh, summer!

OTHER RHODE ISLAND HIGHLIGHTS

These family-friendly attractions don't fit neatly into any geographic category, but they merit inclusion anyway. And in Rhode Island, you're never too far from anyplace else.

☙ Coggeshall Farm Museum

Colt State Park, Rte. 114, Bristol; (401) 253-9062. March-Sept., 10-6; Oct.-Feb., 10-5. Adults, $1; children, $.25. Rates vary for special events.

What was it like to live and work on a New England farm in the 18th century? Find out here, at this working coastal farm located near a salt marsh on Narragansett Bay. These days, rare breeds of livestock are raised here, including oxen, pigs, chickens, and sheep, who roam the property freely. Depending on the season, visiting kids can help shear a sheep, see maple sugaring demonstrated, watch a team of oxen till the soil, and see craftspeople at work. Heirloom herb and vegetable gardens are worked here, too. The best time to visit with kids is during the "Days of Merriment," held in June. Activities include 18th-century children's games. Call for dates and a schedule of events.

☙ Rocky Point Park

Rocky Point Ave., off Rte. 117, Warwick Neck; (401) 737-8000. April, Sun., 11-6. May, Sat. and Sun., 11-6. Memorial Day–Labor Day, daily, 11-10:30; Fri.-Sun., 11 A.M.–around midnight. Park entrance: adults, $2.95; under 8 free. Rides: $5.95 per 20-ride ticket; or for a ride pass, $13.95, adults, and $8.95 for kids under 4.5 feet tall.

Don't call it a bribe. "Reward" them for their patience and good behavior at those Newport mansions with a trip to Rocky Point Park. You would not be the first parent to do so. This 128-acre amusement park, overlooking Narragansett Bay, is one of the largest in New England. With 21 awesome rides including a corkscrew loop roller coaster, plus ten kiddie rides, it's a real child pleaser. It has all the classic stuff, too: a midway, arcade games, fireworks (on holidays), and a carousel. You can even get a real Rhode Island shore dinner in the large dining hall.

☙ East Bay Bicycle Path

Nearly completed as this book went to press, this path will cover 14.5 scenic miles between Providence and Bristol. Attractions along the way include the Loof Carousel, several parks, and Brickyard Pond. There are several places to stop for refreshment along the way, such as Café Gelato in Bristol. Rest rooms are available at Colt State Park and Haines

Park. Need to rent a bike? Try Bay Path Cycles, 13 State Street, in
Bristol.

BLOCK ISLAND

If your description of the perfect getaway features words like "serene"
and "relaxing," and if your vision of the perfect place includes windswept
dunes and sandy beaches, consider Block Island. Many visitors appreciate
it most for what it doesn't have: namely, traffic, fast-food restaurants,
noisy nightlife, and cutesy boutiques.

There's plenty to do on Block Island. It's just that once you arrive
here you won't feel compelled to rush around and do them. The pace is
slow and the pleasures are simple: building sandcastles on the beach, bicycling around the seven-mile-long island, clam digging, kite flying, sailing, and fishing along the beach are popular pursuits.

The ferry ride to the island will put you in the mood, as you watch
Block Island slowly appear on the horizon. Look closely to see if you can
spot the buoys marking the harbor entrance as you get closer to port.
Ferries leave from Point Judith and Newport, Rhode Island; New London,
Connecticut; and Montauk, New York. Even if your ferry accepts cars,
don't bother to bring one. The only proper way to do Block Island is on a
bicycle. (In bad weather, it's okay to take a taxi.)

Block Island is less pretentious than other New England resorts, as
well as less expensive. It's "less" of a lot of things, which makes it more
attractive to families who want a relaxing getaway.

Mohegan Bluffs

These intriguing clay cliffs may be found at the southernmost tip
of the island, off Southeast Light Road. Climb up a path (there are several)
to the 200-foot elevation and gaze out over the Atlantic. To the left you'll
see Saileast Light, a beacon to seafarers since 1874. Wooden stairs will
take you back down to Mohegan Bluffs beach, which is secluded but
pebbly.

Block Island State Beach and Crescent Beach

Off Corn Neck Rd.; (401) 466-2611.

Located along the eastern shore of the island, both of these sandy
beaches are popular with families. The beaches are long and wide, with
white sand that's perfect for castle building. Lifeguards are posted at some
spots; picnic tables and bathouses are available also.

❧ Bicycling

Pedal around this 7-mile-long, 3.5-mile-wide island and you'll see rolling hills festooned with wildflowers, windswept sand dunes, and Victorian architecture. You may also see Great Salt Pond and the pleasure-boat basin New Harbor. Old Harbor is the commercial wharf where most of the ferries dock. At the northern tip of the island, you'll see Settler's Rock and the North Light lighthouse (no longer operating) at Sandy Point. You'll also see numerous freshwater ponds (there are 200 ponds on Block Island) and wildlife refuge areas. Bicycles may be rented at several shops, including Esta's at Old Harbor, (401) 466-2651 (children's seats available), and Old Harbor Bike Shop, (401) 466-2029 (children's seats and childrens' bicycles available).

❧ Boating

Sailboats are available for rent at the Block Island Club, (401) 466-5939. Rowboats are available at Twin Maples, (401) 466-5547.

❧ Fishing

Go fishing from the beach or take out a rowboat. Bait and tackle are available at Twin Maples on Beach Avenue; (401) 466-5547.

❧ Shellfishing

A license is required for shellfishing. Obtain one at the Block Island Police Station on the corner of Beach and Ocean avenues.

◣ RESTAURANTS

❧ Finn's

Water St.; (401) 466-2473. End of April–Columbus Day, 11:30-9 or -10.

Eat indoors or outdoors at Finn's and watch the ferries docking at Old Harbor. You can get a $3 sandwich or a $20 dinner or anything in between here, all day, so kids can choose fun food while adults enjoy a leisurely meal. The number-one kid's choice here is the fish sandwich; adults rave about Finn's baked stuffed shrimp.

❧ Ballard's

End of Water St.; (401) 466-2231. Memorial Day–Labor Day, 11:30-11.

Craving Italian food? Indulge the urge at this waterfront restaurant located at the Ballard Inn. In addition to Italian specialties you'll find clams, mussels, steaks, and steamed lobster—the biggest seller. The children's menu includes fried clams, fish and chips, spaghetti, and something called a "clam steak." Hmm. Eat out on the deck on Ballard's private beach or in the large dining room, where in the evenings there's often a band playing.

⅋ Rebecca's

Water St.; (401) 466-5411. Memorial Day–Labor Day, 7 A.M.–9 P.M. and 11 P.M.–2 A.M.

Want to take a picnic to the bluffs or the beach? Sure you do. Many delis and restaurants on the island offer food to go. We like Rebecca's, where you can get anything from a shrimp dinner to a super sandwich (try the marinated-chicken speidi), packed to go. All you need to add is a bottle of good wine, and maybe a gooey dessert...heavenly.

Massachusetts

Massachusetts Office of Travel and Tourism, 100 Cambridge Street, Boston 02202; (617) 727-3201. Toll-free number for a free vacation kit and calendar of events: 1-800-632-8038.

New Hampshire

Office of Vacation Travel, PO Box 856, Concord 03301; (603) 271-2666.

Maine

Maine Publicity Bureau, PO Box 1057, Yarmouth 04096; (207) 846-0833.

Vermont

State Travel & Tourism, 134 Division, 134 State Street, Montpelier 05602; (802) 828-3236.

Connecticut

Department of Economic Development, 856 Brook St., Rocky Hill, 06067; 1-800- CT-BOUND.

Rhode Island

Rhode Island Tourism Department, 7 Jackson Walkway, Providence 02903; in-state, (401) 277-2601; outside Rhode Island, 1-800-556-2484.

Annual Events

MASSACHUSETTS

January

Winter Carnival, Holyoke State Park, Holyoke; (413) 534-1723.

February

Washington's Birthday Celebration, Old Sturbridge Village, Sturbridge; (413) 347-3362.

March

Saint Patrick's Day Parade, South Boston; (617) 268-8525.
Saint Patrick's Day Parade, Holyoke; (413) 534-3376.

April

Boston Marathon, Boston; (617) 435-4303.
Reenactment of the Battle of Lexington and Concord, Lexington Green, Lexington; (617) 862-1450.

May

Salem Seaport Festival, Salem Common, Salem; (617) 462-1414.
Sheep-Shearing Festival, Old North Andover Common, Andover; (508) 686-0191.
WestFest Arts Festival, Stanley Park, Westfield; (413) 562-5531.
New England Street Performer's Festival, Faneuil Hall Marketplace, Boston; (617) 523-1300.

June

Saint Anthony's Festival, North End, Boston; (617) 523-2110.
International Dory Days, State Fish Pier, Gloucester; (508) 281-2695.
Saint Peter's Fiesta and Blessing of the Fleet, Saint Peter's Square, Gloucester; (508) 283-1601.
Festival Heritage, Battleship Cove, Fall River; (508) 324-2620.
Harbor Festival, Bismore Park, Hyannis; (508) 775-2201.
Water Works Day, Lowell National Historical Park, Lowell; (508) 459-1000.

Amesbury Days, throughout town, Amesbury; (508) 388-3178.
Annual Fly-In and Antique Steam and Gas Engine Show, Municipal
　Airport, Orange; (508) 544-8189.

July

Boston Harborfest, Boston Harbor area and Harbor Islands; (617) 227-
　1528.
Harbor Islands Children Fest, Boston Harbor Islands State Park; (617)
　740-1605.
National Folk Festival, Court Square, Springfield; (413) 787-6622.
Mashpee Wambahoag Powwow, Mashpee; (508) 477-0208.
Boston Chowder Fest, City Hall Plaza, Boston; (617) 227-1528.
Fishtown Horribles Parade, Gloucester; (508) 283-1601.
Old Sturbridge Independence Day, Sturbridge; (508) 347-3362.
Barnstable County Fair, Fairgrounds, East Falmouth; (617) 563-3200.
Feast of the Blessed Sacrament (largest Portuguese festival in the U.S.),
　Madiera Field, New Bedford; (617) 992-6911.

August

Italian Weekend Festival, Our Lady of Loreto Church, Worcester; (508)
　753-5001.
Heritage Days, throughout town, Salem; (508) 744-0004.
Celebrates America/Tall Ships, Heritage State Park, Fall River; (508) 676-
　8226.
Martha's Vineyard Livestock Show and Fair, Fairgrounds, West Tisbury;
　(508) 693-4343.
Westfield Fair, Fairgrounds, Westfield; (413) 562-9555.
Festival Days, throughout town, Dennis; (508) 398-3568.
Gloucester Waterfront Festival, Gloucester Harbor; (508) 283-1601.
Festival of Shaker Crafts and Industries, Hancock Shaker Village,
　Pittsfield; (413) 443-0188.
August Moon Festival, Chinatown, Boston; (617) 542-2574.

September

Spencer Fair, Fairgrounds, Spencer; (508) 867-6877.
Schooner Festival, Gloucester; (508) 283-1601.
Bourne Scallop Festival, Buzzards Bay Park, Bourne; (508) 759-3122.
Cranberry Festival, throughout town, Harwich; (508) 430-2811.
Essex Clamfest, Memorial Park, Essex; (508) 283-1601.
Taste of the Berkshire Hills from Farm to Table, Great Barrington; (413)
　528-9219.

The Big E, Eastern States Exposition Grounds, West Springfield; (413) 737-BIGE.

Newburyport Waterfront Festival, Newburyport; (508) 462-6680.

October

Annual Fair, Belchertown; (413) 323-9710.

Autumn Weekend, Hancock Shaker Village, Pittsfield; (413) 443-0188.

Annual Harvest Bus Tours, Ocean Spray Cranberry Visitor's Center, Plymouth; (508) 747-2350.

Seaside Festival, John Simpkins School Field, South Yarmouth; (508) 394-1525.

Applefest, Wachusett Mountain Ski Area, Princeton; (508) 464-5731.

Harvest Festival, high school, Westport; (508) 636-6504.

Historical Society Walking Tours, Old Colony Railroad Station, North Easton; (508) 238-2655.

Haunted Happenings Week, throughout town, Salem; (508) 744-0004.

Great Pumpkin Halloween Festival, Boarding House Park, Lowell; (508) 459-1000.

Topsfield Fair, Fairgrounds, Topsfield; (508) 887-2212.

NEW HAMPSHIRE

May

Annual Lilac-Time Festival, throughout town, Lisbon; (603) 838-6777.

Historic Preservation Week, Strawbery Banke, Portsmouth; (603) 433-1100.

Memorial Day Celebration, Seashell Stage, Hampton Beach; (603) 926-8717.

Family Day, Main St., New Ipswich; (603) 227-3956.

June

Market Square Day, Market Square, Portsmouth; (603) 431-5388.

High Hopes Annual Hot Air Balloon Festival, Perry Field, Milford; (603) 673-7005.

International Children's Festival, throughout town, Somersworth; (603) 692-5869.

Strawberry Festival, town hall, Windham; (603) 434-7908.

Prescott Park Arts Festival, Prescott Park, Portsmouth; (603) 436-2848.

Mount Washington Auto Road Hill Climb, Auto Road, Pinkham Notch; (603) 466-3988.

Portsmouth Jazz Festival, Prescott Park, Portsmouth; (603) 436-7678.

July

Family Outdoor Discovery Day, White Lake State Park, Tamworth; (603) 271-3254.

New Hampshire State Parks Week (family activities at many state parks); (603) 271-3254.

Children's Day, N.H. Farm Museum, Milton; (603) 652-7840.

Gunstock Crafts Festival, Gunstock Recreation Area, Gilford; (603) 293-4341.

Hayseed Music Festival, Dow Field, Franconia; (603) 823-5640.

Stratham Fair, Stratham Hill Park, Stratham; (603) 436-1326.

Classic Boat Show, Weirs Beach, Laconia; (800) 654-3031.

August

Wildlife Festival, Science Center of N.H., Holderness; (603) 968-7194.

Old-Time Farm Day, N.H. Farm Museum, Milton; (603) 652-7840.

Children's Festival, Sea Shell Area, Hampton Beach; (603) 926-8717.

Annual Children's Fair, Congregational Church, New Ipswich; (603) 878-2420.

Children's Day, Strawbery Banke, Portsmouth; (603) 433-1100.

Family Outdoor Discovery Day, Greenfield State Park, Greenfield; (603) 271-3254.

Lakes Region Fine Arts and Crafts Festival, Meredith; (603) 279-6121.

September

Wool Day, Canterbury Shaker Village, Canterbury; (603) 783-9511.

Deerfield Fair, Fairgrounds, Deerfield; (603) 463-7421.

Squam Lakes Apple Festival, Holderness; (603) 742-2218.

October

Old-Time Shaker Harvest Festival, Lower Shaker Village, Enfield; (603) 632-4346.

Fall Foliage Festival, center of town, Warner; (603) 456-2374.

October-fest, Gunstock Recreation Area, Gilford; (603) 293-4341.

Fall Foliage Festival, Loon Mountain, Lincoln; (603) 745-8111.

Fall Festival, Strawbery Banke, Portsmouth; (603) 433-1100.

MAINE

February

Caribou Winter Carnival, Caribou; (207) 498-6156.

March

Moosehead Sled Dog Races, Greenville; (207) 695-2702.

Rangeley Lake Sled Dog Races, Rangeley; (207) 864-5364.

April
Fisherman's Festival, Boothbay Harbor; (207) 633-4008.

May
Maine State Parade, downtown Lewiston; (207) 784-0599.
Moose Run Road Race and Fun Run, Lakeside Park, Rangeley; (207) 864-5364.

June
Festival of Traditional Sea Music, Maine Maritime Museum, Bath; (207) 443-1316.
Old Port Festival, Old Port, Portland; (207) 772-6828.
Windjammer Days, Boothbay Harbor; (207) 633-2353.
Heritage Days, Norlands Living History Center, Livermore; (207) 897-2236.
Great Kennebec River Whatever Week and Race, Augusta; (207) 623-4559.
Strawberry Festival, on the square, South Berwick; (207) 384-4943.
Military Aviation Air Show, Transportation Museum, Owl's Head; (207) 594-4418.
Franklin County Rodeo, Farmington Fairgrounds, Farmington; (207) 778-4215.
Family Fun Run, Ogunquit Beach, Ogunquit; (207) 646-3032.
Maine Storyteller's Festival, Rockport; (207) 773-4909.

July
Agricultural Fair, Community Park, Houlton; (207) 532-4216.
Oyster Festival, Damariscotta; (207) 563-3175.
Yarmouth Clam Festival, Yarmouth; (207) 846-3984.
Heritage Day, waterfront parks, Bath; (207) 443-9751.
Old Home Days, Crystal Lake Park, Harrison; (207) 583-6001.
Maine Potato Blossom Festival, Fort Fairfield; (207) 472-3381.
Summer Fest, Jalbert Park, Fort Kent; (207) 834-3975.
Great Schooner Race, Rockland; (800) MAINE-80.
Seaside Festival, Fort Foster Park, Kittery Point; (207) 439-3800.
Old Hallowell Day, Main St., Hallowell; (207) 623-4021.
Friendship Sloop Boothbay Regatta, Boothbay; (207) 633-2353.
State Fair, Bass Park Complex, Bangor; (207) 942-9000.
Logging Museum Festival Days, Rangeley; (207) 864-5364.

August
Maine Festival, Thomas Point Beach, Brunswick; (207) 772-9012.

Annual Maine Lobster Festival, Harbor Park, Rockland; (207) 596-0376.
Transportation Rally and Aerobatic Show, Transportation Museum, Owl's
   Head; (207) 594-4418.
Annual Fair, Fairgrounds, Topsham; (207) 729-7497.
State Fair, Fairgrounds, Skowhegan; (207) 474-2947.
Blueberry Festival, throughout town, Wilton; (207) 645-3932.

September
Blue Grass Festival, Brunswick; (207) 725-6009.
International Seaplane Fly-In, Greenville; (207) 695-2702.

VERMONT

May
Kid's Day Celebration, Church Street Marketplace, Burlington; (802)
   865-7242.
Spring Festival, Billings Farm and Museum, Woodstock; (802) 457-2355.
Mayfest, Downtown Bennington; (802) 447-3311.
Bennington County Horse Show, Hildene Meadowlands, Manchester;
   (802) 362-1788.

June
Vermont Dairy Festival, Village Green, Enosburg Falls; (802) 933-2513.
Lake Champlain Balloon Festival, Champlain Valley Fairgrounds, Essex
   Junction; (802) 899-2993.
Annual Discover Jazz Festival, citywide, Burlington; (802) 863-7992.
Ben & Jerry's One-World One-Heart Festival, Sugarbush Resort, Warren;
   (802) 244-6957.
Annual Quechee Balloon Festival, Quechee; (802) 295-7900.
Lake Champlain International Fishing Derby, Lake Champlain; (802)
   862-7777.
Kid's Summerfest, Fairbanks Museum, Saint Johnsbury; (802) 748-2372.
Hand-milking Contest, Billings Farm and Museum, Woodstock; (802)
   457-2355.

July
Summer Festival, Union High School Grounds, Woodstock; (802)
   457-3981.
Green Mountain Chew Chew Vermont Food Fest, downtown railroad
   station, Bennington; (802) 447-3311.
Hot-Air Balloon Festival, Country Club Field, Stowe; (802) 253-7321.

Morgan Horse Heritage Days, Tunbridge Fairgrounds, Tunbridge; (802) 234-5809.

Vermont Lumberjack Roundup, Fairgrounds, Rutland; (802) 525-4404.

Woodstock Summer Festival, Rte. 4, Woodstock; (802) 457-3981.

Vermont Handcrafters Fair, Stowe; (802) 388-0123.

Southern Vermont Craft Fair, Hildene Meadows, Manchester; (802) 362-1788.

Midsummer Festival of the Arts, State House Lawn, Montpelier; (802) 229-9408.

Killington Mountain Equestrian Festival, Shelburne; (802) 422-4302.

19th-Century Crafts Day, Billings Farm and Museum, Woodstock; (802) 457-2355.

August

Champlain Valley Festival, Burlington; (802) 849-6968.

Washington County Field Days, throughout town, East Montpelier; (802) 244-8507.

Vermont State Chili Cook-Off, Mount Snow Resort, West Dover; (802) 464-3333.

Deerfield Valley Farmer's Day, high school, Deerfield; (802) 464-8452.

Great American Buskers Festival (comedy and vaudeville), Burlington; (802) 864-8178.

Bennington Battle Day Weekend, Bennington; (802) 447-3311.

Shelburne Craft Fair, Shelburne Farms, Shelburne; (802) 864-8178.

Children's Day, Billings Farm and Museum, Woodstock; (802) 457-2355.

September

Vermont State Fair, Fairgrounds, Rutland; (802) 775-5200.

Annual World's Fair, Main St., Tunbridge; (802) 889-3704.

Apple Days Festival, town common, Brattleboro; (802) 254-4565.

Foliage Crafts Fair, Topnotch Tennis Center, Stowe; (802) 253-7321.

Old-Fashioned Harvest Market, United Church grounds, Underhill; (802) 899-3369.

Mad River Valley Craft Fair, Howard Bank Green, Waitsfield; (802) 496-3639.

October

Fall Foliage Festival, church vestry, Barnet Center; (802) 748-8246.

Foliage Crafts Show, Sunrise Mountain Lodge, Killington; (802) 422-3783.

CONNECTICUT

May
Springtime Festival, downtown Danielson; (203) 774-8001.
Lobster Fest, Mystic Seaport, Mystic; (203) 572-0711.

June
Bluegrass Festival, Strawberry Park Campground, Preston; (203)
    886-1994.
Saint Andrew Annual Feast, 515 Chapel St., New Haven; (203) 865-9846.
Taste of Hartford Food Festival, Constitution Plaza, Hartford; (203)
    728-6789.
County Irish Festival, Roger Ludlowe Field, Fairfield; (203) 366-3153.
Sea Music Festival, Mystic Seaport, Mystic; (203) 572-0711.

July
Round Hill Highland Scottish Games, Norwalk; (203) 854-7806.
Agricultural Fair, North Stonington; (203) 535-2703.
Annual Ancient Muster, Deep River; (203) 399-6665.
Riverfest, Hartford and East Hartford; (203) 728-3089.
Lobster Fest, Niantic; (203) 739-7641.
Sail Festival, City Pier, New London; (203) 443-8331.
Blessing of the Fleet, Town Dock, Stonington; (203) 535-3150.

August
Annual Italian Festival, Mount Carmel Fairgrounds, Enfield; (203)
    745-7625.
Annual Monastic Fair, Abbey of Regina Laudis, Bethlehem; (203)
    266-7811.
Riverfront Festival, Riverside Park, Hartford; (203) 293-0131.
International Whaleboat Race, Mystic Seaport, Mystic; (203) 572-0711.
Connecticut River Powwow and Rendezvous, Portland; (203) 487-0036.

September
Feast Fest (area restaurants' food festival), Main St., Manchester; (203)
    646-2223.
International Dance Festival, Olde Mistick Village, Mystic; (203)
    536-4941.
Woodstock Fair, Fairgrounds, Woodstock; (203) 928-3246.
Bethlehem Fair, Fairgrounds, Bethlehem; (203) 266-5350.

Waterbury Festival, Library Park, Waterbury; (203) 597-9527.
Annual Four-Town Fair, Fairgrounds, Somers; (203) 749-7320.
Durham Fair, Fairgrounds, Durham; (203) 349-9495.

October

Harvest Celebration Weekend, South Windsor; (203) 528-2396.
Berlin Fair, Fairgrounds, Berlin; (203) 828-3584.
Mystic Seaport's Annual Chowder-fest, Mystic Seaport Museum, Mystic;
(203) 572-0711.

RHODE ISLAND

May

Annual Sail Newport Sailing Festival, Newport; (401) 846-1983.
Rhode Island National Guard Show, Quonset State Airport, North
Kingstown; (401) 886-1430.

June

Annual Children's Festival, South County Museum, Narrangansett; (401)
783-5400.
Strawberry Festival, Smith's Castle, North Kingstown; (401) 294-3521.
Annual Newport Outdoor Art Festival, Long Wharf Mall, Newport; (401)
849-2873.
Annual Waterfront Carnival, Newport Yachting Center, Newport; (401)
846-1600.
Arts Festival, Memorial Square, Narragansett; (401) 789-4079.

July

Arts Festival, various locations, Wickford; (401) 294-6840.
Newport Music Festival, Fort Adams State Park, Newport; (401) 849-
0700.
Green Animals Children's Party, Topiary Gardens, Portsmouth; (401)
847-1000.
Annual East Providence Heritage Days, Pierce Memorial Field, East
Providence; (401) 434-3311.
South County Hot-Air Balloon Festival, URI athletic field, Kingston;
(401) 783-2801.
Annual Black Ships Festival, various locations, Newport; (401) 846-2720.
Annual Big Easy Bash, Stepping Stone Ranch, West Greenwich; (401)
397-3521.

August

Annual Seafood Festival, Minigret Park, Charlestown; (401) 364-4031.

Washington County Fair, Rte. 112, Richmond; (401) 783-2070.

Newport JVC Jazz Festival, Fort Adams State Park, Newport; (401) 849-3990.

Annual Summer Fest and Feast, Main St., East Greenwich; (401) 885-0020.

September

Annual Cajun and Bluegrass Festival, Stepping Stone Ranch, Escoheag; (401) 351-6312.

Rhode Island Labor and Ethnic Heritage Festival, Slater Mill, Pawtucket; (401) 725-8638.

Annual Keep Providence Beautiful Pasta Challenge, One Citizen's Plaza, Providence; (401) 351-6440.

Harvest Fair, Coffeshall Farm Museum, Bristol; (401) 253-9062.

October

Autumnfest, World War II Memorial Park, Woonsocket; (401) 769-4911.

Annual Northeast Surfing Championships, town beach, Narragansett; (401) 789-1954.

Southworth Planetarium, 135
Spirit of Ethan Allen, 178
Sportland America, 225
Springfield Science Museum, 42
Squam Lake Tours, 95
Stamford Museum & Nature Center, 224
State Capitol and Legislative Office
    Building, 204-9
State Capitol Tours, 148
State House Center, 89
State House,The, 9
Steam Train and Riverboat, 212-17
Steve Powell Wildlife Management
    Area, 141
Stone Zoo, 16
Stonedam Island Natural Area, 96
Stony Brook Mill and Herring Run, 65
Story Land, 111-16
Stoughton Pond, 165
Stowe Aviation, 188
Stowe Gondola and Alpine Slides, 187
Stowe Mountain Resort, 191-94
Stowe Recreation Path, 188
Stratton Brook State Park, 208
Stratton Mountain, 169
Strawbery Banke, 77-78
Sugar Houses, 163
Sugarbush Resort, 191
Sugarloaf USA, 154
Sunapee Harbor, 98
Sunday River Ski Resort, 153-54
Surf Coaster, 94-93
Sylvan Way, 121

T.A.D. Dog Sled Rides, 153
Talcott Mountain State Park and
    Heublein Tower, 208
Tanglewood Music Festival, 52-53
Tantaquidgeon Indian Museum, 203
Taproot Morgan Horse Farm, 183
Texas Falls, 182-83
Thomas Point Beach, 140
Thornton Burgess Museum, 57
Top Notch Riding Stable, 188
Topsmead State Forest, 229
Tot Stop, 15
Townsend Lake Recreation Area, 166
Toy Cupboard Theatre and Museums, 46
Trampoline Center, 64
Travelers Tower, 206
Turner Falls Fish Viewing Facility, 48
Two Lights State Park, 136

U.S. Coast Guard Academy, 201-2
U.S.S Constitution and Museum, 14
University of Connecticut Diary and
    Animal Farm, 233
Urban Forestry Center, 80
UVM Morgan Horse Farm, 182

Vermont Historical Society
    Museum, 187
Vermont Institute of Natural
    Science, 171
Vermont Marble Company, 173
Vermont State House Tour, 186
Vermont Teddy Bear Company,
    The, 181
Vermont Wildlife Farm, 183
Viking Queen, 241
Village Carriage Company, 163

Wachusett Mountain, 47
Wadleigh State park, 101
Wadsworth Atheneum, 206
Wadsworth Falls State Park, 215
Walden Pond, 19
Wallis Sands, 83
Washburn-Norlands Living History
    Center, 151-52
Water Country, 79
Water Wizz, 58, 244-45
Waterville Valley Ski Area, 108
Waterville-Winslow Two Cent
    Bridge, 149
Weirs Beach Water Slide, 94
Wayside,The, 19
Wells Auto Museum, 130
Wells National Estuarine Sanctuary, 130
Wenham Museum, 26-27
West Rock Park and West Rock Nature
    Center, 219
Western Gateway Heritage State
    Park, 52
Whale's Tale and Amusement Park,
    The, 104
Whaling Museum, 39
Whaling Museum, 39, 74
Whalom Amusement Park, 48
Wharton Brook State Park, 220
Wheelock Family Theater, 6
Where's Boston?, 9
White Memorial Foundation and
    Conservation Center, 227
White Mountain National Forest, 151